# Lesser Expectations

## CHARLES DICKENS' SON
## IN NORTH AMERICA

## by Vic Parsons

Photos used on cover:
— Hudson's Bay Company Archives,
Provincial Archives of Manitoba,1987/363 R34/30,
Northwest Mounted Police, Fort Pitt, 1884. N67-73 and N13504
— Provincial Archives of Alberta, B1680,
Francis Dickens and Thomas Quinn

**ISBN**
978-1-4602-1437-4 (Hardcover)
978-1-4602-1436-7 (Paperback)
978-1-4602-1438-1 (eBook)

Produced by:

## FriesenPress

Suite 300 – 852 Fort Street
Victoria, BC, Canada V8W 1H8

www.friesenpress.com

Distributed to the trade by The Ingram Book Company

# Prologue

Betsy Kennedy looked about the room she had set aside for the stranger who had arrived only the afternoon before. Her visitor's belongings were partially unpacked from the small trunk that apparently had carried all that he owned. A new pair of trousers was hanging in the armoire.

The bed was unmade. In the shocked haste that followed the tragic event of the previous evening nothing had been put in order. Her husband Sam, their friend Doctor Alexander Jamieson and another doctor had done their best to keep the visitor alive, to no avail. They had borne him up the stairs to the bed to make their new-found friend comfortable. How sad it seemed that the Kennedy's guest had come so far, and with such hopes of success in his new endeavour, only to end so suddenly, without warning.

He had seemed such a gentle and quiet soul, not a hard-bitten policeman who had endured remarkable adventures in hostile lands. So good with her children too, when he read an excerpt from his father's works. Then his eyes twinkled with mirth and he concluded the reading with a comment of his own. "I'm glad my father never wrote anything that was harmful for young or old to read."

With the house in mourning, Mrs. Kennedy had put on black clothes in spite of the June heat. Moving her hand to her dress, she absent-mindedly smoothed a wrinkle, wondering when they would receive word from England, or perhaps Ottawa, Canada, about arrangements for the funeral. Moline, Illinois, was a long way from either of those places to ship a body. And who was to bear the expense? The family of the unfortunate man who after a lifetime of police work was close to being a pauper? Or the government of the country in whose service he had worked for fourteen years? Surely, their visitor's connections would not expect the people of Moline, to bear the cost?

She busied herself with setting the room in order, then noticed on a side table some hand-written notes. The script in hand, she hesitated for a moment, then curiosity won out and she read.

# Chapter 1

*It is the lot of a select few to have been cursed by having great fathers: men whom the adoring world looks to as leaders in the worlds of fashion, politics, trade, and literature or painting. Icons whose words drip with honey and are listened to with reverence or awe, whose pronouncements often go unchallenged except by an element of radicals who barely exist on the margins of society, or by those so backward in their thinking that their minds are encased in cement, fossilized like one of those ancient sea monsters occasionally discovered in the chalk Downs of South England.*

*In this new age, of course, when our homeland and vast empire beyond the seas is ruled by a sovereign who is a beloved woman, and under whose ascendancy Britain has become the greatest power the world has known, I could also include great mothers. My point should not be lost, however. Some may envy those raised in families dominated by a famous parent. Setting the record straight, I would advise those who are jealous to reconsider their feelings. Happy is the child who is destined to overshadow his parent, rather than to be sheltered for life in that smothering, protective bosom that allows little room for personal choice and which sets standards that few mortals can hope to match.*

I speak from experience. I am the third son, the fifth child, of an author of incomparable note, Charles ·Dickens. I have travelled to distant parts of the world, and there is scarce one where that name is not known. There are places, in truth, where the name brings no degree of homage but these are largely populated by illiterate savages who know nothing of literature, whose "art" consists of childlike drawings and whose music is the monotonous batterings of percussive instruments. Even in those parts of Europe where English is little understood, the name Dickens brings privileges not afforded to the general class of traveller. In short, wherever I go I find some men willing to do me favours, fawning to the point of being oppressive. Some say my name is my meal ticket, and I must grant it often, though not always, to be so. Father judged rightly when he referred to himself as "The Inimitable."

Then why do I say that I and others sired by the famous are cursed, you ask? The evils that befall us are of two sorts: First, the name creates great expectations — if you'll pardon the obvious reference — of we lesser beings who have the misfortune to be descended from greatness. Inevitably, I have been expected to play a role — to cause my listeners to fall into paroxysms of delight with witty remarks, to deport myself as my father's worshippers would expect my father to behave, to be cleverer than I in fact am. The sad truth is that I lack my father's talent as a writer and, being of a reserved nature, possess even less of his genius as a lecturer or actor. And when the presumptions of others remain unfulfilled, I am regarded — by those who have placed me on pedestals I myself did not earn nor which I crave — with contempt, as a fraud, for only being what I am and nothing more. In my youth I practised posturing before others but this, while I was at home, only brought scorn and disapprobation from my father and, I could feel it also, from his friends. In reality, I feared his opinion of me, that I could never quite match up, and that fear left a stamp, crushing my own personality. That is one part of the curse.

The greater part is to have had one's life directed by that superior being, the head of the household, and when those commands are not achieved to the satisfaction of himself, our Supreme Judge _ no offense to the Almighty _ they have attracted anger and overtly expressed despair that I would never make anything of myself. I have had little control over my own life and when *pushed and pulled in one direction or another feel constantly as if I have no choice but failure. I have so often felt ground down by the hopes, indeed, the calculations of my father. Perhaps I am being unfair: He sired ten of us — one a poor infant girl who died before her first year was out — and seven were boys. With so many children underfoot and with his feverish devotion to his work it might have been inevitable that he could spend little time with us, and so he saw only bits and pieces of what we were. When he was at home, deeply immersed in his writing, we saw little of him, and when we attempted to speak, usually out of turn as young lads do, we were told to hush. That separation led him to make unfounded assumptions about our talents and thus experience profound dismay at our many failures. It has been related to me that he once said his favourite child was David, and when a puzzled friend inquired about this mysterious David, not recalling previous mention of the lad, he said impishly: "Why, David Copperfield, of course." It was wise, I suppose, not to choose one of the children and stir resentment in the others. But I often think that we were held up to a model of fictional perfection that none of us could possibly match. I suspect he chose outlandish nicknames for us because he found them easier to remember than our real names. Or could it be that he wished to avoid the reality of his own offspring, confirmed in a belief that he would be far more remembered for his inventions than for the pallid accomplishments of his flesh and blood?*

*When I am asked by the pryingly curious of my impressions of father, I almost invariably lapse into descriptions that match and satisfy the expectations of the public. I speak of his love for his children and his creation of special little plays and essays for us, how he alternately wept and raged over perceived injustice, and how his hypnotic personality charmed and flattered persons from all strata of society, even at times those who were the unwitting subjects of his barbs. No one I have ever heard of has questioned his talent, and nor do I, but seeing him up close, in full colour unrepentant life, if you will, brings another image to my mind. All of his sons, myself included, have traded on and benefited from his reputation, so do not be persuaded that my love and respect for him is diminished. Why would we undermine that treasured asset that has brought us personal profit?*

But when I think of father, it is not the public persona that comes to mind. It is the private one, the one that I so often saw at home, vividly expressed in all its fiery autocracy.

I recall, for instance, one occasion soon after we had made the move from close and dreary central London to the open air and the greenery of Gad's Hill. Pa had been enchanted by an estate there in his youth and had purchased the property when it came up for sale in 1855 for less than two thousand pounds. When he was young, Pa had so enjoyed the liveliness of London, and its squalor as much as its glory, in the development of plot and character in his works. He had now had come to realize that the city was something of a cesspool. The reek of decaying garbage, excrement and rotting bodies from overfilled graveyards fouled the air, and he had described the once fair Thames as an open, deadly sewer corrupting the life of the city. Soot from the coal fires and gas lamps hung in the air, clung to the buildings and spread illness in the lungs of the inhabitants. It was a personal discovery that he portrayed and embellished in his serial Little Dorrit. The London he once roamed incessantly and eagerly in search of inspiration for his work now seemed to him to be enveloped in a squalid sea of corruption, greed and snobbery. The bureaucratic Circumlocution Office he invented in Little Dorrit was a summation of the evils he saw in London life and he felt it imperative to preserve us from the evil influence of the city. Now he had decided that his family should exit the unhealthy and socially corruptible environs of the City and we should be permitted space to breathe and develop.

How blessed we all felt at this move, where we could run and play happily through the lush fields, wade and fish in the reedy streams and pester the innocent herds of farm animals with peashooters and slingshots. At first, we used the red brick house on the estate as a peaceful and fresh summer retreat, but over time the dilapidated house was restored and by 1858 it became our permanent family home.

But imagine this tableau, if you will: We boys are on the lawn before the house, engaged in a game of cricket. There is much laughter and good-natured taunting. Many dogs are running to and fro amid the players, barking loudly and joyfully and tripping the lads as they hurl the balls and chase after them. Our sisters stand by giggling and chattering.

*Suddenly there emerges from the back door of the house a bearded, clearly irate fellow, waving a switch. The playground falls silent almost immediately as this man possessed marches purposefully forward, his voice aroar and his eyes blazing and narrowed, taking in the scene which is now a landscape of frozen boys, nervous, whimpering dogs and scattering squirrels.*

*"Confound it," the approaching storm bellows. "How can a man concentrate with this infernal racket?"*

*Cowed, we huddle together, expecting the switch to fall. It does not, but we watch surreptitiously to see if the pressed lips will curl, suggesting a modicum of humour. None is betrayed.*

*Later, our games much subdued, we hear roars of laughter issuing from the direction of his study. Is he amused by the antics of a character he has created? At the panicked expressions on our faces? Or at his own demonic behaviour? No one would dare to ask.*

*Does this anecdote suggest that my love for my father was less than fulsome? I hope it does not, and here is why:*

Father was driven to greatness; we boys were not. Yes, driven is the correct word. As surely as a whip lashes a horse, he was coerced by fear as much as by ambition, for he had experienced something dreadful to him that we had never even contemplated in our conscious sheltered lives, the terror that he could be dragged back into the swamp of poverty that crushed the souls of so many of his countrymen, including our grandpapa and other members of his own family. We did not appreciate that he had in fact achieved that greatness for us as much as for himself, and how could we have realized that when he never spoke freely of that fear to us? We were doomed to be lesser creatures than he from the start.

Perhaps you believe that I complain too much. How bad could life have been, you are thinking? A comfortable family dwelling place purchased by a steady income from father's writings, an abundance of playmates and playthings. The experiences of education and travel of which nearly all other English children of our origins could only dream. No scraping or begging for food and other necessities, like so many of the characters he created. It was not always that way, of course. Father had experienced the disdain of the upper classes and after the aforementioned poverty in his early days, and in his early career, he lived in fear to his dying days that the bubble of prosperity would burst and he would be condemned to the trash heaps of society. But from the time of my first memories we were privileged in many ways. Still, we had little control over our lives, even as young adults. Careers were chosen for us, often haphazardly or tyrannically, perhaps with the ultimate goal of ridding us from his houses, or perhaps more generously as the fairy tales have it, sending us out into the world to seek our fortunes. Father loved travel and moved us frequently. His itinerant decisions were often rashly made, without due regard for the feelings, or even the health, of our poor mother, who endured so much. Her long-suffering resistance to constant mobility contributed in large degree to that terrible breakdown of the marriage, the time when I came closest to hating our father for his evil behaviour toward our beloved Mama.

Yes, he directed our lives as a tyrant of old or as those ancient Greek gods who played mischievous games with unwitting mortals, compelling them to fall in love or to cheat or murder. For my part, it is doubtful that left to my own desires I would have chosen the path that ultimately brought me to a new land. Did I have a choice in my life? Perhaps — if I had been made of stronger stuff. But because the plot of my life was developed when I was too young to know better and to extract myself from it, I would venture to say no, because father, and later my sisters, who carried on after his death as though they were executors of his iron will, directed my fate. Destiny, Kismet, as Lord Nelson might have said, has left me now, still a youngish man, in fragile health, as a contemptible failure in the judgmental eyes of many of my peers. I stand under the shadow of financial ruin and find myself begging bureaucrats and ungrateful politicians for a meagre pension. Moneyless and with few prospects, and sadly, luckless in love. Perhaps if father had been more understanding and flexible my life would not be the shambles that it now appears to be.

But I should not complain too much. Life has a way of throwing up opportunities and now I feel that I might be on the threshold of a new promising livelihood. Even then, it has been father's reputation that has brought about this new chance. Can I ever escape from The Inimitable?

I am getting ahead of myself. As my story unfolds, I leave it to you to judge if my complaints are justified.

# Chapter 2

No one could ever have accused Francis Jeffrey Dickens of good timing in his itinerant life. Frank's birth in January 1844 had come at a difficult time for his famous father. Charles felt beset by financial worries. Sales of the latest Dickens epic, *Martin Chuzzlewit*, had not met expectations. *A Christmas Carol*, published just before Frank arrived, had been a great popular success but the profits were lower than anticipated, partly because of Charles's prideful insistence upon sparing no expense in its publication. Furthermore, pirate publishers and stage producers had cashed in on the Christmas tale, creating their own variations of the story. Charles, ever mindful of his copyright, had spent seven hundred pounds sterling on legal fees to fight off the interlopers. Normally restless and energetic, Charles had then entered a period of sterile depression in his writing and he felt pecuniary pressures were closing on him. Even before the nadir of his literary output, there were signs that the wellsprings of inspiration were running low. While working on his Christmas classic, the author would unexpectedly burst into tears, and then laugh hysterically. His bizarre behaviour alarmed his family and longtime friends like John Forster feared for his sanity.

For the first time since Charles had burst upon the English literary scene as a writer adored by lord and commoner alike, he lived in fear of bankruptcy. The author's personal success and fame were regarded by his kin as the pot of gold at the end of the rainbow. Charles's father John had continued a lifetime of profligate spending, trying to cash in on his son's growing reputation and leaving Charles to pay his mounting debts. Now the new baby Francis entered the family drama, the fifth child of Charles and his wife Catherine Hogarth. Another hungry mouth had to be fed and a young body clothed. Each childbirth left Catherine increasingly despondent and each time it took longer for her to recover her spirits. Charles, searching in his mind for scapegoats, began to think of Kate's fecundity, lethargy, intellectual torpor and post-natal depressions as hindrances to both his work and economic stability.

So Charles regarded his expanding family with mixed feelings. He was sufficiently proud of the new arrival that the baby was named for Sir Francis Jeffrey, a prominent Scottish literary critic and judge who profoundly admired Charles's work. His lordship would be the baby's godfather. But Charles also expressed something akin to disdain about the child to his friends.

"Kate is all right again, and so they tell me is the Baby. But I decline (on principle) to look at the latter object," he wrote to a friend who inquired after the health of the mother and infant.

The author did repair to one of his favourite hostels, the Star and Garter in Richmond, with a trio of literary cronies to drink to the health of the newcomer. Whether it was to escape his sorrows, or celebrate the occasion, was left unclear in the minds of his companions.

Not long after Frank's birth, his father decided he and the family needed a change of scene. He packed them off to the continent, where they settled in Genoa for several months. The family could live in Italy cheaper than in England, Charles thought, and some of the financial clouds that overshadowed his creativity might dissipate under the Italian sun. Catherine knew that Charles, as ever, would set a furious pace in Europe, and complained mildly that it was too soon after Frank's birth for her to be travelling abroad, but in the end, of course, Charles' will prevailed.

America had been ruled out by Charles as a destination. After his visit two years previous with Catherine, Charles had grumbled the Americans were "coarse and mercenary" and he was angry at their reluctance to pay royalties on his works even though his writings proved as popular across the Atlantic as at home. Upper Canada he liked for its liveliness and being a "haven of Britishness in the maelstrom of Yankeedoodledom" but Charles had been irked by the rabid Toryism he encountered among the elite in the capital of Toronto. These crass provincials emulated the despicable class prejudices that were irritating enough to him in the Old Country.

At first the plan was to leave new-born Frank behind with Granny Hogarth while the rest went to the continent. But then plans changed and the new babe was brought along. Charles now seemed to look more fondly upon the infant. While the family was in Genoa, Charles wrote *The Chimes*, which included the plump storekeeper Mrs. Chickenstalker. Charles, who invented nicknames for all his children, chuckled when he decided that would be a fitting nickname for his little toddler, who seemed to follow the local domesticated creatures intently. When Frank was fourteen months old, Dickens wrote that the youngster was "a prodigious blade, and more full of queer tricks than any of his predecessors had been at his time of life. He is decidedly a success — a perpetual grin is on his face."

Although as an author Charles Dickens peopled his works with likeable children, his own brood was never sure which persona would appear to them. Would he be the loving funny father who delighted in little pranks, plays and demonstrations, and made sure all his children had parts to play in his specially written dramas? Or would Charles appear as the stern, demanding and disapproving patriarchal ogre, who complained sharply about the noise the children made while he was writing, or his boys' shortcomings at school or at work, or snapped peevishly at their mild-mannered mother?

The sons were sent away from home — even out of the country — to attend boarding schools, and young Francis was no exception. Charles had decided early on that Frank was the cleverest lad and therefore, not surprisingly, the most like himself. Charles's initial fondness for his third son soon waned, however. Frank continually failed to meet his father's exacting standards for punctuality and tidiness. A robust child at birth, Frank dismayed his father by being smaller in stature than expected, and he developed a stammer. At age nine, Frank was sent with his younger brother Alfred to attend a school run by two English clergymen in Boulogne, France. They were joined later by brother Sydney. The school provided lessons in French, fencing, dancing and German in addition to the usual subjects, but the boys found it uninspiring and their learning suffered. Perhaps the fact that they were only home on summer vacations and usually — though not always — at Christmas dampened their enthusiasm.

Later in life, Frank would reflect on why his father went to such pains to ship his sons off. True, it was common practice for the aspiring middle class, of which the Dickens family was definitely a part, and it could be justified as an enhancement of the children's future prospects to have a foreign education, including the opportunity to learn other languages. But Charles seemed to find it difficult to show his love for his sons. While he was concerned with their well-being, perhaps he did not have the energy, because of his many other pursuits, to get close to them. Certainly, Frank's knowledge of French was indeed to benefit him in his later career. But Frank would rather have spent more time with his mother and father, from whom he felt increasingly estranged.

The children were all home at Tavistock House in London in the early 1850s, however, when Charles arrived at their home roaring with triumph. He was carrying some wrapped books under his arm.

"Now there are two published authors in the house!" he declared with delight.

The puzzled children gathered around as Charles tore the wrappings from the volumes. He held up a copy.

"You see, your mother's cookbook!" Catherine, rarely demonstrative, quietly beamed with pleasure behind him. *"What Shall We Have for Dinner?"*

Young Katey, the younger daughter and always the most acute and observant, frowned.

"But Papa! It says: By Lady Maria Clutterbuck."

"Ah, little Lucifer Box," Charles replied with a smile, using Katey's family nickname. "My little bright star, always illuminating those things that others do not see. What we must consider, dear Katey, is whether ladies of social standing will consider purchasing a book written by Mrs. Catherine Hogarth Dickens. Even the Dickens name, brilliant as it is, might be insufficient to tempt them to the expense. No, ascribing it to a 'Lady' gives the book a shine, a bit of polish that it would otherwise lack. And since there is, in fact, no Lady Clutterbuck, it will leave a mystery for the higher classes to gossip about — which of their number is the anonymous authoress. The puzzle will tempt others to peer into its pages seeking out clues to the writer. But Mama, and we, too, will know the truth, won't we?" He winked at the children.

Frank and the other Dickens children found the Christmas and New Year's respites and the summer vacations from school always delightful. Especially around Christmas, Charles would break from his writing and create little skits to be performed by the children. Charles in those weeks was frisky as a young pup, generous, forgiving and hospitable, as joyful as the redeemed Scrooge after the visits from the ghosts. Prominent visitors always seemed to be spending time at the Dickens home. William Makepeace Thackeray, Alfred Tennyson and Mark Lemon, the editor of Punch, paid their respects. The guest the children were most excited to see was Hans Christian Andersen, anticipating to be regaled by his children's tales. One summer, Andersen stayed two weeks at the Dickens home. Unfortunately, Andersen's English was incomprehensible. Most of the time the family did not know if he was speaking English or Danish. The confusion led the gleeful children to invent a mixed English-Danish non-speak, which invariably resulted in gales of laughter as the listeners attempted to translate what was being said.

When Frank was thirteen, the entire family underwent a crisis that left a lasting imprint on his own life.

Charles, who for years had divulged to select friends discontent with his marriage, was smitten by a young actress, Ellen Ternan. Charles had first met Ellen in Manchester in the company of her mother and two sisters when he and all the Ternan women had acted in a production of The Frozen Deep, a play by his friend Wilkie Collins.

This development set off a chain of events that would eventually result in divorce from Catherine. To justify his new relationship with Ellen, Charles had begun to find reasons to avoid his wife and he undermined her among the children. She was an unfit mother, she suffered from mental incapacity, she was lethargic and dull, he complained.

"Poor Catherine and I are not made for each other, and there is no help for it," he had written to John Forster in 1856. "It is not only that she makes me uneasy and unhappy, but that I make her so, too — and much more so."

Charles had decided in his own mind that Catherine was to blame for the slothfulness and profligacy displayed by the lads. He was almost manic in his energy, while Catherine was slow, lacked self-reliance and gumption. She had failed to induce in the boys a spirit of independence, because of her own indolent nature, Charles decided. Young Frank was singled out by Charles as the prime case of the negative influences of Catherine on her children. The lad had begun to sleepwalk and a mild hesitation in his speech developed into a severe stammer, especially noticeable when he spoke to his father and other persons of strong character, or when he felt under stress. Charles used this unsettling change in Frank as simply another excuse to berate Catherine, accusing her of hiding his son's disability from him. To Charles, Frank seemed frail, anxious and nervous. A waverer, indecisive, not like him at all. "The boy stammers so horribly as to be an afflicted spirit," Charles grumbled. All this disturbed the demanding father immensely, especially so when friends would mention how much Frank resembled his sire, in physical appearance, gestures and mannerisms. Charles resented Frank's incapacity.

In an attempt to cure Frank's stammer, he locked himself up with the boy for hours and compelled him to read Shakespeare aloud. When the boy failed, he was berated for not trying hard enough.

In a letter to his friend Angela Burdett-Coutts confiding his unhappiness with his marriage, Charles complained that Catherine had never cared for the children. "If I stood before you at this moment and told you what difficulty we have to get Frank, for instance, to go near his mother, or keep near his mother, you would stand amazed," he wrote.

Then Charles, without warning, had moved from their shared bedroom at Gad's Hill Place to an adjoining room in October 1857. To prevent Catherine from entering his quarters, he had the door between the rooms sealed up. For some time now, Charles had spent much of his time away from home, acting in plays and giving readings.

Early in the new year, a package had arrived at Gad's Hill. Catherine, supposing it to be a gift from Charles, opened it. There was a bracelet and a card inside. It began: "Dearest Ellen...Affectionately, Charles." Those were the only words that mattered to Catherine.

Catherine, face contorted in grief, howled and sobbed. Red-haired Katey heard the commotion.

"What is it, mother?" Catherine showed her daughter the card. Fierce and hot-tempered, Kate resolved to confront her father.

"No, child," said Catherine. "This is for me to do."

When Catherine insisted on speaking to Charles about the bracelet, he snarled.

"It's simply a gift for an actress I have worked with," Charles said. "It means nothing. It was delivered here by mistake. You must take the bracelet to Ellen. She lives with her mother. You must talk to them, to prove that you trust me."

Catherine left the room, weeping. She would not resist but would do what Charles asked. Kate wanted to know what her father had said.

"No, Mama," Kate said, outraged. "You shall not go. It is sheer lunacy. What has got into father? Why, this…this girl is younger than I am!"

But Catherine did go, and then she packed up and left the house.

Young Kate was in a fury. The other Dickens children were mystified and devastated in turn. The upheaval in the household shook all of them to the core. Father was remote and bitter, frequently leaving them in the care of Aunt Georgina, Catherine's sister, as he raced about the country and beyond, to the continent, undertaking a gruelling pace of acting in plays and doing readings of his works. His temper was short with the children and he sought to justify his separation, then divorce, from Catherine with public diatribes that confounded his friends and turned some of them against him.

Frank was dismayed and could not understand why his father was treating his beloved mother so reprehensibly.

"F-f-father," he stammered. "What has come between you and mother? Why can't you stay married?"

"This is none of your business, boy. It's my affair. In truth, your mother is an incompetent parent. She hid your stammering and your poor health from me."

Frank was heart-broken. Challenging his father was a fearsome prospect at the best of times. Only Kate had ever dared. So, he walked away, shaken, without further protest, large tears rolling down his cheeks. He had felt very close to his mother, and Charles had now made him feel responsible for the separation. He became a sad, introverted youth, blaming himself, stunned by the ferocity of his father and the apparent rapidity of the family breakdown. How had mother hidden his disability from Charles, he wondered? What had he done to cause the breach between his parents? His father had seen him as often as he saw the other children. How could he not notice the affliction?

Charles met with much public criticism. Thackeray, once a frequent guest with his daughters Anny and Minny at the Dickens home, sent Catherine a message of support. When Charles attacked Thackeray in print, Charles Jr. risked his father's wrath and boldly defended Thackeray. Mark Lemon, the editor of Punch and a longtime Dickens friend, was asked to be a trustee for Catherine in the divorce discussions. When he agreed, Charles cut off that connection. The family and friendships were in disarray, split by arguments that Charles seemed bizarrely determined to bring to the attention of the public, as though the family drama was one of his fictional creations. Charles printed his own letters in his magazine to justify his actions, and wrote to newspapers in New York, alleging that Catherine had abdicated her duties as a mother. Home life was chaos. Charles dashed madly about the house, throwing papers and books around, shouting at the children, ordering the boys to bring boxes of his precious correspondence from the house so that they could be burned.

Daughter Kate bore the brunt of his criticism at home. Arguments raged constantly between Kate and Charles, while the other children cowered in fear in the corners, or shrank into hiding places to avoid the maelstrom. Frank found himself miserable most of the time, when he was home keeping to his room, trying to concentrate on his studies, but weeping at the most unexpected times. When he spoke, his stammering was worse. Only the fact that the boys were often away at school preserved them from greater turmoil.

"You don't give a damn what happens to us, do you?" Kate screeched at her father. "You are a selfish brute. Well, I'm not staying here longer than I can help it. Charley Collins and I are getting married."

That stopped Charles mid-rant. He gasped for breath, unbelieving. His beloved daughter, taking up with the ne'er-do-well brother of Wilkie Collins? He could not have it. Charles Collins was a mediocre painter whose artistic talents were widely disparaged. He had no prospects and was not a suitable match for a Dickens girl!

"You will not marry that man," he roared, when he stopped sputtering and stamping his feet and regained some coherence in his speech. "Charley Collins is an ignoramus, a fool, a talentless oaf who will take you nowhere in life. Besides, he prefers the...uh, *company* of men to women, if you take my meaning. I will never permit a daughter of mine to enter such a disgraceful union."

"How dare you talk to me of disgraceful unions," Kate screamed back. "Look to your own connections. Do you realize that I am older than your precious Ellen? I will marry Charley, no matter what you say. He is a sweet man, considerate and is steady in his work. He may not possess your genius but you are no example for him as a husband. If you have not gone mad, then you are as contemptible a man as has ever walked the roads of England."

With that, she stormed from the room and left Gad's Hill Place. Frank, who had overheard the confrontation, clung to her arm, begging her not to go, afraid that now there would be no one in the house who would dare stand up to their father. And so it was. With Kate out of the house, any outspoken opposition to Charles at home was over. Only Catherine's sister, Aunt Georgina, and occasionally sister Mamie, would moderate Charles's temper. The other children feared the frenzy of their father's activity, his furious moods and rages. Over time, they came to accept the breakup of their parents' marriage, though they often took the opportunity to visit Catherine. Charles made no objection to the continuing connections between Catherine and her children but he never saw his wife again.

Frank came to fear his father's wrath more than ever, however, chiefly because he was so unpredictable. And Charles blamed himself forever for driving his beloved young Katey from the house and into what he always believed to be an unsuitable marriage.

Charles and Catherine finally had legally separated in 1858, and Frank was packed off again to school in Hamburg, where he was to learn languages and prepare for what was expected to be a career in medicine. But Frank was weighed down by depression and his confidence had ebbed. His stammering was worse than ever and he had periodic episodes when his hearing was impaired.

Young Frank's studies did not go well, and finally in despair he wrote his father.

"Dear Papa: I write to tell you that I have given up all thoughts of being a doctor. My conviction that I shall never get over my stammering is the cause; all professions are barred against me. The only thing I should like to be is a gentleman-farmer, either at the Cape, in Canada or Australia. With my passage paid, 15 pounds, a horse and a rifle, I could go two or three hundred miles up country, sow grain, hay, raise cattle and in time be very comfortable."

Charles alternately raged and roared with laughter at the letter. So, this is the thanks I get from a boy whose stammering I spent countless hours trying to cure! And Frank a farmer? The entire notion was preposterous! And what knowledge would he bring to those far-off lands that would give any confidence of success? He let a friend know what he thought of Frank's proposition.

"I perceived that the first consequence of the fifteen pounds that he would be robbed of it — of the horse, that it would throw him — and of the rifle that it would blow his head off," Charles wrote. "Which probabilities I took the liberty of mentioning, as being against the scheme."

Frank sobbed when he heard his father's response. "How could father be so cruel?" he wailed. His reputation, with his father at least, had plunged from being the most astute of the seven Dickens boys to the least self-reliant.

Instead of accepting Frank's desperate appeal, Charles thought about bringing the youth into his own literary activities. He would groom Frank for an important role in his new enterprise, the weekly journal *All the Year Round*. This two-penny magazine would carry, among other works, instalments of Charles's new work, *A Tale of Two Cities*. By the time Frank was sixteen, his father decided he was capable of taking on an office job.

At first, Charles was delighted at Frank's progress. "He has a natural literary taste and capacity, if I'm not mistaken," Charles told friends. "I believe young Frank enjoys his endeavours and will do well in this work."

His confidence in the young man was soon shaken, however. Frank's abilities failed to progress and he proved a flop at office work.

His money-handling mistakes meant lost revenues for the magazine, his inefficiency resulted in lost subscriptions and his lethargy resulted in work being rushed at the last minute. The boy's untidiness offended Charles as well; the father had always had a penchant for order in his work and could not tolerate sloppiness. "I just don't understand you, boy," Charles thundered at Frank one day after the lad admitted to another workplace error. Charles considered stopping Frank's allowance when he began to pile up debts reminiscent of other Dickens kin. The lad became a negative yardstick by which the other boys were measured. When Charles mentioned he was disturbed by son Edward's extraordinary "want of application and continuity of purpose", he added that it would have come as a surprise had he not witnessed it before in Frank.

Charles encouraged Francis to take another road. He could write the British Foreign Office examinations to try to obtain a post in the imperial offices. Frank, after all, had some knowledge of languages and had expressed an interest in living abroad. Once again, however, Frank failed. His results in the tests were poor. Charles, now desperate to put this errant child on a path to self-sufficiency, looked to the military. Walter, the second of his sons, had gone to India to serve with the East India Company and then the 42nd Highland Regiment. Although Walter had displayed the inherited Dickens tendency of overspending and falling into debt, he nonetheless had earned praise as a military man, becoming a lieutenant before the age of eighteen. Now Frank thought of India as a way of escape and asked Charles about the possibility of joining the Bengal Mounted Police. The author approached friends and acquaintances in hopes of finding Frank a position.

# Chapter 3

*There were occasions when I felt closer to my father. One holiday he took Alfred and I rowing on the Medway and laughed and teased us mercilessly as he urged us on with our oars. Again, on Christmas Eves in London, he would take us to a favourite toy shop in Holborn and watch with a smile as the clerk showed us how to operate the workings of the playthings. At these times he was almost like a child himself and examined the objects so that one would think he was purchasing them for himself.*

*In my late youth. Father enlisted me in a project which made me feel for the first time that he considered me an equal.*

*At the end of October 1860, in the neighbourhood of Gad's Hill, there had been frequent reports of a ghost. Local folk walking in the autumn darkness near Larkin's monument had been unnerved by a low, rasping wail from local fields and the nearby cemetery that sounded to them like the spirits of the damned. Only fleeting glimpses of a white floating spectre were made, but these were enough to assure passersby that a tormented phantom had established itself in the area. Who did this anguished lost soul represent? locals wondered. A highwayman hanged by the roadside two centuries before? A victim of religious persecution in the Reformation? An ancient Christian* convert martyred by Roman soldiers? A woman slain by a jealous husband? The speculation mounted and news of the haunting spread across rural Kent.

By then, the worst of our family tensions had dissipated and Father was once again in better humour. When the story of the ghost reached his ears, he was determined to solve the mystery. He encouraged me, now sixteen, and my eight-year-old brother Edward — nicknamed Plorn — to join him in the hunt for this wandering spectre.

"Come, Chickenstalker," he said after tea one evening. "Tonight we will go stalking ghosts. Let us lay this phantom to rest, or die trying." He chuckled.

I regarded him with caution and was relieved to see that he meant the last remark humorously.

"Do you believe in ghosts, father?" I asked.

"Why, of course, Frank," said Papa, peering over his spectacles with amusement. "I've written about them, haven't I? Do they not appear vivid and alive?"

He looked at young Edward, seated beside Andrew Gordon, a companion he had invited to tea. He spoke in a solemn tone.

"And what of you, Plorn? Do you feel sufficiently like a man to join us in this most worthy endeavour?"

Young Plorn gulped. He looked at his friend, who bent low to the table, trying to avoid being seen.

"Can a ghost kill, Papa?" the timid Edward asked.

Father stroked his beard, leaving an impression of deep thought.

"I have encountered many ghosts in my lifetime, Plorn, and I can honestly say that none have ever threatened my life. To be sure, they can be a frightening lot, especially when they rattle their unworldly chains and create quite an unnatural fuss. But never have they caused me to fear death. Some ghostly maidens who have perished from unrequited love, in fact, are downright pleasant to see, if you see beyond their tattered shrouds and doleful expressions. I have heard of men going mad in the presence of spectres, of course, but those poor devils already have guilt on their conscience, and young innocents like yourselves would never bear such burdens, would you? Ah, yes, Plorn, you must join us."

He looked at the boy beside his son, who had ducked below the table's edge. "And you come too, young Master Andrew. The rewards of finding a living — I should say, an 'existing' — ghost far outweigh the perils."

He smiled with satisfaction. I sat without comment, wondering what Pa was up to, but my eyes — I am sure — darted from my father to the faces of the younger lads, and back. Young Edward and his friend looked at each other with mixed feelings of fear and excitement.

Father rose from the table and went to the back of the house to speak to the housekeeper, Mrs. Cornelius. He returned wearing a heavy coat, a tweed cap, leather boots and carrying a loaded shotgun.

"Dress warmly, lads," he ordered. "It will be chilly tonight. If you are shivering, I want it to be from honest fright rather than from the mundane autumn cold."

"Will a shotgun be of any use against a disembodied spirit, father?" I asked, pulling on my coat.

"Hmmm," Pa appeared to reconsider. "Likely not. I've never heard of a ghost being killed by gunfire. No unearthly corpses have ever been displayed to my recollection. But we'll carry it anyway in case we need to sound alarm or call for help."

He gave me a kitchen carving knife and told me to sharpen four long spear-like sticks for myself and the other boys.

"Fat lot of good pointed sticks will do," I mumbled, "if a shotgun is of no use."

Our group of phantom hunters set off under a rising October moon which occasionally hid behind drifting clouds. We first went to the location of the last reported sighting of the ghost. It was in a farmer's field, next to the cemetery. We crept along a hedgerow without a word spoken, eyes moving side to side, at any moment anticipating a horrifying apparition. Father, energized by the hunt, led the way, climbing over fences and stiles, pushing through hedges and splashing through puddles left by the previous day's rain.

The rest of us, looking out for a spectral ambuscade, raced to keep up. I helped the smaller ones over the difficult obstacles. I felt foolish carrying a pointed stick but I was not going to spoil the party and decided to humour

Father, who evidently thought his hunting companions should carry some kind of weaponry, ineffective though it might be.

We had searched the fields and hedgerows for about an hour, when from the heavy shadows cast by the moon's glow there came a wheezing superhuman noise. Something low to the ground, white, thrashed through the underbrush. I tried to train my eyes to spot movement in the shadows when a cloud passed over the moon. I was following my father by about ten paces and the two young lads were right at my back.

"Did you hear that, Pa?" I whispered. Although I was a skeptic, my heart beat faster.

"I did," said Papa, who crept closer to the sound for a better look.

The wraith, emitting ghastly wails, was lumbering through the bushes, coming straight toward us. Plorn tried to stifle a scream, then fell to the damp earth, cowering, afraid to raise his head to look at the approaching ghost. His little companion turned tail and ran off in the opposite direction as fast as his young legs could carry him, stumbling over stumps, branches from the bushes whipping his face as he raced away, imagining that every stick that clutched at his clothing was the grasping claw of an evil demon. I must confess, that though I had scoffed at the notion of ghosts, much to my surprise I began waving my pointed stick to ward off the unexpected. My skepticism was being put to the test as the wailing and wheezing phantom drew near.

I noticed that Papa had levelled the shotgun and was ready to fire. Now I saw that he had begun to shake. From fright, I supposed. This astonished and unnerved me. I had never before seen Father afraid of anything. Overcoming my own growing fear, I gallantly rushed to his side to help fend off the supernatural being.

Once there, I realized that Father was not trembling with fear but shaking with laughter.

"There's your terrifying apparition, that has had the entire county in an uproar," he said, as tears rolled down his cheeks. He roared aloud now, relishing the moment. Plorn raised his head, wondering if Father had been driven insane by the horrible sight. He sunk low to the ground again and covered his ears. He had no desire to see or hear his now-demented father.

As the moon reappeared from behind the clouds, I saw that the white shape was no ghost at all, but a lone sheep that stood breathless and wheezing in the shadows.

"Poor old sheep," Papa said. "Too old for meat, too scabby and matted for wool, too asthmatic to keep up with its fellows. It might as well be a ghost."

As Father and I laughed heartily, Plorn lifted his head again to discover the source of the merriment. Then, he bravely stood up and moved up beside me, his eyes wide as he gazed upon the noisy sheep. Little Andrew was nowhere to be seen.

"Chickenstalker, stay here with Plorn, and guard this poor animal," said Papa. "I'll look about to see if this is the only spectre we'll encounter this night."

No other beings, earth-bound or supernatural were discovered. Father thumped me on the back and took Plorn by the hand as we three headed back to the house. There we found little Andrew cowering by the front entrance.

"Good work, Chickenstalker," Father laughed. "Perhaps you have a talent for police work."

Later, as he told the tale to the rest of the family at Gad's Hill Place, Papa magnanimously poured me a large portion of rum and water to celebrate the successful resolution of the ghostly mystery. I felt for the first time that he had accepted me as a man.

# Chapter 4

"Come in, Chickenstalker." Charles Dickens beamed at Frank as the nineteen-year-old stood at his father's office door. "Sit down. I have wonderful news to impart."

Frank entered, warily. "Yes, father."

Charles finished writing a note, then put the paper aside and turned to his son.

"Through the good offices of a friend, I have secured you a position with the Bengal Mounted Police. It is an attractive opportunity that will offer you a good living in future."

Frank stared wide-eyed at his father. Though he had mentioned the idea, he had not expected it to be pursued by his busy father. He began to wonder if he had the ability to be a policeman in a foreign land.

Charles noted the fear of the unknown in Frank's eyes and hastened to build his argument.

"Your brother Walter is there, and has now spent six years in India, so you will have company. He has done well in military service, and I have no doubt that you will fare likewise. It will be a great comfort to have Wally close to you."

"B-b-but, Pa," Frank tried desperately to keep his stammer under control. "I h-h-have no talent for police work…"

Annoyed, Charles interrupted. "No more than you have talent for office work?" Sarcasm dripped from his lips. "I'll hear no more. Our friends have gone to great lengths to secure a posting for you. You will be trained as a policeman. Some instruction in military discipline will be good for you. You will return to England a better, more confident young man ready to tackle whatever life throws at you."

Frank stopped his futile protest. All he could do would be to enrage his father further.

"I have booked passage for you from Portsmouth to Calcutta. It departs in November. I will give you a small living allowance to maintain yourself until you are established in Bengal. I trust you will use it wisely, unlike some of your spendthrift brothers. Even Wally, who has done us proud, overspends his money and I have to cover his debts. Enough, now, you may go."

Frank, bewildered, turned to the door.

"What?" exclaimed Charles. "Not a word of thanks?"

The ship from Portsmouth anchored in the deep channel of the Hooghly River off Calcutta in early January 1864, carrying passengers from the dreary English winter into the steamy tropics of Bengal. Exotic odours drifted across the waters from the city and boatloads of peddlers, eager to sell fruits and vegetables and more enticing wares to the new arrivals, were soon heading toward the ship. Along the riverbank small groups of half-naked bathers washed themselves in the murky water. Frank, not quite twenty, stood excited, and more than a little anxious, on the deck. He squinted in the morning sun toward the sprawling city where his new career would begin.

Frank had left his family behind before Christmas and the long voyage had taken weeks, sweeping down the west coast of Africa, around the windy Cape of Good Hope and northeastward across the Indian Ocean. The ship had passed close enough to the shores of Ceylon that travellers could smell the spicy odours from fragrant trees. Charles had paid 117 pounds to the Peninsular and Oriental line to cover Frank's fare and puffed up the anticipation in his son's anxious mind by creating a scenario of the joyful reunion Frank would have with Walter on the distant shores of India. The young man regretted leaving his family at that time of year but he knew his father's patience with him was nearly exhausted and so made no further objection to his time of departure. In an introspective frame of mind, young Dickens smiled at the probable antics of his father at Yuletide. This time, Granny Dickens would not be there — she had died in the autumn — but Charles would still insist that the traditional plays be put on by his children for visiting family and friends. Christmas dinner for Frank, however, had been a shipboard banquet with the captain and selected passengers. The vessel's master, learning that the young traveller was a son of the famous Dickens, had invited Frank to his table.

Frank was urged by the diners to give a reading of his father's Christmas works. At first, he declined. It was the first time he had ever been asked to read before such a large audience of adults. There would be high expectations for his performance. He was a shy youth and he fretted that his stammering would take over and turn his public dramatic debut into an embarrassing spectacle that would be painful to himself and a burden to listeners. Worse, he feared not being worthy of Charles' brilliance. Not until a Mr. Williams, seated nearby, enticed Frank into sampling some brandy, did he build the courage to face the challenge. To his own surprise, the liquor settled his nerves and his efforts earned him delighted applause.

Despite being the focus of attention and the new-found respect from his fellow voyagers, Frank could not help but feel he had been banished at the best time of year for the Dickens family. He consoled himself with the thought that soon he would be with Wally for his birthday.

Walter Landor Dickens was only three years older than Frank, but the young brothers had not seen each other for years. Wally had gone to India shortly after the quashing of the Sepoy Mutiny of 1857 to take up a post with the East India Company, an opportunity secured for him by Charles's aristocratic friend, Angela Burdett-Coutts. With fighting ended, the Colonial Secretary had decided that the best way to ensure stability in the sub-continent was to increase the representation of British-born troops in the army. The six-to-one ratio of Indians to British that had held under the rule of the company before the mutiny was changed to two-to-one now that the British government was taking full charge of the country. The result was a strong demand for recruits from Britain. Serving with the 42nd Highland Regiment, Walter had been posted to the hills of Bengal, north of Calcutta. Charles was proud of Walter, who had readily taken to the military life and seemed destined to move even higher in the commissioned officers' ranks. He was even prepared to overlook the fact that Wally, like most of the other Dickens males, had a baffling habit of piling up debt. Charles, to preserve Walter's reputation and office, had forwarded money to his second son to cover mounting bills, one hundred fifteen pounds in 1861 alone.

Wally's successful career, and the news that India's police and military establishments were being reorganized in the aftermath of the Mutiny, had prompted Charles to encourage Frank into service in India. Once Charles had decided the destiny of his misfit son, Frank was put through a hectic regime of horsemanship, taught the rules of military etiquette, and a variety of other activities that the author deemed to be suitable pursuits for an officer. Suddenly, a parade of generals, admirals and senior policemen descended upon the Dickens home for dinners and receptions. India was a place where a British soldier of even limited means could live a luxurious life, waited upon by servants, where the cost of living was cheap, past failures easily forgotten and where a man with some education could pass as a monied member of the gentry. And Bengal was the heart of British power in India.

The reorganization of British administration also included the replacement of the system of district magistrates, often absentee, apathetic or corrupt, by police superintendents. Young Frank was expected to report to one of these officers by mid-February. He would start on probation as an assistant to a district superintendent, third class. There would be a long learning process ahead in India before the tenderfoot would be assigned to take on significant duties. The jump from a proper London business office to a posting as a police officer was enormous in a country where the customs were so much at odds with those in England. And each time Frank believed he was beginning to understand his role, he would find that the cultural chasm gaped wider than he anticipated.

Eyes gleaming, Frank lined up for the first launch to be taken ashore. He had inquired of Mr. Williams, whose home was Calcutta, where he might find the headquarters of the 42nd regiment. His fellow traveller sized up the earnest Frank, decided the naïve lad would be overwhelmed by the foreign experience of the streets, and offered to take him there.

Williams swept his hand along the Calcutta waterfront.

"This river is a branch of the mighty Ganges, sacred to the Hindus," he said. "The Ganges is at once the salvation and the curse of Bengal. Salvation because the silt it carries replenishes the soil for agriculture; a curse because its floods and the monsoons that roar in from the Bay of Bengal often lead to destruction, famine and death. You will witness its moods, if you stay long enough, I warrant."

"It is so hot," Dickens exclaimed. "How can you bear this?"

"Hot?" Williams chuckled. "My dear young Dickens, you truly are a griffin, aren't you? This is the wintry season in Calcutta. In two months, the day time temperatures will be over a hundred degrees, with no relief. You have yet to experience 'hot'."

"What's a griffin?"

"It's the term they use here for a newly arrived Englishman," said Williams. "Well, you have a lot to learn. A word of advice: Stay out of the sun at mid-day. The mornings and evenings are pleasant enough — well, save for the plagues of voracious mosquitoes at sunrise and sunset — but you must avoid the heat of the day. At least until you learn what hot is."

On the quayside, two Indian servants clad in turbans, white cotton trousers and jackets gathered the bags of Williams and Dickens and put them in a black horse-drawn carriage with a shade that hung over the passenger's seat. Frank was glancing about, eyes beaming with curiosity, taking in all the sights, sounds and smells of the bustling harbour. Soon, he was besieged by a clutch of young boys, begging for money, food or whatever else they could get. Frank had seen beggar children like this in London, running along beside respectable gentlemen with their hands out for a farthing, but the English counterparts were easily dismissed. These supplicants were more numerous and persistent, hanging and pulling on his clothes and holding their hands right in the face of their target. Frank appeared beyond his depth when he was rescued by one of the Hindu servants who rushed over with a buggy whip and waved the beggars away sharply.

The carriage drove through the streets, crowded with stalls, shoppers and merchants selling rice and lentils, exotic fruits and vegetables, clothing, glassware, clay pots and metal goods. Frank was especially taken by a thin man in a white loincloth, with twin baskets swinging from each end of a bamboo pole. The baskets contain fragile glass bottles filled with water, and the bearer wore a turban with brightly coloured flags. He shouted to gain attention from potential customers, Frank marvelling that such a deep powerful voice could emerge from such an emaciated old man.

"Holy water from the Ganges," Williams said, noticing how the young man swung his head to follow the water carrier with curious eyes. "At least that is what the seller will tell you. And most Hindus will believe him. I am more skeptical."

Frank was aware as they rode along that the carriage was being watched closely. There was curiosity in the eyes of the watchers. But he sensed another emotion he had not felt before. It was not until he looked closely into the eyes of a young man, bent over under a heavy bale of cotton that he realized that it was hatred. Then he shuddered, remembering the scene from *A Christmas Carol*, when the Spirit of Christmas Present had showed Scrooge the two beggar children. Ignorance and Want, Frank recalled. "Beware them both!"

His thoughts were interrupted when a scrawny, half-naked man in his mid-twenties wearing a turban leaped onto the running board on Frank's side and stretched out his open palm, appealing for money.

Williams, without a moment's hesitation, put his foot into the man's chest and shoved hard.

"Down, damn you," Williams cursed, as the carriage rolled on, leaving the beggar sprawling in the dust by the roadside.

"You'll learn in time to deal with these people," Williams growled. "You have to watch them. They'd just as soon slit your throat for a few rupees as give you the time of day."

Frank felt a mix of bewilderment and unease.

"You'll need a valet," Williams said. "Every young gentlemen officer needs someone to look after their needs. Please do me the honour of finding one for you. There are many fine, experienced Hindu men who could do the job for you, but they rejoice in seizing on newly arrived British lads thinking to mould them into Indian ways. There's something to be said for learning the ways of the country, I'll grant, but you must take care not to be youthful prey for the sly old tiger. Above all, you want someone you can trust at all times, even with your life. I can provide you some possibilities.

"Now I will tell you something you must always remember," he continued. "We are here in India on sufferance. The peoples of the sub-continent are accustomed to being under the thumb of conquerors — Greeks, Persians, Moguls, Portuguese, French, British — we come and go. Do not deceive yourself. The Hindus, Mussulmans, Parsis and Sikhs neither like us, nor admire us. They will flatter you for your power and your knowledge, but it is always on the surface, and their moods can change as soon as you show yourself to be vulnerable. And who is to say they are wrong? We might do the same if we were under their thumb. We have the upper hand now. In time, that will come to an end, of that I am certain, and so are their wiser men. So, because of their history and divisions we will be tolerated unless our oppression of them becomes too severe. The people of lower caste fear those who are of higher caste as much as they fear their conquerors. Indeed, we British are like a caste in our own right. The people of the lower orders are not more poorly treated by us than they are by their own higher castes and landlords. And we will take advantage of their caste divisions, and their many religious and tribal differences, and build practical alliances with willing partners, until some far-seeing leader can convince the Hindus, followers of Mohammed, Sikhs, Brahmins and untouchables, the whole damned lot, to put aside those things that divide one from another."

"But what of our military might? Can't we control the country and put down rebellion as it rises?"

"Ha," Williams snorted. "India was almost torn from the empire in the recent mutiny by ragged and untutored common foot soldiers. I myself lost a son and scores of friends. How long do you suppose our tens of thousands spread thinly across the country, and situated chiefly in the cities, could withstand the rebellion of tens of millions if they ever came to be of one mind?"

At the gate to the regimental headquarters, an enormous turbaned guard, standing well over six foot, scanned the two Englishmen in the carriage and then let them pass into a broad, stone-cobbled courtyard. Kilted soldiers shouldering guns were striding in pairs across the plaza. The carriage came to a halt and Williams said something in Bengali to the driver, who nodded impassively.

"I will wait inside the lobby for you," Williams said. "I can help you acquire proper lodging and food for the night. Then you can arrange a meeting with your brother in the morning."

Frank jumped from the carriage and eagerly dashed toward the marble lobby. Inside, it was refreshing and cool compared with the blistering and steamy heat outside. A mustached and uniformed British clerk sat at a desk, while a second soldier stood by as a sentry.

"I'd like to know the whereabouts of my brother, Lieutenant Walter Dickens of the 42nd," Frank said, trying to sound self-possessed despite the excitement building inside him. "I'm his brother, newly arrived in Calcutta this morning. I'm to report to the Bengal Mounted Police next month but I would like to spend some time with him, if possible, before the commencement of my duties."

"Dickens, Dickens…" The seated soldier was thumbing through pages of a register.

The sentry grunted. "Sir, if I'm not mistaken, there was a Dickens…"

"Oh, yes," the clerk said, glancing at the sentry and pushing back his chair. "Well, young Mr. Dickens, if you would like to come with me."

The clerk led Frank through a hallway into second office, where he sat alone for a while. They would be searching the record to find out where Wally was stationed, he thought.

After fifteen minutes, the clerk appeared with a major who spoke with a gentle Scots burr.

"Corporal, Mr. Dickens arrived with a friend, did he not? Fetch 'im please."

The clerk left and the major guided Frank to a chair in his office. Williams arrived in the room.

"Mr. Dickens, 'tis with great regret that I must inform you that your brother passed away unexpectedly a month ago. A letter was immediately dispatched to your family but you must have left England before it arrived. Lieutenant Dickens's death was a great loss to his comrades, as well, of course, to yourself and your family."

In shock, Frank tried to speak but nothing came. His face turned white and pain surged through his temples. This was only a nightmare, he thought, trying to shake himself awake. A feeling came that he was really in that room but was watching a scene from one of his father's books. He felt a hand on his shoulder but had no idea of whose it was.

"Lieutenant Dickens had been posted to a station up-country and fell ill. He returned to Calcutta on sick leave, and stopped by the hospital to see some of his brother officers who were similarly afflicted. He seemed well, and was talking cheerfully about being invalided home to England, when he suddenly became quite agitated, gripped his chest and collapsed. Blood poured from his mouth in a great rush and he was dead in an instant. We still don't know the cause, but we lose far more good soldiers here from a multitude of diseases than we do in combat. Aye, it's a damnable country, this is. And it's a dreadful thing to relate, but so common…so common…Mr. Dickens?"

Frank didn't hear. His head had rolled back in a dead faint. The major rushed to his side.

# Chapter 5

George Williams had taken a fatherly interest in young Frank, so disoriented and lonely after he received word of the unexpected death of Walter. Williams had grown accustomed to the death of close friends after all his years in India, but he had a particular emptiness in his soul because his oldest son had died in the opening salvos of the Mutiny of 1857. He knew Frank would need some emotional help to get over the shock. Williams took the new arrival to his home to rest for a while until Frank was formally inducted into the Bengal Mounted. When he felt the time was right, Williams took Frank to the Park Street cemetery in Calcutta where Walter had been buried.

The young man stood before the grave in silence, staring forlornly at the freshly turned dirt and the simple wooden cross marker painted with his brother's name and rank .Frank felt as though his world had been shaken to the core. Did Father know yet, he wondered? Walter would have died when Frank was at sea and it might have been very difficult to get messages to him. In fact, Charles did not learn of his son's death until February 7th, the date of his own birthday.

Frank shuddered. So many Britons seem to end their days here. Would this be my fate as well? he wondered. He found it difficult to leave this dismal place, until Williams came over, and putting his arm around the young man, led him back to the carriage.

Williams had sent a message that he would stop by to pick up Frank at the barracks of the Bengal Mounted Police. Their destination that sweltering evening was a celebration held by a Hindu business acquaintance of Williams.

The young man was waiting for him at the gates as Williams' carriage rode up. Dickens looked smartly dressed in his police uniform with the blue shoulder sash and gold-plated badge over clean white cotton, topped by a white pith helmet. The young man had attempted the wispy beginnings of a mustache, which reflected golden highlights in the late afternoon Bengali sun. He was not tall, but Frank was slender and carried himself erect and Williams nodded approvingly. Dickens had clearly learned some discipline in his early training with the Bengal police. Williams hoped these lessons, this burgeoning confidence, would stay with the newcomer; he had seen so many lose their self-control as their time on the sub-continent lengthened.

"Good day, Mr. Williams. I'm looking forward to this evening in your company," said Dickens as he clambered aboard the carriage. "I received your message but, tell me, who is the gentleman we are visiting tonight?"

"I simply know him as Dutta," said Williams. "That is all you need to know. The full names of these people have so many deuced syllables I just lose track. Apparently, names can tell you where they are from and their caste, if you know about such things. But for me, Dutta is sufficient."

As they rode along, Williams expanded. "He is a pundit, Frank, a learned Brahmin who taught me what little Hindi I know and speak so poorly. He is a fine man, well regarded both in his own community and British circles as well. You will enjoy his company. Dutta is an unusual man of his caste, a free-thinker. He is open to dealings with we the oppressors and has broken away somewhat from many of the hide-bound restrictions against relations among the various castes of Indian society."

As they rode along and twilight closed in around them, Frank informed his friend that he was to be posted soon up-country, in a rural area northeast of Calcutta. Williams regarded Frank with concern.

"My advice is to be fully aware of your surroundings whether on or off duty. Learn some of the local language so that you have a sense of what is happening around you. That, or take on an interpreter whom you can trust with your life. Calcutta has been an adjustment for you, hasn't it? Well, life outside Calcutta is even more of a challenge. You will be completely reliant at all times on your comrades and those around you. Beware of treachery, Frank."

Williams fell silent. A vision of his assassinated son, killed by the troops he led, passed through his mind. Betrayal, he thought. Young John Williams had been a good officer, fair and considerate to the men under his command, but when causes beyond his control resulted in rebellion, he had been swiftly swept away. Williams was bitter, but as bitter against the ruling classes of the East India Company and the British Raj as he was against the low-caste sepoys who had taken John's life.

While Williams seemed lost in thought, Dickens was looking around him as they passed through the noisy streets, the air perfumed by the rich oily smell of ghee and grease, the array of tables, couches, glassware, foodstuffs, knives and other implements offered for sale. Dickens was by now accustomed to the bazaars but his attention focused on a stall surrounded by a crowd of squatting peasants and their children that offered entertainment resembling a Punch and Judy show.

It was the repetition of what seemed to be the word "Damn" that first caught his ear. Then he noticed that one of the principal puppets was a swaggering European, carrying a large club, clad in uniform much like his own, and seemingly slurring his words. The puppet would suddenly dash across the stage, waving the stick and bringing it down hard on the other characters clad in native dress. At each blow, the crowd would hoot angrily, and would shout out epithets when the European bully staggered back to his place on the other side of the stage. Frank looked at Williams for an explanation.

"That's the way they see us," Williams said with a grimace. "Live high, drink too much, thump the servants, cursing all the while. It's a caricature, to be sure, but unfortunately there are sufficient of us who behave that way to lend credence to the show. I tell you, most of the people won't be sorry to see our backs."

The carriage soon turned through some gates into a large square courtyard that was surrounded on three sides by living quarters and on the fourth, opposite the gates, by a family temple. The temple was behind thin cloth veils but Dickens could make out an image of Vishnu surrounded by chandeliers and large candles.

Servants helped Williams and Dickens out of the carriage and led the horses away. Some guests, both British and Indian, had already arrived. Soon, they were approached by a tall, light-skinned Hindu of middle-age wearing a white cotton jacket and trousers.

"Mr. Williams," he said. "How delighted I am that you could come this evening." His English was accented but flawless.

Both men put their hands together and bowed in greeting. The host turned his attention to the young man.

"And this must be the Mr. Dickens you spoke of. I am Dutta. I am honoured and humbly welcome you, sir, to my home."

Frank doffed his helmet and stretched out his hand to take the other man's but noticed Williams was shaking his head. Dutta was bowing. The young policeman quickly put his fingertips together and followed suit.

Dutta led them to a garden in the middle of courtyard. "Sit. Rest yourself here and take a cooling drink. The entertainment will soon begin. If you will excuse me, I must see to the other guests but I would be delighted to converse with you both later."

As Dutta left, Williams whispered to Frank. "Dutta will not shake your hand. Don't take it as a slight. Most Brahmins think of we English beef eaters as pariahs. Dutta is a practical man and is much more open to consorting with us. But he still feels the need to undergo ritual purification after consorting with us."

Despite his connections with the British occupiers, Dutta was no toadie to the foreigners. He had been among the most vocal supporters of Rani Rashmoni, who had commanded that a great chain be stretched across the Hooghly River to block British ships from disturbing the activities of the local fishermen. Several small boats had been run down by the larger vessels, with the fishermen cast into the waters, their livelihoods gone. The British authorities had paid no heed until the Rani forced their hand. Because of her great popularity among the people, the British were reluctant to take action against her. Dutta had been one of the delegation sent by the Rani to negotiate passage times for the trading and military vessels that would not interfere with the fishing of the peasants. This, indeed, was how he had first become acquainted with Williams, and though the two men, both widowers, were from different worlds, they became friends.

Dickens looked around the courtyard. There were perhaps fifty guests, about evenly divided between Europeans and Indians. Most were older but there were other young officers in uniform and a scattering of young white women attired in heavy dresses and parasols. The women glanced at Frank as he entered, and whispered to one another, giggling. A pair of servants walked among the guests carrying bowls, dipping leafy branches in rose water and sprinkling the perfumed attar on the visitors.

A quartet of musicians entered the garden and began playing. One bowed away on a saringi, a kind of violin, while another beat the rhythm on a tabla. The others played on tambura and sitar, the music starting slowly, melodically, and building up to a fast paced crescendo, the tabla player's hands blazing so fast at the finish that they appeared to Frank as a blur. The music at first was discordant in Dickens's ears and the voices sounded to him like wailing, but the effect was hypnotic, and Frank found himself closing his eyes and swaying to the mellow twanging as each tune developed.

Then some male dancers entered, with graceful yet powerful movements imitating the actions of animals, a crouching, stalking lion, a peacock displaying his magnificent feathers before taking flight, the tremendous power of the elephant and the entrancing swaying of the cobra. They moved to the rattle and crash of several drums and the accompaniment of a chorus of singers. Dickens lost track of time, contact with his surroundings. The sun had gone down now, and the evening was refreshingly cool. Large torches with aromatic herbs had been lit to drive away the incessant mosquitoes of sunset. Then abruptly, there was a pause in the music. Servants brought around baskets of fruit. Some were familiar to him — apricots, figs, grapes, pears and apples, but others — guava, custard apples and jackfruit — he had not tasted before. The retainers also brought jugs of araca, a powerful, fiery liquor distilled from palm wine and sweetened with dried grapes, and nipa, a milder and sweeter wine. Fragrant aromas of curry and other spices were filling the courtyard from the cooking areas on the other side of the living quarters. The entire atmosphere seemed like a dream.

The break concluded and eight young women entered the garden, lithe bodies draped in colourful saris, waving fans of red silk with golden fringes. They wore anklets with brass bells that tinkled as they swirled about the garden in circles, beaded necklaces and dangling brass bracelets and earrings, waving streamers of silk flying above faces that were heavily made up with cosmetics, accentuating their dark eyes and handsome features. The music started up again. They began the dance with expressive and subtle movements of their fingertips only, then their hennaed hands floated with incomparable gracefulness, until their arms and shoulders and then their whole bodies joined the dance. Frank, dazzled, thought of the ripples spreading outward when a stone is thrown into a pond.

After the first performance, one young woman emerged from the group and began a dance that started slowly but gathered in intensity and speed, the music racing along, until in one motion as she spun she took an egg from her sari and placed it in the streamers twirling about her, the object held in the banners by centrifugal force. She widened her circle of dance, coming closer and closer to the rapt onlookers, until her legs brushed against Frank's trousers and her full breasts flashed by his eyes. Dickens, feeling uncomfortable, and imagining that all eyes were upon him, slid his chair back, thinking she had come so near accidentally. He did not want to become the centre of attention by clumsily interfering with her graceful motions. But as she swept around the circle of the admiring audience, she again grazed his legs. He moved again, startled by the audacity of this young dancer and looking to see if the touch had been noticed by others but apparently it was not. The slight contact happened a third and fourth time, the dancer's brown almond eyes focused on him as she came nearer. Then the tempo of the music slowed and came to a halt, the streamers collapsing as the young dancer gathered them to her bosom. With a quick flip of the streamers she caught the egg in the air. She bowed as the audience burst into enthusiastic applause, then crouched, cracking the egg on the ground and spilling its contents. The performer rose to her feet, and scanned her admiring audience with flashing eyes, then, with a haughty glance in Frank's direction, left the garden.

"That is Dutta's daughter, the delight of his eye, and of many a young Hindu gentleman, too, I'd wager," said Williams, whispering to Dickens. "Now I think the meal will be ready. You will find it superb, Frank, though perhaps a little spicy. Dutta never fails to impress."

After the dinner, Dickens was chatting with some guests when Dutta approached and led him aside.

"So, you are a son of the great Charles Dickens. I am honoured that you could come and when you are in correspondence with your father, I would consider it a great favour if you would pass along my respects."

"You know my father's writings?" Dickens asked, dismayed.

"Of course, I read all I can, and Mr. Williams has been kind enough to share his copies with me. I fear that I have gained more from my contact with your friend than he has from me. I was expected to teach him Hindi, but I believe I have learned more English than he has learned of my language."

"I am stunned and gratified that you are acquainted with father's work, sir," Dickens said.

"My dear young man, you must not assume that we who are so far removed from the centres of European civilization are all illiterate savages." Dutta smiled and Frank detected sarcasm. "Unfortunately, there are too many of your countrymen who, may I be so bold to say, display their own shortcomings by considering our society to be backward and ignorant. In truth, we have a written language in our country that goes back far beyond the antiquities of Greece and Rome. There are many literate, intelligent people here, and others, also literate, who misinterpret the ancient scriptures for their own ends, just as I suspect some people do in your own England. But, yes, I am well acquainted with your father's work and I am hopeful that, like your father, our writers will tackle some of the absurdities and misguided social constructions that plague our own society."

Frank pondered Dutta's remarks. He felt it would be impolite to mention the caste system, of which his host was a beneficiary.

Dutta seemed to read his mind. "Yes, I understand that I am one that stands near the top of our hierarchy. But I also know that if our collection of quarrelsome feudal states and divided religions and classes is ever to stand and to proudly..." He paused briefly, searching for words, then carried on: "contribute to the *glories* of the Empire, we must put aside those things that divide us."

Williams had come by to thank Dutta and to tell Frank his carriage was ready. When the two men left, Dickens sensed a pair of almond eyes was watching him from behind a pillar of the house.

As the neared the barracks, Frank mentioned the dancer again.

"You said she was Dutta's daughter, Mr. Williams. Might I inquire her name?"

Williams smiled. "Her name is Darshani. It means 'beautiful', I understand. And she is, for a Hindu girl."

They rode in silence for a few minutes.

"A word of warning, Frank. Do not get involved with a native girl. There are many risks. Dutta, as agreeable a man as he is, would not approve. Besides, there is a ready supply of British beauties available for courting, and their fathers would not be averse to their daughters being wooed by a son of the great Charles."

Darshani. Frank found often himself mouthing the name. Those stunning brown eyes invaded his sleep. The twirling colours of her dance, and the light agility as she spun in circles, her eyes on him as she brushed past his legs. The rich, brown hues of her skin and the round fullness of her breasts and hips evident through the swirling silk had captivated him completely. He found himself drifting off into dreams of Darshani when he was on duty or receiving instruction or on parade.

He resolved to see her again. He would call on Dutta with a copy of one of his father's books. A gift to a gracious host.

Frank arrived at the gate one afternoon when he was on leave. A turbaned servant showed him into the garden and he strolled about, examining the glorious array of flowers and the ripening fruit on the trees. Dutta appeared and expressed surprise and delight at the unexpected visit.

"I wanted to give you this copy of one of my father's books, in grateful thanks for your recent hospitality," Frank said. "My father had given it to me himself, but I can always acquire another."

"How wonderful, Mr. Dickens," responded Dutta. "I shall treasure it always. And how are you adjusting to Bengal? Do you find the heat and humidity overwhelming? Many Englishmen do. The climate, and the mosquitoes, and our strange customs and foods, often drive them home rather prematurely, I fear."

"I'm a young man and determined to stick it out," said Dickens. "True, there are many things that I must adjust to. In that regard, Mr. Dutta, I wonder if you would do me a great favour. I know that you instruct Mr. Williams in languages. Could you do the same for me? I have some proficiency in European languages, so I believe myself to be a satisfactory student. I would be prepared to pay a fee."

"I would be honoured. And in exchange, you could tell me the latest news from England and of the literary endeavours of your father."

A servant approached and spoke to Dutta in Bengali. The Brahmin replied. Dickens caught what he thought was the word Darshani.

"I apologize, Mr. Dickens. I am called away on business. But you have taken some pains to come here, so stay awhile. Rest in our garden. My daughter will bring some refreshments."

Dutta disappeared, and Dickens wandered among the flowers. He heard the swish of garments and Darshani appeared, her eyes modestly downcast, followed at a distance by an older woman, her amah.

Dickens felt his heart begin to pound wildly. His faced flushed and he took short, rapid breaths. Darshani approached with a platter of fresh fruit.

"Please, Mr. Dickens. Sit, and have some fruit. You will find it most refreshing. You must have some tea, as well. We have some newly arrived from Darjeeling."

So she spoke English, more deliberately and with a stronger accent than her father, but very well. As she offered the platter, her eyes shifted from the ground to Dickens's face, fleetingly, but enough to register with the young officer. Her breath smelled sweetly of caraway and another exotic spice he could not determine. His composure had completely melted and he was only able to stammer thanks.

Her dark eyes were so expressive, so excruciatingly perfect, that Frank felt he could not bear leaving this new paradise he had found. He searched for something to say.

"S-show me your garden," he stumbled. "What are these flowers here?" he asked distractedly, waving his arm at a nearby bush.

Darshani looked at him and giggled. "Why, Mr. Dickens, those are roses! Are they not the emblem of your country?" she teased.

Dickens emitted a nervous laugh. "Why, so they are!" He pretended to examine them more closely.

"Beautiful," he said.

He was conscious of those eyes on his face. He wanted to reach out and clutch her to his yearning body. She looked away, remembering that she must be proper, especially when dealing with the white rulers. Now, the amah, sensing the attraction between the two young people, and feeling a degree of alarm, cleared her throat and advanced upon them.

"We can talk freely," Darshani said, a smile on her face as she nodded toward her chaperone. "She does not speak English."

Darshani had just begun leading Dickens through the garden, the amah trailing behind a few feet, when Dutta appeared. He and Frank sat down to tea, with Darshani retreating some distance away and the teacher told the young officer what to expect when he rode upcountry in Bengal. Soon, it was time to go.

Dutta turned to his daughter. "Mr. Dickens will be coming here often to take language instruction," he remarked.

Darshani said nothing but bowed to her father. Her lips were turned in a triumphant smile and there was a shine in her eyes.

# Chapter 6

Over the following weeks, Dickens spent much of his free time at Dutta's mansion taking language instruction. Learning took second place in his mind to the expectation that he would catch a glimpse of Darshani and that they might have a few moments together. This happened often enough that they were able to form a close friendship, although the amah was always nearby. On one occasion, as Darshani served him tea while Dutta was detained, Frank decided to declare his feelings.

"I care for you deeply, Darshani," he whispered.

"And I for you," she replied, taking extra time in pouring his tea. "But I am promised."

"Promised?" His cup shook and hot liquid spilled on his uniform.

She brought a cloth and dabbed his tunic, her hand lingering on his sleeve. The amah was startled and as watchful as a cobra about to strike.

"It is arranged," she said shortly. "A son of a family with long connections to ours. I was promised at birth but have not yet met my husband to be."

Tears filled her eyes and she said nothing more, but retreated into the living quarters.

Frank sat back in his chair, shaken and empty. He did not recall the rest of the lesson that day, nor how and when he returned to his barracks.

"I have been posted to Berhampore, upcountry," Frank Dickens informed Dutta when he next came for lessons. "I leave at the end of this week and will not be back for some time. The duties are very heavy there and the district superintendent has not been well, so I will be expected to help him carry out a significant part of his responsibilities."

"I will miss our meetings, Mr. Dickens," his host said. "You are a good student. I am certain however, that this is a wonderful opportunity for you. You will feel somewhat at home there, in spite of the searing heat. The city was the first British capital of Bengal and Krishnanath College there was built by your administrators. It is styled after Oxford University, I believe. The area is very fertile and our finest Indian silk is produced there."

Dickens noted that Dutta did not mention another fact that was on the minds of the British officers, and that worried him.. Berhampore was the site of the first attacks of the mutiny of 1857. But Dutta continued talking.

"I have noticed you have developed something of an acquaintance with my daughter. I do hope you can obtain leave to return for her wedding. It will take place in six months time and I would be honoured if you could attend the celebrations after the private religious ritual is complete."

Throughout the last lesson, Frank could only think of the young woman: "Darshani, my beautiful Darshani. You are lost to me. Can I bear seeing you with another?"

Dutta bowed deeply to Dickens on his departure. "I sense you were not with us today in your lesson. Your mind is on your move and your career, no doubt. May the gods be kind to you, then."

Frank turned to leave and Darshani rushed to the gate. With her father's narrowed eyes looking on quizzically, she gave the policeman a small red silk purse.

"Open it," she said.

Inside, there was a painted egg and a fresh rose.

Speechless, Frank nodded and mounted his horse, saluting both his friends. Then, choking back his emotions, he wheeled the animal about, jabbed spurs in its flanks and rode off quickly without looking back.

The monsoons began soon after Dickens had moved to Berhampore. The harbinger was a line of white fleecy clouds that moved in from the Bay of Bengal in the south. The heat and humidity combined to enervate all activity. Dickens and his British colleagues felt oppressed by the climate. Then masses of black, heavy clouds moved in from the south, accompanied by powerful, gusting winds. Finally the rain came, falling in sheets and the winds grew ever stronger, bending coconut palms almost to the sodden earth. Great swaths of lightning sparked overhead. The roadways became treacherous and impassable, filling with water, and new streams formed everywhere, sweeping away soil, trees and crops, even unfortunate animals. It seemed nothing in nature could resist the deluge. The police barracks were invaded by all manner of creatures trying to escape the wrath of the storms — swarms of ants and gigantic centipedes, toads and lizards, cockroaches, and scorpions and poisonous snakes. For many days the rains fell, and then it stopped.

When the rain abated, the police again went out on patrols of the district. Trevelyan, the local superintendent, asked Dickens to lead a patrol in the villages close to the Ganges. During the monsoons, there was little property crime. People were too busy coping with the raging waters, there were few travellers on the road so the Thugs, the strangling bandits, were less active, and most people remained close to their homes. The confinement would sometimes lead to an occasional murder committed by one overwrought family member or neighbour against another, but by the time the police could arrive the perpetrators would have fled or community revenge would have been exacted and nothing was reported to the supposed authorities. The superintendent's main concern was to estimate the damage that might have been inflicted by the storms and whether there were pockets of peasants in dire need of assistance.

By the coast, there had been severe damage caused by surging waves rushing in from the Bay of Bengal over the low-lying land, washing away soil and leaving behind pools of salt water that poisoned the earth. In the jungle areas and mangrove swamps around Sundaraban, the flooding seas had forced many wild creatures out of the forest. The most dangerous of these were Bengal tigers that prowled the outskirts of villages, terrorizing local people who feared going into their fields to repair the damage wrought by the monsoons. Several villagers had been killed by the marauding beasts and the retelling of the horrific tales magnified perhaps a score of deaths into attacks by the hundreds.

In the area where Dickens was stationed, ocean flooding was not the problem. The ground was higher, more rolling, as the topography became more hilly toward the north, eventually culminating in the foothills of the Himalayas, which could sometimes be glimpsed in all their majesty from the palaces of Berhampore. Here the threat to life and the bane of the peasants were the rampaging flood waters that rushed down from the higher hills and the plains toward the Indian Ocean, tearing away the good soil, the seed that had been planted, the cattle, horses and fowl, and homes unlucky enough to be perched close to the changing channels of the flowing torrents. In a bad year, and there had been several in the previous decade in Bengal and the neighbouring provinces of Bihar and Orissa, the loss of crops, animals and stored food meant starvation for many who lived on the edge of sustenance. As the monsoons ended, people emerged from their thatched hovels to see what remained and were stricken by the damage. Fields that had been planted with food crops were barely recognizable, altered by the raging streams. This led to disputes among landowners and their tenant sharecroppers over where the bounds of their holdings lay. These confrontations sometimes had to be settled by the police. As corpses of dead animals rotted in the returning hot sun, diseases spread quickly and many died.

As Dickens rode along with an interpreter and two Hindu policemen, he noted the damages to each village, estimated populations, erosion of the soil, stinking fetid backwaters where pools lay motionless and stagnant, breeding grounds of mosquitoes, and thus the source of malaria, dengue and yellow fever. Many people were desperate, and he tried to steel himself against the continuing pleas for help in a language he could not yet fully understand. Some would crowd his horse, singling him out as the man in control, hands outstretched in supplication, until his men rode in with whips, beating the beggars back. What could they give these unfortunates that would be of any value and could satisfy them all? They hardly carried enough food, and coins were useless to most of those who were devastated by the floods because there was nothing to buy.

Down by the eroded bank of one stream, he saw the corpse of a dead horse, now rotting in the sun, the stench overpowering. He saw movement, a flash, and took out his binoculars. An old woman, clad in dirty rags, was hacking away with a knife at what little remained of the flesh, the leavings of the vultures, wild dogs and maggots. A group of vultures stood watching, hopping in to pick at the carcass when the woman's back was turned. She would spin around angrily, hissing as she threatened the other scavengers with her knife. Dickens felt pity and he and his men approached the emaciated woman.

"Give her some naan," he said to one of the others.

The officer reached into a saddlebag and produced some flatbread, and offered it to her.

The crone approached warily, her knife in one hand and a jute bag of bones and raw, rotting meat in the other. She grabbed the bread greedily and gnawed on it, then stuffed the remainder in her bag. Then she approached Dickens. He gagged and covered his mouth at the stink she emitted, but stayed where he was, thinking that she was going to thank him. Instead, when she was close, she slashed out with the knife, the blade missing his leg but cutting the side of his horse, who reared with the pain.

"She is mad, sahib" the interpreter said, and the two other men raced at her with their whips. "We can kill her."

"No," said Dickens, struggling with his horse. "She is mad with hunger, I agree. Let her go, she is not responsible for her actions."

He dismounted from the horse and examined the wound. "Only a graze, nothing serious. I will put some ointment on it now."

The interpreter watched.

"Most of the ryots — the tenant farmers — hereabouts grow indigo for the zemindars, the landlords, who then sell it to British agents and they send it to England," he told Dickens. "When there are crop failures, the indigo must still be produced but it comes at the expense of food for the peasants."

Dickens stood back, examining the side of his horse, but taking in the interpreter's words. He looked at the young man, the product of an illicit liaison between a British soldier and an Indian woman of lower caste. This fellow seemed so self-assured and intelligent, a superior young man, yet most of the British officers Frank knew treated him with contempt.

The interpreter continued: "There is much resentment among the ryots but they do not know where to direct their anger. They are punished by the zemindars if they do not plant some of their land in indigo, and they seldom see a white man's face in these parts. Still, they know it is the white man that wants the dye, so sometimes they lash out."

Back in Berhampore, Dickens submitted to Trevelyan his report on the district.

"I should like to see how indigo is made," he told the superintendent, as he handed over his document.

"Just the right time, Dickens. The harvest begins now, after the end of the rainy season. You will have to stay up late or rise early. The harvesting is done at night. I will arrange something."

Trevelyan had set up a tour of an indigo factory owned by a local landlord. The zemindar's foreman, Mahmoud, showed Dickens around the work buildings.

"The shoots which provide the dye must be harvested quickly and at night, to provide the best quality," the foreman told Dickens, as Trevelyan watched. "We call in all the ryots in the local villages to work on the harvest. All the shoots are placed in those large stone fermentation troughs over there, we fill them with water and then we allow them to sit in the hot sun for at least two days. The shoots turn the water a dark blue."

Mahmoud led the two policemen to another set of troughs that smelled of ammonia. He held a torch close to the water in the smaller troughs. It was pitch black.

"Now, we drive off the water. The solution is put in those large metal vats you see over there and they are baked slowly until all the water is gone. What is left behind is a dried blue powder which is what is collected, sold to the agents, mostly British, and then sent to England for use in dyeing cloth."

Mahmoud left to direct some peasants bringing in another load of shoots.

"I've invested in these indigo works," said the superintendent. "One can make a damn fine living from the investment. A happy supplement to the rather modest income of a policeman, Dickens."

Dickens grunted. He could see that possibility. But he remembered the gaunt old woman, kneeling by the dead horse, desperately hacking off bits of putrid flesh. The widow of a ryot, no doubt. He would not invest his money in indigo.

Dickens lay naked on his bed. He had suffered the last few days from prickly heat and the humidity was so oppressive he could not sleep. He could hear the incessant whine of mosquitoes searching for ways to get through the netting that covered his bed. Sleep came only when exhaustion completely overcame him, and then in small interludes. He prayed for a breeze from the mountains in the north and then it seemed that his wish was granted. The winds had shifted and he could feel the temperature, the humidity in his room dropping as gushes of cooling air poured through his open window. Grateful, he fell asleep.

On the edge of a forest, Dickens saw the most beautiful creature he had ever beheld. A small and graceful antelope with brown almond eyes, covered with handsome brown fur and white spots, stood grazing among the trees. Its long ears twitched about, alert for the sound of an enemy. As Dickens watched, he became aware of another presence, an evil force, lurking in the long grass. He could not make it out but soon realized it was an enormous tiger, larger than any he had seen before, stalking the unsuspecting prey. He felt a sense of outrage that this stunning little creature should be in danger. He drew his sabre and advanced on the big cat, determined to fight it to the death to save the antelope. But it was too late. The tiger had pounced on the pretty creature, ripping out its throat and disembowelling the poor animal with a sweep of its huge paws. Dickens rushed upon the tiger, which now was tearing great chunks of flesh away from the bones. He slashed again and again at the monster, his sword cutting through its powerful muscles and enormous head. The tiger ignored this human, crying with anger, that was hacking at him. The sword strokes were having no effect and the cat continued ripping the remains of the antelope until nothing was left. Then the tiger raised itself up and loped into the forest, without any sign of damage or distress. Dickens sank to his knees sobbing, hurling the sword away and rubbing his hands frantically in the gore left by the tiger, as though he could somehow restore it to life.

He awoke with a start. The sun was up and he could hear noises of villagers preparing for another day.

Six months after his departure from Calcutta, Frank Dickens returned to the city on leave. He left his quarters after settling in and rode to Dutta's mansion, where a servant bade him enter.

A few minutes later, Dutta appeared. Dickens was shocked at his appearance. The usually neatly dressed man looked dishevelled and had lost a good deal of weight. His face was unremittingly sad and worn, and his expression changed little when he saw who was calling. He greeted Dickens formally, his words as welcoming as ever but it was evident from his posture that he took no joy in seeing the young Englishman. Dickens had the impression that here stood a broken man.

"Pandit-ji," Dickens exclaimed. "What has happened to you? I came here expecting to see joyful preparations for your daughter's wedding and I see you are terribly ill. Is there anything I can do to help?"

"There is no wedding," Dutta said in a dull voice.

For a brief moment, Dickens felt his heart exulting. Had the arrangement fallen through? Would Darshani be free? Would Dutta, would Anglo-Indian society, allow them a courtship?

Dutta cleared his throat.

"I have had the cholera. I was close to death and wish that I had indeed died. I will never be the same man. The fever, the pain, the exudations of my tortured body, robbed me of my dignity as a human being. But somehow, I was spared death, which has given me no relief, but only greater sorrow than I have ever felt before."

"My poor Mr. Dutta," said Dickens.

"This dreadful scourge swept through my household…"

"Darshani!" Dickens voice cracked. He felt his stomach heave.

"Dead, my friend. Oh, my beautiful daughter," he wailed. "She nursed me to exhaustion and then the accursed cholera took her away from me. She fell ill in the evening and by the next afternoon, she was gone. My last child. Oh, my friend, how can this be?"

Dutta shuddered with grief and Frank, tears streaming down his face, went to embrace the Brahmin whose strength was gone and who now appeared to be a feeble old man awaiting his own fate.

"Her last words were, 'Father, remember me to my young man.' Since she had not yet met her husband-to-be, I believe she meant you, my good friend."

# Chapter 7

Poor Williams. The man who had been such a friend and mentor to me when I first arrived in this cursed country had died suddenly while I was upcountry. It was as if he was determined to personally affirm the declaration he often made, that Bengal was a graveyard for Englishmen.

He had taken quite a shine to me, I think because he had lost his son in the recent mutiny. I was often invited to his home for dinner and the relationship grew warm. I began to think of him as my father in India, the replacement for my own Pa.

How lonely I felt when word came that Wlliams had gone. India seemed to me a place of death. Darshani had died of plague, followed soon after by her father, whom I believed suffered from a broken heart. There was brother Wally who had been taken before I even arrived.

And one of the first letters I had received from England was from Anny Thackeray. I had torn it open eagerly, only to find to my surprise and sorrow that her father had passed away suddenly and without warning. I had always had a tender feeling for Anny, though she was older. She had seemed like a cousin to me since her happy summer visits of bygone years in Kent.

"Dear Frank:

"Perhaps you have heard from your family about our recent tragedy. Father passed away suddenly on Christmas Eve after an unexpected seizure in his brain. It happened just four days after you left and it has taken me all this time to compose myself to write you about it. Poor Father, he had suffered so much during his life, what with Mother's depression, and the loss of our dear baby Sister.

"You had been on my mind for some time. Perhaps you did not know that Father was born in the very city where you are now. Grandfather was with the East India Company in Calcutta nearly sixty years ago. And now you tread the same streets that my Father and Grandfather trod…

"I would like to share with you a mysterious dream I had the night that Father died. Father and I had climbed together up a long hill, which was shrouded with clouds at the top. We became separated in the mist and I could not hear him calling, so resolved that it would be best if I made my way down by myself. I was certain he would find his own way to the bottom of the hill, where we would be reunited. Unfortunately, when I arrived at the bottom, Father was nowhere to be seen. I awoke with a start, and there was a knocking at my bedroom door. I opened it, and there was Minny with a doctor and housekeeper, come to tell me the dreadful news that Father had died overnight. I have always believed that dreams reveal to us the course of life, and I hold this memory as evidence of that truth.

"We were all very grateful that your papa came to Kensal Green to pay his respects to our Father. It was sad that our Fathers had lost their close connections of earlier days. We know that your Father suffered greatly with the loss of your Granny Dickens and then of poor Wally. He seemed so disconsolate at Father's funeral, straining mightily to hold back the tears and staring into the tomb as the coffin *was lowered. It must have been quite the unhappiest Christmastide that Charles has ever endured. Do not fret, dear Frankie. I am told by Katey that Charles is back at his writings and readings, as energetic as ever.*

*"With great affection,*

*Anny.*

Whenever I reread Anny's letter, her relation of the dream foreshadowing the death of her father shakes me to the core. It recalls to me the nightmare I had before I learned of the fate of Darshani.

I must tell you of the last time I had occasion to meet with George Williams.

The continuum of tragic events in my life made me feel closer than ever to Williams. He was my sole anchor in those sad times.

One night he asked about my early life.

"There is something I've wanted to ask," Williams said, while pouring me a glass of port. "It's just my idle curiosity, so if you would prefer not to answer I'll accept that. I've always wondered what was it like growing up in the household of a world-famous man?"

I stared at the wall. It wasn't the first time I had been asked about this, of course, and on most occasions I'd brushed it off with a cheerful response. Somehow, it seemed to me that George was entitled to the truth.

"I don't mean to intrude in private matters," Williams apologized, seeing the expression on my face. It was clear he worried that he'd touched a raw nerve.

"No, no. I've been asked that as you might imagine, and every time the answer seems different. I suppose it really depends how I feel at that moment."

I swallowed the port to steel myself for the recall of hard memories and Williams refilled my glass.

"I have mixed emotions about my Papa. He was like two men. He could be jovial and full of good humour one moment and within minutes turn morose or angry and judgmental. I would say we children, especially the boys, feared him at those times. Father's word was law in our household. I sometimes think that those who are the most ardent reformers in public might be the most tyrannical authoritarians in their private lives. Yet we adored him at

*Christmas, and he wrote a book especially for us, The Life of Our Lord, that incorporated all facets of his incisive wit and delightful commentary. He left instructions that it not be published until all his children have died. We loved that book. It was our own special gift from our father.*

*"This is not to expose my dear father as a hypocrite," I went on. "His tendency to criticize our faults was simply due to the fact that he expected much from we who were born to a comfortable life. He wanted us to be successes in our own right. And when we failed in that responsibility and duty he could not countenance that failure.*

*"When I'm asked to read from his works I feel as if I am transformed from the person that I am to a being of much greater intelligence and wit. There's a spirit that rises in me that I frankly do not display in daily life."*

*"Come now, young fellow, don't sell yourself short."*

*"None of we boys have matched what Papa has hoped for us. I suppose one might say that unlike Pip, our expectations are diminished. Yes, lesser expectations," I repeated myself, pleased with the ironic reference.*

*"Father was so energetic, often travelling England or the continent, a demon possessed by work, constantly making notes and listening to conversations, driven by his nerves, haunted by his past and fearful of the future. He was shaken to the core by the unexpected death of Thackeray, with whom he had a tense rivalry .*

*"If we ever interrupted his work, there was the devil to pay. He matched us against himself and found us wanting. We were lazy, spendthrifts, misfits. I fear I have been a disappointment to him, like my brothers, but if I were to beg for mercy, that plea would be based upon my youth."*

*I swallowed more port and held out my empty glass. The liquor was going to my head.*

*"Father has always looked after our debts, provided an allowance while expecting us to find our own living. We took that too much for granted. He was compelled to pay for the hare-brained schemes and plottings of Grandfather Dickens, even paid an allowance to the shamefully abandoned wife and children of my Uncle Augustus who fled England for America. Lord knows, we children should have behaved better, respected the hard work that went into providing for us all, I know that now.*

"He treated my mother barbarously, you know, leaving her for a younger woman. I find it hard to forgive him for that."

"And you, Frank. How has he treated you?"

"I try to believe that what he did, he intended in a kindly, supportive, instructive way. I am a nervous person, as you know, still am around authority. I have sleepwalked, I stammer, as you have noticed on occasion. It began when I was about age seven and it recurs under stress. I do not know whether my affliction stems from a feeling that I could never quite meet the standards that Papa has set for me. Whatever the cause, his way of dealing with it was cruel. First, he blamed poor mother for somehow implanting that anxiety in me. 'Why was I not told of Frank's affliction?' he roared at her, as if she had tried to conceal it from him. Yet I was around the house, did he not notice? I believe now that he was trying to build a dark mythology in order to justify his impropriety with others, his own guilt over his decision to end the marriage with our kind, sweet mother, she who had been an island of calm and patience in our tempestuous household. I am bitter that he used my disability as one of his infamous excuses to break up the marriage. It was an unfair burden placed upon my young shoulders by a father who cared more for his own carefully prepared rationalizations than for his children.

"Then his methods of correcting my stammering and my weak physical constitution were brutal. Every day, no matter how I felt, I was compelled to drink a glass of dark porter. Today, that might not seem a punishment, I admit, but as a young lad the taste revolted me at first. In truth, I came to like that daily dose overly fondly, almost looked forward to it. I was also ordered to spend an hour each day with father in his study when he was home, reading aloud works of Shakespeare and other classics. My father expected me to read with the same clarity and lack of hesitation that he did. It was humiliating. I would stumble over phrases and mispronounce words and the more he impatiently pressed me to continue the worse I would read, the more my stammer would return. The other children and my mother could hear him raging when I failed. I would be in tears, sobbing, trying to read the orations of Hamlet with the fluid style and flair of Papa."

"That sounds cruel," Williams interjected. "But there was success, was there not? You seldom stammer today."

"True, but I cannot help but wonder if there was a kinder, more effective way. Would I have grown out of it over time? Papa has ridiculed me before others for my ambitions and chastised me openly. I went to work in the office at his magazine at his request, but confess I was not his best assistant. I was not well organized and my shyness led me to hate dealing face to face with his business acquaintances. But again, I defend myself by pointing out that I am young and organization and confidence are skills one learns."

"So they are," said Williams. "So they are." We both lapsed into silence.

"And yet...and yet," I started again, "There were wonderful times too. I remember a cold winter, so bitter that the Medway froze from Chatham to Gravesend and we could skate the full five miles on the ice. We laughed and teased Pa as his beard , dampened by the moisture from his breathing, froze to his coat, and he roared with delight too. Then there were the plays he wrote for us. Perhaps it was not that he was a hard father, but that we were, as a group, too soft, took too much for granted. My sisters, Kate and Mamie, were much more self-assured and accomplished than any of us boys."

More silence, as I pondered whether I had been unjust to Father in my account.

I begged leave. "I'm off again for Berhampore at first light."

Williams stood and gave me a firm handshake as we parted.

"Look me up again when you are next in Calcutta," he said. What sad words those are to me now.

# Chapter 8

As a police officer in Bengal, much of Frank Dickens' preoccupation was with indigo, a lucrative crop that was dispatched to British mills to produce blue cloth for European and American buyers.

Indigo was produced by a cruel tinkathia system that forced peasants, through their Indian landlords and British planters, to plant a crop on meager land holdings, at the expense of food crops like rice or millet. And if the peasants resisted, the landowners often had the poor driven from the land by hired gangs, with their skin-and-bones cattle stolen, to be left penniless and landless so their families would starve. The cruellest landowners prospered, while those who had some empathy for their tenants barely survived.

In rural Champaran, in the province of Bihar, violent protests began in 1868 that spread eastward into neighbouring Bengal. The system gave the zemindars the authority to demand of the ryots, that they plant three-twentieths of their land in indigo. This was never to benefit the tenants. Indigo for them was usually a money-losing proposition, perhaps even a sentence of death in the lean years. An elaborate system of heavy taxes sanctioned by the British governors, as well as fines, bribes and charges ensured that the zemindars and their contracted planters would profit, but their tenants would lose, be unable to make their costs and fall deeper in debt to the landlords. The ryots were prisoners, never able to free themselves of debt and afraid to challenge authority because enforcers could take away the land where they grew food to support families. What choice did they have? And in years of drought — there were many when Dickens served in Bengal — there would not be enough water for food plants, but there had to be enough for indigo, cotton and jute destined for export.

The Bihari peasants had been pushed too far in the fourth year that Dickens was in India. He, and others, in the Bengal Mounted Police had been warned to prepare for rebellion.

Dickens had been dispatched in 1868 to the village of Baidjabati on the banks of the Hooghly north of Calcutta to assist a police superintendent who feared that unrest over indigo plantings was now spreading to Bengal.

Frank was twenty-four. He was tanned and fitter than he had ever been. He had sprouted a red-gold mustache that made him look older and wiser than his years would allow. He had never, however, grown accustomed to the searing heat and humidity of Bengal in the summer months. What illnesses he had suffered were attributable to this inability to adjust to the climate. Still, his health had held up remarkably well for someone who had always been regarded as sickly by his family and acquaintances in England. Many comrades had fallen ill, some had perished, laid low by cholera, malaria, typhoid, enteric fever. "Liver", the endemic disease carried by insistent Bengali mosquitoes, that turned white faces and eyes yellow and shortened lives, had passed him by, for which he gave thanks. He again remembered Williams' comment that "Bengal is the graveyard of the Englishman." There was also plenty of evidence to support Williams' declaration among Dickens's fellow officers.

The officer Dickens reported to was a Superintendent Robert Forsythe, a military man of many year's experience on the sub-continent and a veteran of the Sepoy mutiny in 1857. He was an impatient man, overly fond of the bottle, scornful of what he considered to be the soft academy-educated British officers sent to serve under his command and brutal to his Indian underlings. He sized up Dickens as he oversaw the erection of barricades in the streets of Baidjapati.

"Pah," Forsythe spat. "'ow old are you, boy? I requests a senior man and they send me a wet-behind-the-ears novice. Well, you must do, I s'pose. The mob of ryots are closing in so we have little time to prepare. I suspect a volley will send 'em packing. Dickens, you'll take the left flank. I'm commanding the middle, and Malcolm over there is handling the right."

Dickens turned to take his position.

"A moment, sir," said Forsythe. He produced a bottle of gin. "A swallow or two to give you courage. And contempt, and rage. Never underestimate the benefit of rage in a soldier. Never play the gentleman in war, Mr. Dickens. You must think of these people as wild animals that must be tamed, and if they are not, you and your men will pay the price of hellfire."

"You said 'war', superintendent. Is this not simply a police action?"

Forsythe scowled. "When the bullets fly and bodies fall, it don't matter what it's called, do it? A cesspool by any other name smells like shit. That's what the poet says, right?"

Forsythe shoved the bottle at Dickens. Following the senior officer's lead, Dickens swallowed from the bottle.

"More, Dickens, more. Don't be a namby-pamby. Courage demands more fuel."

Dickens took another gulp. Forsythe abruptly tipped the bottle higher so that the flow from the bottle was faster than Dickens expected. He coughed as the liquor spilled from his mouth down the front of his jacket. The senior officer roared with laughter. Cowed by Forsythe's brutal manners, Dickens wiped his mouth with the sleeve of his tunic and handed the bottle back.

Later, as Dickens saw to his defences, he noticed a well-dressed Hindu man followed by a train of servants talking to Forsythe. The conversation was animated.

"Who is that?" he asked a British corporal.

"Don't know his name, sir, but he is a local zemindar, a landlord. A lot of indigo is produced on his land. Like as not many of our mob out there are his tenants."

Dickens watched through his glass as the visitor took out a large purse and handed it to Forsythe. The superintendent reached in, pulled out a handful of coins and examined them closely. He closed the purse, smiled and shook the zemindar's hand, then tucked the purse into the saddlebag of his horse.

There was noise of an approaching throng down the road. Hundreds of peasants, half-clad in white cotton, barefoot, and carrying an array of makeshift weapons was approaching. The streets were clear except for the mob. Its members collected rocks, waved large knives, forks, pikes, spears and sickles as they advanced on the barricades of British and Indian police and soldiers. The crowd shouted angry threats at the defenders and waved their weapons, until a strikingly tall man emerged from the centre and took two paces forward. He began speaking loudly in Bengali, too quickly for Dickens to make out the words but it was evident that he was appealing to the commander of the force before him. His supporters shouted out encouragement and cheered his words.

Forsythe, with a menacing grimace on his face, ordered his troops to ready themselves, then aim. He raised his sword above his head.

Dickens ordered his flank to do likewise. "If it comes to firing, first a volley over their heads," he said.

"Shoot to kill," Forsythe yelled, dropping his sword. "Fire!"

Dickens looked on in shock as gunfire erupted. In the centre and the right flanks, scores of peasants sprawled on the dusty street, their blood seeping into the ground. Cries of agony and panicked screams filled the air as the ill-armed ryots fled for the safety of the nearby buildings. Forsythe's men were loading again.

On the left flank, the mob flinched and ducked as the first volley passed over their heads. Many fled but some rallied and chose to charge as Dickens's men paused to reload. A handful of the attackers came within a few steps of the kneeling and standing troops, hacking and slashing with their weapons, before they were beaten off with a second volley from Forsythe's men. The entire throng was now fleeing in panic down the streets, raising a dusty cloud as they ran, shoving and pushing one another to escape, followed by sporadic fire from the troops.

The commander ordered his men to fix bayonets and advance on the mob, driving them from the village. Then, his face red with rage, he came to Dickens.

"Damn fool," he shouted. "What did you expect to gain by a warning shot? Don't you know this cursed lot would rather die on the streets than die in their fields or perish from starvation. They're desperate and would think nothing of slitting our throats."

Dickens stammered. "I th-th-thought a warning would drive them off. W-w-what good are they to the zemindars if they are dead?"

"Hah," said Forsythe. "There are thousands like them, desperate to take their place. The zemindars are only too happy to rid themselves of unruly scoundrels and take on ryots who are pliable, accepting of the needs of the landlords. These fellows are bound for death, and whether it be from our guns, or starvation, or at the hands of their own petty tyrants, it matters little."

Dickens looked at Forsythe with disgust. He had become bolder now.

"And if the zemindars are happy to line pockets to keep their peasants under control, you are most pleased to oblige?"

Forsythe's face turned a deeper crimson but he maintained control.

"You're Charles Dickens' spawn, are you not?" he said, emphasizing each word with a sneer. "I see you've brought the soft-headed notions of your father to plant in India's shallow soil. Well, sir, they will not sprout here as in England. This is a different place. This is not even your civilized Calcutta. It's rural India and life here is as remote from the cities as is life in London. I'm astounded that in your four years here you have not yet grasped the essentials of how to rule an empire."

Dickens turned away. For the remainder of his stay in Baidjapati he avoided Forsythe as much as he was able. He was happy to escape back to Calcutta.

The last time he saw Forsythe, the superintendent stood beside Frank's horse.

"I'll be sending to your superiors an evaluation of your conduct while here, Mr. Dickens. Sad to say it'll not be as praiseworthy as you might like."

Dickens turned his mount to join with the travelling party for Calcutta.

"One more thing, sir," said Forsythe. "To show I've no lingering hard feelings, I offer you some pretty advice: Invest in indigo. It's a damnably profitable business, all losses borne by the growers and no risk to yourself."

"Never," said Dickens. "I'll not profit from the misfortunes of others."

Forsythe roared with laughter and slapped Dickens' horse hard on the rump.

The bloodshed at Baidjapati left a deep mark on Dickens. He was enticed by comrades to drink more, often brandy laced with laudanum, which enabled him to forget that horrific scene. It was not that he was a stranger to death — his years as a policeman in India had exposed him to the victims of starvation, the murders perpetrated by the remnant of Thugs who still operated in the remote parts of Bengal, and to disease. But he had seldom witnessed in one place the enormity of it, the deliberate brutality, which had been perpetrated in the dry streets of that small village. As he spent more time in a state of intoxication, his health worsened. Never capable of dealing with the debilitating climate of Bengal, his sufferings from the heat and humidity grew more intense. Dickens became more depressed each month he spent in India and yearned to leave forever. Time passed slowly, painfully. But he feared the scorn of his father if he should give up his commission and return to England.

Letters from his sister Kate were a lifeline for him. He awaited eagerly the next missive from his older sister, the sibling whom he felt was most like him in appearance and temperament. Katey was a habitual correspondent, and virtually every ship that anchored at Calcutta from England carried a letter, limp from the humidity, but replete with news of the family and the home country. In the spring of 1870, Katey wrote that she was most concerned about their father's health.

> "Father suffers greatly from insomnia, terrible headaches and stabbing pains in his eye, chest and stomach," Katey wrote. "His body, once vigorous, shows visible signs of exhaustion and weakness. Yet, against advice, he has once again taken to the stage to give readings of his works, and he is transformed on those occasions into a vital, young man, his countenance changed, his flashes of wit fresh and vigorous. All of this is greatly appreciated by his audiences who clamour for more, but when he dismounts from the stage he is closer to a state of collapse than ever.

> "In the times when he feels the need to talk about personal matters, he tells me of terrible visions. He again sees the coffin of Thackeray lowered into the tomb. "Poor Thackeray," he says, "I had only reconciled with him days before his death." He imagines the awful thump of the first clods of earth shovelled into a grave. His eyes shriek with panic then, he shudders and his mouth opens but nothing escapes. He had gone last year to see physicians and they advised him to stop touring, but then his recourse is to lock himself away in his study and work without rest from dawn until dusk. His works have become increasingly morbid, without redemption in them, tales lacking in humour, of death, greed and betrayal.

> "Last Christmas, I have not yet related to you, we played the old memory game. Do you remember that, dear Frank? We were all laughing and carrying on in our family custom, when it came to be his

turn, and Father said: 'Warren's Blacking, 30 The Strand.' He then burst spontaneously into tears, and could not be comforted. I had never seen him so sad, and all of us were confounded by the mention of this place, of which we know nothing. I asked John Forster about it, as one of Father's oldest friends and executor of his will. John is the possessor of an auto-biographical fragment written by Father. He con-fided in me that this was a terrible place where father was compelled to work as a young lad, without hope of redemption, of a future. Grandfather Dickens had been imprisoned at Marshalsea for his debts and Father was taken from school to earn a livelihood to help pay those debts off. John says Father felt aban-doned by our grandparents then, cast away by his own father and mother. I now comprehend why he has always been so angry at those of his family who run up obligations they are unable to meet. What marks that place must have left upon his soul! And hence upon us as well!

"Once again, Father has taken up stage perfor-mances and in them he seems almost possessed, as though each reading or role might be his last. Our little brother Harry has travelled with him to cater to his needs. A few months ago, Father put on an enactment of the murder of Nancy by Bill Sykes that was most dreadful and horribly graphic, playing both parts with an intensity that cannot be expressed in words. Harry says that women fainted in the audience at the screams that emitted from Father's lips and he came down from the stage, drenched in sweat, his voice broken, tears dripping down his cheeks. Harry had to support him because he was near a state of collapse. Do you think poor Papa has gone mad?

"In March, Father had an audience with the Queen. Her Majesty bade him sit in a chair, while she stood. Whether that was due to her respect for him, or out of concern for his health, I cannot tell, but no one I have spoken to has ever heard the like.

"Be assured, Dear Frank, that Father sends his love to you. He is proud of your service. Our Mother also sends her affection as always. Of the Other Woman, I have heard nothing of late, and feel certain that she cares not one whit what happens to any of us, including Father. Your brother-in-law Charley, who is sadly having another bad spell, also sends his greetings.

"Your loving Sister,

Kate."

The news from home did not improve Frank's depression. Following his daily duties he drank even more heavily, squandering much of the money he had saved. Secretly, now, he would take little flasks with him while on patrol and would sip them away from his comrades. He was becoming dependent on brandy or gin to keep him going during the day. Moody, and with his growing indulgence in self pity, he began to think of Bengal as his own Warren's Blacking.

In May, 1870, Frank was ordered to take a patrol north of Calcutta. Once again floods, followed by severe drought had punished the countryside. The water along the route of his patrol was all spoiled, courses dried up and ponds polluted by the corpses of dead animals. Not even the local peasants could recall when the heat was so extreme. Riding north toward the distant hills, Frank became increasingly light-headed, then he was stricken by severe headaches. He stopped his horse, his head reeling, and then toppled to the ground, retching violently, before losing consciousness.

Frank had suffered a case of dehydration and sunstroke that was so debilitating that he had to spend weeks inside or in the shade. His doctors declared him an invalid. He could not bear to go out in the sunlight and his duties were restricted to office work, and even then for only a few hours a day. Recovery was gradual but Dickens appealed for leave to return to England for a few months to regain his health and visit his family.

Before a decision came, Frank received another letter from Kate. Charles had announced he was giving his last public performance and then retreated, feeble and exhausted, to his home at Gad's Hill. Kate had visited and casually remarked that she had her own ambitions to become an actress, which Charles, as the protective father, adamantly advised against. When Kate left to return to London, Charles burst into tears. "I wish I had been a better father, Kate, a better man," he moaned, weeping on his daughter's shoulder.

"For my part, I forgave him," Kate wrote. "I would urge you too, Frank, to write and abolish any grievances you might hold. I have no doubt that you, like the rest of us, harbour them. Now is the time for us all to be generous."

He sat down to write a letter to his father but could not concentrate with his head throbbing from the sunstroke. He put it aside for another day. But before he had completed his letter, more mail arrived. There was a new message from Kate, marked urgent.

Charles was dead.

# Chapter 9

*It is difficult to express the profound depression that I feel after reading the latest news from Kate. Of all the sadness I have been compelled to bear, this is the heaviest of burdens. My wonderful father is gone from this earth and I have not seen him once these last seven years.*

*This has not been my fate alone. Father had seen to it that most of his children were virtually banished from his life. Poor Wally and I to India, Edward and Alfred "transported" to Australia, Sydney to a life on the high seas. Only Charlie and Harry have escaped the mixed blessing of exile from England. What father would have taken such pains to see his sons scattered about the globe, likely never to be seen again?*

*But I must reflect whether I am fair in my estimation of Father. I loved him greatly, and yearned for his approval; yet I also feared him for the way he treated me. I cannot blame him for my shortcomings, surely, but I am convinced that he made them worse at times — my stammering, my sleepwalking, my inability to concentrate.*

*I have to remind myself that his tendency to criticize was simply due to his earnest wish that all of we boys become achievers in life. He expected a higher standard from we who have been raised in comparative ease. He wanted desperately for us to succeed, and when we failed in that duty he could not accept that failure.*

*My own life so far has been one of privilege when matched against his early years. I had not been aware of the terrors that haunted him until my sisters informed me in their letters. No doubt those terrible events shaped his own existence in ways that I can only begin to contemplate, and so have been transmuted into our own lives. I have to make my peace with his memory.*

*Pa had been in declining health for years, made worse by the driven exertions of his writing and his manic, dramatic stage appearances. He has apparently not been the same person since that dreadful railway accident of five years ago. Despite his own severe pain from injury, he went forth among the victims, aiding the injured and comforting the dying as best he could. His actions were heroic and were much praised. I can only hope that I might behave so valiantly if I am placed in a similar circumstance.*

*Katey writes that shortly before his death, Pa said he wished he had been a better father. How could Kate do other than reassure him, to comfort him in his despondency? She certainly had her own grievances against Pa — the way the separation from our mother was handled, his warnings against her choice of husband. Yet she was able to forgive and urged me to do the same, so I must. Whether I can forgive myself for not living up to his expectations is another question.*

*Forgive me if I bound from post to post like a ricocheting billiard ball, but my emotions are so much in conflict.*

*Although I have failed to inherit Pa's literary inclinations, I have written a poem which relates to our father-son relationship. It cannot equal his mastery of language, but the tear-stained page upon which it finds form should convey, I hope, how earnestly it is intended:*

> *Cursed be the Sons of Famous Fathers, giv'n birth;*
>
> *The Pride of Lions renowned throughout the Earth.*
>
> *For when those Cubs inevitably go astray,*
>
> *The World stands back, affronted, in dismay.*

# Chapter 10

Frank Dickens had returned to England via the newly built Suez Canal, a marvel of engineering that considerably reduced the long voyage from Bengal. When he arrived in London, he learned from sister Mamie that his father had ordered in his will that an investment trust of 8,000 pounds be established for Catherine, with the income to be ultimately distributed to the Dickens children after her death. Charley was well-fixed and master of his own fate; Charles, Sr., had left all of his share and interest in the weekly All the Year Round to his oldest son. But Frank resented the notion that younger Harry was one of the trustees. He was the youngest of the surviving Dickens children, not quite twenty-one, while Frank was twenty-seven. Frank was most indignant that a thousand pounds had been left to Ellen Ternan, and another eight thousand to Aunt Georgina, Catherine's younger sister, who had lived as part of the household since she was fifteen. His mother, entering her late fifties, continued to receive the six hundred pounds a year that had been a part of the separation agreement between Frank's parents. There was a further trust fund established for the children from money remaining after Charles' debts and funeral expenses had been settled.

Soon after his arrival in London, Frank was summoned to the office of John Forster, his father's close friend and the executor of Charles' will.

Forster eyed the young man with his usual critical eye, then produced a package.

"Your father bequeathed this to me, but there was a note attached, and I believe that he truly intended it for you. He was proud of your service in India, as much as he was mystified by your failure to thrive here in England. But take it now. You may find it to your liking. It is a wonderful inheritance."

Carefully Frank tore open the package, heavy for its size. He caught his breath when saw what it contained. Inside was his father's first watch, attached to a fine gold chain. He studied it in the dim light, touching it gently, almost with reverence. Also included was a small gold locket attached to the chain. Inside was a miniature of Catherine Dickens and a small braid of her hair. Frank picked it up, and kissed the locket.

There was a letter accompanying the watch. Frank unfolded it, hoping it would contain the message of love and acceptance that he craved from his father.

"Dear Francis:

"*L'exactitude est la politesse des rois.* Louis XVIII of France wasn't much as kings go, but he was never more perceptive than when he made this observation. Your inability to be punctual has worried me, Chickenstalker, and so I thought this watch would be a suitable portion of your inheritance. You will never be a true gentleman until you learn that punctuality and promptness will earn you credit among your peers and likewise your superiors.

"I have missed you all these years, my son, but it has been more important to me that you establish your way in this world. I'm sure you will return from

Bengal a sturdy and proud young officer, brimming with confidence and prepared to deal with whatever life decrees. This is my wish for all my boys. You must learn to apply yourselves to your work, eschew idleness and fear debt, and be a credit to your family. As a policeman, you will have learned to take nothing on its looks; take everything on evidence. I can offer no better advice in life than that.

"Your affectionate Pa."

Even in his last message to me, Pa could not resist the temptation to scold and lecture, Frank thought.

Frank hastened to his mother's house in Fulham. Catherine rushed happily to meet him and brought him to the drawing room, where they sat for tea. She was dressed in black, the room was dark and chilly and Frank could see that his mother had gained a great deal of weight. Her initial delight at seeing him quickly faded away into the depressed state of mind that he remembered after her separation from Charles. Her hand shook as she poured tea and some spattered on the carpeted floors.

"Are you well, mother?"

"Oh, yes, Francis. As well as ever." He had missed the gentle Scots burr of his mother's placid voice.

"Mother, I fear father left you not too much to live on. He owed you so much, raising us, putting you constantly on the move, which I am certain harmed your health."

"Now then, Francis. I have enough and a bit to share with my children besides. He has provided for me and I am as happy as I might be in this house. So, let's not hear of any complaints on my behalf, child."

"Did you see him before his death?"

"No," Catherine replied, thoughtfully sipping her tea. "Not since our separation. But let us talk of other things. When will you return to India? I hope you will spend some months here so we can become reacquainted."

"Mother, I do not intend to return to India."

"Do you not?" She looked at her son, her eyes mild and her manner non-judgmental. "Well then, Francis. I look forward to seeing you here more often. I'm so pleased."

Frank felt angry. His mother had been expunged from his father's life. When Charles was dying, Frank's sisters had sent instead for Nelly Ternan to come to his bedside.

He became even more furious when he heard a rumour going the rounds in London.

"There is an outrageous slander that Nell gave birth to a child and Papa is the father.," Frank told brother Charley. "This suggests we have an unwanted half-brother who might be at a point to claim part of the estate."

"Oh, that word has reached my ears too," Charley replied. "But one can't stop up the mouths of all the gossips in London. Nell has made no further claim. Let it rest. It is a price of fame."

"Well, I, for my part, will challenge this lie with all my being."

Next was a visit to his Aunt Georgina. Georgy was more like an older sister to Frank. She had been seventeen when he was born and was a constant in the lives of the Dickens children as a housekeeper, organizer, advisor and friend. Charles had described her in his will as "the best and truest friend man ever had". She had a strong personality and was a real match for Charles, despite her younger age. Now that Charles was gone she wielded great influence in the family.

"I shall count on you a great deal, Frank," she said firmly. "Your younger brothers admire you for your service in India. I fear they are not as well disposed as you are toward hard work and honest living. They are content to rest on their father's legacy. I expect you to be an example for them."

Frank resented the pressure of her expectations. He felt weak and vulnerable, depressed and overwhelmed by the events of recent months.

In spite of Aunt Georgy's admonitions, Frank now launched himself into a life of riotous living, indulging a lust for rich food and wine, gambling and the fair-weather companionship offered by high-living male and female friends. Like Micawber, he soon found that a consistent pattern of expenses in excess of income can lead to misery. Soon, his savings from Bengal exhausted, he was borrowing advances against his trusteed income and his mother, running up debts, and cadging money from a shrinking supply of willing lenders.

In a pub near Covent Garden he encountered some men he knew from India. One was John Skeffington, a former junior officer with the Bengal police.

"Are you still in police work?" Dickens inquired.

"No, old chap. I'm a broker now. I do well in making money for my clients. Still investing in India, though."

Frank was interested. "In what?" he asked. "Gems? Cotton?"

"Cash crop. Indigo," replied Skeffington. "The best place to invest your money. Can't lose, old man. The whole system of production is set up that way. Backed by laws and penalties. Exported for use in the mills here. I could invest some for you, if you'd like. No trouble at all. I have many references, clients who are delighted with the results they've had."

Dickens swallowed some beer.

The wish expressed by Charles in his will — that his children should try to guide themselves by the teaching of the New Testament "in its broad spirit" — came to mind.

"No. I had to deal with some uprisings that resulted from that damned tinkathia system. I saw the evils of it firsthand. Unjust, I'd say. Terrible effects on the natives. I vowed never to invest in it."

Skeffington scowled. "Well, have it your way, old chap. These fellows here have no such qualms and they've done well by it. Here's my card. Let me know if you change your mind."

As Frank's resources dwindled and it became difficult to borrow funds, he began to rethink the pledge he had made in more idealistic times. Indigo production seemed an almost universally profitable business. A fool-proof source of easy money. What would Father say about making an investment in such an exploitive industry? Frank thought. The poor tenant farmers of Bengal were not better off than the children in English workhouses and factories. But Frank was growing increasingly desperate and others had become rich, so why shouldn't he? He approached brother Charley and asked for one last advance. Charley, though skeptical, agreed but warned him there would be no more from the trust.

Skeffington was delighted to hear from Dickens and quickly made an investment for him. "Sound as the Deccan, the granite backbone of India," the broker said with a grin.

But fortune eluded Dickens, or so the brokers reported. Drought in Bihar had killed most of the plants on the plantation where Frank's money was invested. What little survived was torn from the ground by angry mobs enraged that this crop produced for the foreigners' blue clothing was given preferences over the food they needed for survival. True, the rioters had been severely punished, the broker told Frank, but it was too late for this year's crop. And now there were rumours that scientists in both England and Germany had found the secret to making artificial indigo dye. All Dickens's money had been lost. Was it unscrupulous dealers, drought or flood, corrupt landlords, incompetent or lazy farmers that failed his own investment? He would never learn the truth.

Frank's decision not to return to India in his post of District Superintendent was firm. He prepared a letter announcing that he was resigning his commission and ignored demands from the authorities in India. To ensure that he was not persuaded to assume his duties, he went underground. At the moment his assigned ship left port for India, he was in the company of a pair of Cockney trollops.

By chance, Frank encountered his older brother Charley on the streets of Marylebone. It was one of the few events he would recall through the alcoholic stupor that engulfed him in 1871.

"Where the deuce have you been?" demanded Charley. "Mamie is worried sick. Aunt Georgy is furious. Mother is ill with concern.

You've missed your passage and very likely lost your officer's commission to boot."

Frank grinned and placed his right hand on the breast of one of the young women he was leaning on. She ignored Frank's liberty but looked startled at the sudden appearance of this unknown angry man berating her client. Charley was appalled.

"India be damned. Bengal be cursed," Frank slurred. "I shall never look on the majesty of the Raj again."

Staggering, he took out his father's watch and scanned its face. "Not to worry, dear Charley. She weighs anchor at four, it's only noon."

"But three days late, Frank! Damn you! What would Pa think?"

"Papa is well past worrying, dear brother. And why should you be concerned? You will face an early demise if you try to redeem the many sins of your brothers. Or, indeed, the sins of your many brothers. As father remarked, we are a crowd of wastrels and layabouts. Let me be. I have spent nearly eight years in hell, with violence, death, plague and starvation on every hand. And now I have nothing. Let me have some peace."

"Frank, you have talents but you have squandered them. I thank God that your younger brothers, who admire you so, have not witnessed your true character." Charley turned on his heel and strode away.

Frank watched for a moment, then waved his hand dismissively. He snorted with contempt and then guided the women up the stairs to his broken-down lodgings.

Three years of poor investments, liquor and loose living followed. These times were made even worse when younger brother Sydney, who had attended the school in Boulogne with Frank, died aboard HMS Malta in 1872. The news compounded the grief Frank felt about other losses: Walter, Williams, Darshani and his father. Sydney, whose nickname had been Ocean Spectre, was another brother who exhibited the Dickens family predilection for unpaid debts. At one point, Charles had even forbade Sydney to show his face at Gad's Hill, so furious was he about his son's profligacy.

By 1873, the Dickens family had had enough of Frank. His antics, reported back to relatives in excruciating detail, made Mamie and Kate resolve to find honest employment for Frank through their social connections. A posting abroad, they felt, would remove an embarrassment to them.

Mamie, as mild-mannered and practical as Katey was hot-tempered and rash, had called on her sister to discuss a family matter of some urgency and delicacy. Mamie had taken charge because Katey was still mourning the death of her husband Charley Collins who had recently died after a long battle with stomach cancer.

Three years had now passed since Frank's return from Bengal. Three years of dissipation. He was now penniless and had compiled debts that were beginning to fall due to the family. In some respects, Frank's wastefulness weighed more heavily upon his soul than his disappointed sisters could have imagined. His unfortunate investments left him penniless. His erstwhile friends quickly deserted him when the money was gone. Frank's desperation overcame his pride and he went to beg for Mamie's help. His earnest pleas, on those occasions when he presented sober, softened her heart though she let it be known that she expected better behaviour from her younger brother in future. Mamie had explored every connection she could think of to no avail, even asking friends in America to use their best efforts to find employment for Frank. No one appeared willing to take the chance that Frank would give up his indulgences.

Finally, she had made some progress with a highly placed admirer of her father.

"You must remember Freddie Blackwood," Mamie reminded Kate.

Blackwood was now Lord Dufferin and had been a lord-in-waiting for the Queen in his younger years. He was a member of the House of Lords and a longtime friend of the Dickens sisters. A short but energetic, literate and adventuresome man, he enjoyed great personal popularity. Blackwood had helped Charles arrange the author's final American tour. He had described Charles as "a teacher of the duty of gaiety and the religion of mirth." Blackwood knew little of Frank and would have been appalled at the general gloominess and lack of discipline of Dickens' third son had they been closely acquainted. But he had been charmed by the Dickens girls and would go to great lengths to do them favours.

"Last year, you'll remember, Freddie was appointed Governor-General of Canada," Mamie continued. "Now, I hear that the prime minister there — John Macdonald, I believe — is planning to send a police force to patrol the Canadian West, which is infested by roving bands of wild Red Indians and unscrupulous Yankee whiskey traders. With Frank's experience in police work, and Freddie's influence, he might be able to obtain a suitable posting as an officer."

"But Frank has spent all his inheritance!" exclaimed Kate. "How would he raise the money to outfit himself and pay passage to Canada, even if he is so fortunate as to be chosen?"

"This is my purpose in stopping by," Mamie said. "I'd like each of the brothers and ourselves to set aside a little money to cover his costs. If we all share the burden, it won't be too heavy. Goodness knows, we are paying his bills now at any rate! This could give Frank a chance to get back on his feet, learn some self-discipline, and it will get him out of England. You must agree that he has become a costly embarrassment to the family here."

# Chapter 11

It was fall of 1874 when Frank Dickens boarded the SS Hibernia in England with a mix of excitement and trepidation. The discipline required in a policeman was still lacking after the dissolute life he had led for nearly four years in London. He retained his fascination with the fleshpots and taverns of the cities he visited. But there was a seed of impatient eagerness in him that compelled him to ship out for Canada even before he had confirmation of his appointment as a sub-inspector with the North West Mounted Police. Not to mention that his brothers and sisters had made a generous offer to cover his debts if he would leave the country.

Frank was annoyed that the final word on his appointment had not come. After all, it had been June when he sent a letter asking about the status of his application. Upon his arrival in Quebec City, he proceeded to Ottawa, picked up a pre-arranged travel allowance of $200 at the government offices, and took the train on to Toronto. He had ordered his belongings to be forwarded even though his final approval as an officer was not yet in hand.

Toronto was too tempting for him when he arrived there on October 22nd. He had recalled his father's description of the city and its rampant Toryism, but that Charles had also remarked with approval upon its energy. Toronto was conservative, but Frank had enough experience to know that even in the soberest of cities he could ferret out places where sinful pleasures were available. In Ottawa, he had acquired a timetable for travel from the police comptroller. The plan was precisely set out: He was to travel by rail to Chicago from Toronto, then on to St. Paul, Minnesota, overland to Pembina, North Dakota, on the Red River, and thence by river boat to Fort Garry in the new Canadian province of Manitoba. From there he was to travel by wagon to the White Mud River and meet up with a Sub-Inspector Frechette on November 2nd. They were to ride together to the police headquarters at Swan River in the northwest corner of Manitoba for the winter.

Calculating that the free time he would have in Toronto would be the last until he was subject to the rigours of military service and a Prairie winter that was still beyond his imagination, Dickens indulged in more than his share of intoxicants. Two days behind schedule he caught the train for Chicago. He chastised himself for his foolishness and took no more alcohol until he reached Pembina. He arrived in a cold spell in late October and Dickens had never felt a chill as bitter as that of the Prairies. Like all frontier towns, Pembina contained more than its share of rogues, swells and desperadoes, wonderful characters whom Dickens found enchanting. He again succumbed to temptation, easily taken in by new-found friends and took what he considered to be a modest amount of brandy to ward off the frigid winds of late fall. This was a momentary lapse, but it launched him into a wave of comradeship with the peculiar people who populated the local saloons. It was three days before he realized with alarm that he would be unable to make the planned rendezvous with Frechette. He would plead illness as an excuse and headed immediately to Fort Garry, hoping that his travelling companion might also have been delayed. He could certainly not afford to be dismissed from his appointment, without adequate resources, and so far from home.

At Fort Garry, he rented a driver, horse and wagon and lit out immediately for White Mud, near Portage la Prairie. However when he arrived, Frechette — tired of waiting and anxious to meet his own deadlines — had already left for Swan River. Dickens and the driver, both unfamiliar with the road ahead, returned to the fort on the banks of the Red River. He had now spent all $200 of his advance and had run up extra expenses of $58. As he arrived back at Fort Garry, he met up with Lieutenant-Colonel George Arthur French, the Irish-born police Commissioner.

French eyed his new officer skeptically. "And how is it, Mr. Dickens, that you missed your connection? No matter. No point in continuing on to Swan River now. The E Division you were expected to join is already overstaffed by three officers and D division at Dufferin is short one. You might as well stay here with me for the winter and we will head for Swan River in the spring."

Dickens viewed his chance encounter with the commissioner as a stroke of luck. The longer-established post would be more comfortable surroundings for his first winter in the Canadian west than the rough and tumble, hastily erected quarters at Swan River. All might have gone well had Dickens not claimed extra expenses for the $58 he had spent on gear, feed for horses and the driver to catch up to Frechette.

Much to his surprise, Dickens's claim had been forwarded to senior levels, the office of the Minister of Justice in Ottawa. Worse, rather than it being settled with him directly, the correspondence was referred back to French. The commissioner, who had been appointed by the former prime minister, John A. Macdonald, was already regarded with hostility by the new Liberal government of Alexander MacKenzie. French was seen as a beneficiary of Tory political patronage, and found himself engaged in constant struggles with Ottawa to meet basic needs of the police. A minor skirmish over questionable expenses was a confrontation with headquarters that French did not need.

French called Dickens in when the reply arrived from the minister's office. The letter said Dickens had shown no sufficient reason for his late departure from Toronto.

"I will read you this portion," said French. " 'The time wasted in Toronto in disobedience of such positive instructions caused clearly the loss of connection. The Minister of Justice directs that the extra expense incurred in the abortive attempt to overtake Mr. Frechette be borne by Mr. Dickens personally.' So, what do you have to say to this, Mr. Dickens."

"I believe it to be an unfair allegation, sir. I should like to contest it."

"Yes. Well, sir, I have enough difficulty dealing with those nincompoops in Ottawa that I do not need further battles. I will recommend that a portion of your expenses, say, ten dollars, be compensated."

Dickens would not let his complaint die. There were several more exchanges before he finally wrote: "The reason that I was unable to overtake Sub-Inspector Frechette was that after leaving Portage, one of my horses was so fatigued that it was impossible to proceed further in pursuit of the party. The letter from the minister is herewith returned." He signed the letter with a flourish: "Your most obedient servant."

Privately, French roared with laughter at Dickens's impudence. As an artillery officer who had established the Canadian militia gunnery school in Kingston, he would not have tolerated insubordination from Dickens if it had been his authority that was challenged. But, in dealing with the hated bureaucrats from the new government such boldness should not go unrewarded, he thought. He explained to the ministry accountants that Dickens's tardiness had in fact benefited the force because the D troop needed another officer. Dickens was compensated for part of his expense and the issue died. But Frank's apparent resistance to orders had been registered in higher circles and would not be forgotten.

One of Dickens's early acquaintances when he met up with French was Dalrymple Clark. Clark was the paymaster for the police force and a nephew of former prime minister Macdonald. The two men, hoping to escape the boredom at Fort Garry during the long winter, would ride into Winnipeg when they had leave. The rapidly growing village at the junction of the Red and Assiniboine rivers now had about two thousand inhabitants. There was no running water, sidewalks, streetlights or sewerage for the swelling population, but there were thirty saloons, an abundance of muddy and booze-fuelled brawls, and newly arrived first-class madams from the east. And considering that two police recruits died at nearby Dufferin over the winter from typhoid, somehow the supply of alcoholic beverages seemed safer than the dicey water supply.

Clark and Dickens were drinking one evening in one of the saloons known to locals as the "Bucket of Blood" when two swells swaggered in. They eyed the clients and pulled up stools to the bar where they ordered drinks. Clark nudged his companion.

"The fellow on the left with the receding hairline, trimmed beard and curly dark hair…that's the mayor, Frank Cornish. He was once the mayor of London, Ontario, until the other councillors called out the militia to ensure a fair election. Once they got it, he was ousted and he came out here and soon got himself into local politics. He's an Orangeman and a rowdy devil. Mighty handy with his fists for an educated man, a lawyer."

"And a poor judge of character, too, I'd warrant. Who is that boorish young fellow beside him?"

Clark snickered. "That brawny lout's young John Ingram, his chief constable. Only in his early twenties. Fastest fists in the West, they say. And he likes his women. Some say he owns a share in all the town's brothels. That gives the houses some shelter from the long arm of the law. The two of them are the biggest carousers and instigators of brawls in the city."

Dickens looked at his friend with amazement. "And who polices the police?"

"There are two constables, Murray and Byers, who suffer terribly from Ingram's recklessness. They're dedicated fellows who've been close to quitting on several occasions, I'm told. But Cornish has his followers, or if he doesn't, he invents them. In the last election for mayor, there were 308 names on the voter's list and 331 ballots were counted for him. Seems he transferred his Ontario election techniques to this part of the world. And he's not about to get rid of his companion Ingram."

Clark sipped his drink, and chuckled.

"There's a tale about Cornish. As mayor, he is also the chief magistrate for the city. Not long ago after a shocking display of public drunkenness he was told by some of the upstanding citizens of Winnipeg that he had to do something about his offensive conduct. He was setting a poor example. A mayor, they argued, should bring credit to his community."

"And?"

"As chief magistrate he went into the court, charged himself with disorderly conduct and pleaded guilty. Then he fined himself five dollars, which of course, was paid to the magistrate, that again being himself. As the witnesses to the affair were about to leave, he said to himself: 'Wait a minute, Cornish, is this your first offence in this city?' 'Why, yes, your honour,' he replied. 'Well, then, since it's your first offence, I'll remit your fine,' and he handed the five dollars from his right hand to his left. As the astounded witnesses looked on, Cornish the magistrate said to Cornish the rogue, 'Go thou, and sin no more!' Then he rose, pocketed the five dollars and walked out of the court without so much as a glance in the direction of the gaping onlookers."

Dickens nearly fell from his chair, laughing.

"And did his behaviour improve?" he asked.

"Not on your life," said Clark. "Oh, the devil, we have visitors."

Cornish had heard the laughter, recognized Clark and came directly over. He stood over the two policemen. Ingram stood by, rubbing his fists menacingly.

"So, Mr. Ingram, we have visitors from our brothers in the law," he sneered.

"Yes, indeed, Mayor Cornish," said Clark. "This is Sub-Inspector Dickens who is also with us until the spring when we move on to Swan River. As you see from our dress, we are on leave, enjoying the good beer."

"That's good, Clark. Because I'd hate to think you might be wastin' your time on official business here. We are a well-policed city, thanks to our fine Johnny Ingram here. Never beaten in a brawl. We need no assistance in police work from your sickly, raw recruits." Cornish stared hard at Dickens as he said this. "Well, good evening to you."

"And stay outta trouble, hear?" warned Ingram. "I'm hopin' for time off t'night."

Cornish and Ingram returned to the bar, the mayor slapping his comrade's broad back. The two Mounties finished their drinks, then moved on to another saloon. The ambiance of the Bucket of Blood suddenly left something to be desired.

As spring 1875 broke, Commissioner French announced he would proceed with D troop to Swan River, the remote and spartan outpost that had been selected as the police headquarters because it was on the planned route of the new transcontinental railway.

Dickens had found the standard issue saddles used by the police to be shoddy and uncomfortable and resolved to order one for his own use while on duty. He also found the outer gear worn by the police to be lacking, not warm enough in the winter and lacking the quality of waterproofing required to ward off drenching prairie downpours. He called a couple of fellow officers to his quarters and suggested that they, too, might like to place orders through him.

"I know of a London saddler, A. Davis on The Strand, which furnishes excellent gear," he said. "He is recognized with a special appointment to the East India Forces, with whom I served in Bengal, and so I know of the quality of his gear through personal experience."

Two of his colleagues agreed, and so the trio of junior officers ordered saddles, valises, saddlebags, bridles and other gear from A. Davis. The order, however, did not arrive until after their departure for Swan River.

D Troop departed Fort Dufferin, south of Winnipeg, on May 20. French, a no-nonsense officer, had become famous in the force for his long, rapid and determined marches.

"We'll be in Swan River by May 24 to celebrate good Queen Victoria's birthday," he shouted.

Before they left, French had the troop lined up and took out a copy of the Order Book Maxims for the Guidance of Constables. He wanted the members of the new force to conduct themselves by the book. He read each of the points in a loud clear voice:

"One, Constables are placed in authority to protect, not to oppress, the public.

"Two, to do which effectively, they must earnestly and systemically exert themselves to prevent crime…"

Dickens looked about as French read out the maxims. This was the first time he had seen all the men together in uniform. They looked a fine lot now. He wondered how long it would last. There were rumours of numerous desertions from those troops who had moved further west.

French continued. "Be impartial in the discharge of duties and discard all political and sectorial prejudice.

"Be cool and intrepid in the discharge of duties in emergencies and unavoidable conflicts."

Dickens mind focused on French. He was an impressive-looking, ramrod-straight man, educated at military colleges at Woolwich and Sandhurst, and tough in discipline. He had added his own rules to the ones he was reading out now: There would be a five-dollar fine for every time a man was caught swearing. That was the equal of five days pay for the constables. And his tolerance for liquor was very limited.

"Never strike but in self-defence, never treat a prisoner with more rigour than may be absolutely necessary to prevent his escape." French declared.

"Treat with the utmost civility in words, manners and tone of voice, all classes of the public. Cheerfully render assistance to all who may require it."

When French was finished, he ordered the officers and NCOs to inspect the gear of the constables. There was not to be a bullet out of place, a bar of soap missing. They were to carry one blanket, one towel, the soap and a comb, overalls and a pair of shoes, socks, a coat and cape, sixty rounds of ammunition in assorted and specific pouches, a butcher's knife, oil rags and a sponge for cleaning weapons, a curry comb and bristle brush for grooming the horses, and a picket rope, nosebag and hobbles for the animals. They had .450 Adams revolvers strapped to their belts and a .577 Snider-Enfield carbine deposited in a bucket on the right side of the saddle. When the officers were satisfied all the men were appropriately equipped, French gave the order to move out, riding well ahead of the parade in a gruelling pace that the mostly inexperienced constables found near impossible to match.

The troop soon caught up with a procession of Red River carts that had left before them carrying supplies destined for Swan River. The wooden wheels of the carts groaned and shrieked like lost souls as they rumbled along the muddy and deeply rutted trail. There would no secret to anyone within miles that a convoy of the wagons driven by Metis freighters was on the move. Dickens was astonished at the omnipresence of the thick cloying muck that clung to the wheels, the horses hooves and the boots of the men, spraying about as the wheels of the carts rolled forward.

He spotted Alphonse Dupont, a half-French, half-Saulteaux driver that he had met at Dufferin, and struck up a conversation. He wanted to know what the man thought of Swan River. Dickens had to lean close to hear the freighter's answer over the screeching of the wheels.

Dupont laughed. "Don't know how come you chose dat place," he chuckled as the cart screeched along. "Too far nort', not the open prairie. A cold windy place. No whiskey men there. Isn't that why de police come? To stop the whiskey business? How you gonna patrol places where whiskey traders are in winter, when snows come, heh?"

The May evening was still warm as the men stopped to make camp. Dickens was startled to see that Dupont was stripping himself completely naked and placing his clothes deliberately on the ground over an anthill.

"What the devil is he doing?" an astonished Dickens asked Clark.

"Poor chap has lice," said Clark, with a grin. "That's the halfbreed way of getting rid of the little buggers. The ants come out of their holes and raid the clothes for lice and their nits. I'm told it works quite well, but I just hope I never have to test the validity of the practice. Quite undignified, isn't it?"

Dickens felt an irresistible urge to scratch all over his body.

The exhausted men arrived — as pledged by French — in time for the day of celebration. The commissioner was appalled at what he found. The post was erected on the brow of a long, isolated treeless escarpment, blasted by the worst of the prevailing north and west winds. Buildings were strung out at least half a mile along the hill, instead of being clustered together, making the place virtually indefensible. The only shelter against the winds was provided by huge granite boulders left by Ice Age glaciers which had covered the area ten thousand years before. The barracks and other buildings had been erected in late fall, using unseasoned wood, which warped and shrank throughout the winter in an area where the average temperature was minus 20 degrees in January. The men, suffering miserably from the cold, were engaged in an almost constant struggle to plug the gaps in the walls and roofs that opened each time the wood in the buildings shifted. Often, they had to brush drifting snow off their bunks and floors before settling down for the night. Mud had been used in the fall as additional covering for the roof, and now with the spring thaw, great clumps of wet muck fell through onto the floors, the beds and the furniture.

Now that spring had arrived, the men found that the hill was also a breeding ground for garter snakes which, though harmless, found every available hole and hiding place. A constable would sometimes rise in the morning to find that he had been sharing his bed with a number of snakes that had slid into the barracks in search of warm places to energize their cold blood. The Queen's day would be no holiday. Instead, French ordered a hunt of the snakes, and by twilight, the men had collected over 1,100 of the squirming reptiles.

The E troop stationed at Swan River had turned out enthusiastically to cheer the arrival of their D troop comrades. The newcomers soon learned why. Friendship and celebration of the monarch's special day had nothing to do with the happy mood. Rather, there was an expectation of fresh provisions arriving with the men led by the Commissioner. The Swan River troops had subsisted on bread and dried pork at each meal from the beginning of April. The notion that something to vary the diet would come with the new men was reason alone for rejoicing. Now the old supplies of rancid and mouldy pork, which would have been disposed of if there were some alternative meat, could be burned or otherwise destroyed. The cooks tried to trade the old meat to the local natives for freshly killed game, but the Indians and Metis turned up their noses, offended by the rank-smelling meat.

Dickens surveyed the scene with bemusement. His troop had arrived resplendent in their red serge uniforms and pillbox hats. The men at Swan River wore all manner of clothing, some buckskin lined with fur, some homemade cloth caps, trousers and shirts. Others covered themselves with buffalo robes and Hudson's Bay blankets, and sported cowboy hats purchased in the United States. It was not easy to distinguish the police from the Metis, or even the local Indians, by their dress. The official garb was worn only on parade and at formal occasions. There was not an official issue pillbox or helmet in sight most days.

He found Frechette, the officer he was supposed to have met the previous fall.

"You're a damned lucky devil, Dickens. The police clothing we were issued is useless," Frechette complained. "It is entirely unsuitable for the weather here. You will die if you stick to regulation. The pillboxes are fine for city parades but stand up to no weather. When it is hot, they do not provide shade. When it is cold, they provide no warmth. When it rains, they are like sponges and do not keep your head dry. The white helmets, though heavy, are of some use: They are good to hold water or oats when you want to give some to your horse. And now the cold is ending, the snakes are multiplying, and the plague of insects begins — mosquitoes, black flies, horse flies, no-see-ums, stinging wasps, lice..."

"You have spent a hard winter," Dickens observed dryly.

"Pah," said Frechette in disgust. "You go out on patrol, you have to beware of snow-blindness when the sun shines, getting lost when it storms, and frozen, damp clothing and frostbite on all other days. There are no smart-dressed women to delight the eye and ear, and other parts of the body. You have to report sick to get liquor, except for some God-awful brews made in secret. We hide them under the floorboards. You didn't hear this from me, but when the men are paid in the next few days, do not be surprised if many will desert. Some have already left because they weren't paid. For others, the only reason they stay is they have no money to leave. I myself will leave when my enlistment is up."

French saw immediately that there was a problem with morale. He ordered buildings to be torn down and reconstructed and to be made weather-proof. If nothing else, a dose of hard work would keep the men occupied and their minds off their other troubles. He wrote a letter to Ottawa requesting that a piano be sent and that books be provided for a library to keep the men occupied. He proposed to set up a band. The predictable response from Ottawa was that would be a good idea, but the men would have to provide their own instruments. He immediately instituted a daily drill in full dress and was outraged to discover than many of his men had lost or mutilated parts of their uniform.

Rules for consumption of liquor were drawn up. Officers would be issued special permits in order to obtain alcohol. Those who abused their privileges would have them withdrawn. French was not a teetotaller, but believed the police could not achieve a prime objective, the control of illicit liquor in the territories, without showing restraint themselves. There would be no liquor deliveries, or other parcels, to Swan River during the winter, when supplies and mail had to be brought in by dog team and space on the sleds were restricted. French believed that a winter of idleness would only lead to drunken excess among the men and this had to be curbed.

The saddles and other gear Dickens and his comrades had ordered from London had arrived in Winnipeg during the summer but were held there until duties on the imported goods were paid. Frank was incensed. Already his standard issue equipment was wearing out and his saddle was uncomfortable and unstable. He and his friends were stunned to find that the customs officers had added duties amounting to half the total bill. The customs men expected prompt payment. Those extra charges were the equivalent of a month's pay for each of the men.

Frank protested to French. He would not pay such outrageous levies, he told his commanding officer.

"I'm not surprised, Dickens," French said. "I feel you have a good case that you are using this gear on government business. But this is a battle you and your fellows will have to fight on your own. You know that I personally am not regarded with favour by the new government and its new class of bureaucrats. My intervention would likely only weaken your case."

Dickens wrote the customs headquarters in Ottawa, insisting that the equipment was to be used on public service and therefore should be exempt from duty. Months passed as complaint and counter-assertions were made but by the following spring the duties were waived and the saddles were delivered. Along with them came a letter to senior officers warning that duty must in future be paid on items for private use. There was, however, no definition of private use.

In early December 1875, an unexpected guest arrived in Swan River. Major-General E. Selby Smyth, the British commanding officer of the militia, had been ordered by the government to assess the quality of the officers and men with the North West Mounted Police. Smyth was a strict disciplinarian and a humourless man who was feared rather than respected by the men he commanded. French, who had developed his own opinions of the men under his command, resented the intrusion of this stranger. He knew the appointment reflected the jaundiced view that the government held of his own abilities.

Smyth always seemed to be present at the men's activities, whether they were patrols, parades, work details or recreation. He watched like a hawk, scribbling little notes on a tablet of paper he kept in the pocket of his uniform. French told his men that they should carry on as normal and pay no attention to Smyth unless he addressed them directly. Out of Smyth's hearing, however, they often grumbled at the general's spying and aloofness.

In mid-December, a dog train with supplies and mail arrived at Swan River. Sub-Constable Maunsell, a junior recruit, was sorting through the mail when he noticed a parcel in contravention of French's orders. It was addressed to Frank Dickens. He was examining the heavy package when French walked into the mail room in search of his own post.

"What is that parcel, Maunsell?" French asked. "Who is it addressed to?"

"Sub-Inspector Dickens, sir," Maunsell answered sheepishly.

"Bring Mr. Dickens here immediately."

Maunsell returned with Dickens in tow.

"Dickens, I have given very explicit orders," said French harshly. "No parcel deliveries during winter when it is difficult and costly to bring them here. Do you recall that order, sir?"

"Y-y-yes, sir," Dickens said, attempting to control his stammering. There was little of Dickens' earlier bravado evident now. "I recall, sir, and will not repeat the offence."

"See that you don't," said French. "If my officers break the rules it is very difficult to ask more of the lower ranks. Now, go about your business. Maunsell will bring you your mail."

French turned to leave, then noticed that Dickens, in obvious eagerness, had made a move to retrieve the package.

"One moment, Dickens. What exactly is in that parcel?"

Dickens stood erect. His face had turned deep red and his hands were shaking. "It's a Christmas package, sir."

"What?" French barked.

"B-b-brandy, sir."

French snarled incoherently. He turned to Maunsell. "Take it outside and destroy it. Now! I won't have my orders undermined." He glared at the forlorn Dickens.

"One more thing, Dickens," French said, hands on hips. "Each of the officers is entitled to permits for brandy, for medicinal purposes only, it is to be understood. When the time comes for orders to be placed, you will not make use of your permit but will allow it to expire. Do you catch my meaning, sir? Do you?"

Dickens' face flushed even more as he stared at the wall ahead of him. He struggled with the words. "Yes, sir."

Maunsell put on his winter coat, went outside and placed the parcel on a chopping block. He retrieved an axe, hesitated briefly when he thought about good brandy going to waste, then brought the blunt end down heavily on the package. The bottle inside shattered and a clear amber liquid ran out over the wooden block and into the snow.

Smyth happened by at that moment. Curious, he ventured over.

"What is this?" he asked Maunsell.

"Illicit liquor, sir. The colonel asked me to destroy it."

Smyth peered at the label on the torn and shattered package. He could see it was addressed to Dickens.

A few days later, Smyth and French met in the Commissioner's quarters.

"Well, sir," said the major-general. "I am impressed by the general quality of your constables. They are eager to please and you seem to have taken a rather rowdy bunch of rascals and turned them into policemen. My congratulations on that score. My chief concern is whether they are being well led. To my mind, too many of your officers are decayed gentlemen. I myself think you would be better off with hardy and well-trained Canadian farm lads. Your gentlemen officers feel as if they are entitled to privileges. Most, in fact, have over-estimated their skills. They are poor value, French, and most should be encouraged to leave the force. Better to act now and avoid future difficulties."

"These are difficult times to be rooting out those who are less qualified, general," said French. "We are already under staff. A lot of men who rallied to the flag have learned the reality of police work on the frontier and have since departed, whether with our blessing or through desertion. We need to hold on to the men we have until new recruits join up. I would rather give our current officers an opportunity to improve."

"Be realistic, French. Some of them are damned hopeless cases. Take your Sub-Inspector Dickens. He is not a strong man, either physically or mentally. I see from his file that he is continually challenging decisions made in Ottawa, those disputes over expenses and the duties on saddles. What you need above all are disciplined men who will obey authority without question. I gather, too, that he is a drinker and will try to circumvent your decisions. Very bad habits, sir, and, worse, a dismal example for your men. I consider him to be a poor officer of no promise, and that's what will go in my report."

# Chapter 12

After Swan River, Frank Dickens was moved from one post to another for several years. The dressing down at the hands of French at Swan River penetrated his psyche and he could not rid himself of the torment. Instead of reforming, he went to extreme measures to satisfy his cravings.

In late 1876, with Sitting Bull and the Dakota people he led fleeing across the border after the Battle of the Little Big Horn, the Northwest Mounted Police were directed to bolster their forces at Fort Walsh in the Cypress Hills. The hills were just north of the American border, an idyllic site where for generations the people of the plains met peaceably to enjoy the shaded forests, the fresh cooling waters, and the abundant game and food that could be harvested.

Frank Dickens was among those sent as part of the contingent to ensure that fighting did not break out among the refugee Sioux fleeing the American blue coats and the native Cree and Assiniboine who frequented the area. Pressure was being put on the food resources of the hills.

Around the fort there had grown up a small settlement of about 500 Metis people, and assorted hangers-on who provided an array of services to the police and the locals.

Dickens was posted to Fort Walsh in May 1878 and stayed two full years. Walsh had grown to be quite a substantial settlement at that time, boasting three hundred families. As in many frontier communities, some of the residents had a rather dubious reputation. The little town, situated on Battle Creek in a pretty dale in the hills, boasted two hotels, one of which subsisted entirely upon earnings made from the perpetual poker games played in the lobby. Dickens soon made the acquaintance of W.J. Casey, an Irishman and onetime member of the police force who had established a billiard parlour in the village.

There were also five thousand native people in the vicinity, including many of Sitting Bull's Sioux. Although the police took great pains to keep liquor out of the hands of the local Indians, and would prosecute blatant whiskey traders, it was well known that alcohol could be easily had in the town. It was also well known that some of the worst offenders when it came to liquor wore the uniform of the Queen.

Dickens soon learned that there was a laundry, set somewhat apart from the village, run by a woman named Annie Harris, known to the locals as Nigger Annie. Word was that the serving of lubricants, and other services, too, were available at the laundry. Oddly, Annie was never charged with bootlegging or other offences, even though the whole town knew what was on offer.

Every time Frank wandered in the direction of the laundry, Casey seemed to be at the door of his billiards room.

"So, then Frank, are ye off to be starched and pressed again?" Casey inquired with a sly grin.

"The water in this valley is undrinkable," Frank replied. "One must seek out alternatives. I'm sure people will die from bad water. As my father once wrote, 'Picturesqueness and typhus are fast friends.'"

Casey approached. "How is it, me friend, that when you return from the laundry, your clothing is no cleaner than when you left? Everyone thinks you should have the cleanest outfits in the valley, the number of times you head to Annie's."

"Now, isn't that my business?" Frank replied.

"Sure, tis so, but mind my friend. I have heard some of the senior officers comment on the lack of discipline of a few of the men, yourself not included, I'm sure. I hold no brief for those gentlemen but I want to give ye a fair warnin'."

Frank looked Casey in the eye. "I've had bad news from home. My poor mother is ill and may not have much time left. I was away in India when my father died. And there is nothing I can do about it. When I'm on duty, I can keep my mind off this. But during my time off, it weighs heavily on me."

"Sad it is, to be sure. Now, just wait a bit. I'll shut down the parlour, and join ye for some poteen, then."

In August 1878, when Frank Dickens was posted at Fort Walsh he had his first encounter with the Cree chief Big Bear. Dickens had gone to Sounding Lake, between the Battle and Red Deer rivers, with police Commissioner Acheson Gosford Irvine, and officers Dalrymple Clark and Cecil Denny for the distribution of annual treaty payments to thousands of Cree, Assiniboine and Saulteaux. They met there with David Laird, the lieutenant-governor of the territories, Edgar Dewdney, the Canadian Indian Commissioner and Superintendent James Walker, in charge of the police contingent.

Frank had travelled there with a party that included Elliott Galt, secretary to Dewdney, who shared a tent with Dickens and with whom he paddled across the Saskatchewan River. The group was plagued by swarms of mosquitoes that not only harassed the men but tormented the horses so much that they ran off and were not found until the following evening. Then dense fog settled in on the prairie and the travelers were disoriented for several days. When the party finally reached Sounding Lake, much later than expected, they found the various Indian bands waiting for them impatiently. Frank was delighted to learn, however, that he had been chosen to lead the escort for the senior authorities.

The site of the meeting, situated in what had once been the best buffalo hunting country of the northern plains, had been recommended by Big Bear. Many bands led by other chiefs had arrived. And now there was an expectation among the white authorities that the Cree chief, greatly respected among his people, was about to take treaty, a move he had resisted so far. Why would he have selected the site if he was not about to sign, they thought. So the government representatives were dismayed when Big Bear arrived with only two or three of his band's lodges with him. The rest were hunting in the south, he told them. Walker, incensed, grumbled aloud that Big Bear was feeding his reputation as the most troublesome of the prairie chiefs.

Dickens was startled when he first saw this man whose name struck such consternation among the authorities. He had expected a stalwart warrior, tall and inspiring. Standing before them was a short character in his mid-fifties, with long black shaggy hair, an unattractive face, with deep scars on a barrel chest. He wore a tall bearskin cap, with long eagle feathers that helped add something to his physical stature, but around his ankles were strips of fur that looked like skunk, and he carried a bouquet of sweet-smelling prairie herbs.

Big Bear carried himself proudly — haughtily and defiant some of the white men said — but his biggest impression was made when he spoke. His voice was deep, rich and hypnotic in his own tongue. One moment, it could blare loud and powerful as a trumpet, and the next could be gentle and caressing as a soft spring breeze. He spoke no English, but when he talked all eyes stayed on him as if drawn by some mystic force. Indeed, his people believed he came from a line of shamans and his medicine was strong. This power, in the white men's eyes, was what made him a dangerous man.

"Quite an impudent fellow," Laird said. "He arrives with only a few lodges from his own band, yet claims to speak not only for his own followers but for all those who have taken the treaty."

This was only the start.

"Why would I want your paper money?" Big Bear told Laird and the others through the interpreter. "This is useless to me. I can't eat it. It will not keep me warm, unless I toss it on the fire, and then only for the flash of a firefly's belly."

The assembled chiefs laughed.

"Why should I accept the white man's promises? My people need real food. The government must pledge to provide sustenance for all the people. I will not sign the treaty now, but will wait four winters. Four is a holy number to my people. This time will show me how the people who signed the paper are treated by the councillors of the Great Mother. Then, if I am satisfied that the Great Mother has cared for all her children, I will sign".

The lieutenant-governor turned to Walker and the interpreter with dismay.

"The gall of this man," Laird said, motioning to the interpreter not to transmit his words. "This damned devil is not only not going to sign, he might lead some of the others away." Then he replied to Big Bear.

"I have no authority to change the terms of the treaty that the other chiefs have signed."

Big Bear listened for the translation, then responded firmly, repeating so there would be no doubt. "My people need to know they will be cared for when the buffalo are gone. The great herds of buffalo I saw in my youth are already a pitiful sight. My people need the food, clothing and shelter that the great herds once gave us. This is the most important thing to us. True chiefs must pity the poor, and help those in difficulty. I have spoken." Then he turned abruptly and left, followed by many of the assembled warriors.

"Big Bear is leading more people away than he came with," Walker observed.

Laird's patience was exhausted and he broke up the gathering. Back at his camp, there was a sudden burst of gunfire and bullets whizzed over the lieutenant-governor's tent. Young mounted warriors, angry at Laird's insistence that he could not improve the terms of the treaty, rode through the camp firing in the air, menacing the police wagons.

Walker summoned Dickens. "This demonstration cannot be tolerated. We will go to Big Bear and put a stop to it."

The two policemen and an interpreter marched through the Cree camp to Big Bear's lodge. The three men were surrounded by Cree men, women and children, ominously silent, watching to see what would happen next.

Big Bear was seated in his lodge with his family when Walker arrived.

"You must put a stop to this now, Big Bear. The lieutenant-governor will not stand for it."

The chief looked at Walker's face, flushed with anger. He marvelled at how the faces of the white men turned a deep red when they were enraged. He considered the words of this irate policeman. It was several tense minutes before he answered.

"These are not my people, but I will ask them to stop."

On his way out of the lodge, Big Bear stopped and gave a penetrating look deep into Dickens's eyes. The policeman felt uncomfortable but was transfixed. He could not look away from the chief's gaze. For his part, Big Bear felt uneasy at the sadness in the younger and quieter Red Coat's eyes. The chief shuddered. He had a premonition. This man would be important to him at some time in the future, he knew. At a time of great peril for both of them.

# Chapter 13

The penetrating look that Big Bear gave me at Sounding Lake has affected me deeply. He has a reputation among his people of being a soothsayer, a leader who can predict the future. I wish I could speak to him man to man and ask what he saw in me. Instead, in moments of reflection like this I fear what might come to pass.

This is an inhospitable land. The bitter cold of the winters makes life almost unbearable at times and I shake every time I am required to make a patrol in that season. Getting lost in a howling blizzard, separated from one's mates, is one continuing danger. Then the summers on the plains go to the other extreme. We ride in our heavy uniforms in blistering heat that while — not as excruciating as Bengal — recalls to me the sunstroke I suffered there. I often fear a recurrence. There are the persistent swarms of biting insects — mosquitoes, black flies, midges, deer flies — that are a constant part of late spring and summer days.

Almost worse is the boredom. The days that pass, end on end, without anything to occupy oneself. The limited selection of books is read over and over, searching for new insights that fail to appear. We play cards occasionally — whist, vingt-et-un, casino, but soon tire of that recreation.

The combination of these things can almost drive one mad.

I do not even mention the possibility that a hostile tribesman might lie in wait for an easy target riding over the plains. That is the kind of danger we take for granted.

No wonder that so many desert the force; the greater wonder might be that more do not.

I walked by a mirror at Walsh the other day and I struck me that my image is less than flattering. In India, as a young recruit I once cut a fine figure in uniform, in spite of my receding chin. That day, I saw myself in a different light. I am of less than average height, stoop-shouldered and full stomached. My retreating hair exposes a broad ruddy forehead. There are now flecks of gray in my bushy reddish beard and mustache, and the whole partly conceals a blotchy complexion with a purplish hue that deepens when I am under stress.

Then, the name of Chickenstalker that Father gave me in a jesting, kindly way, has become something of a laughing matter to my less amiable comrades-in-arms. My deafness has increased over the years, but I am sure that I sometimes hear rude fellows contemptuously making clucking chicken noises when I walk by, with others grinning away like baboons.

Much of my description I blame upon the anxieties and extremes of my career, both here and in India. Am I feeling insecure, sorry for myself? No doubt. But here I have few friends and virtually no contact with family to bolster my spirits. At least, Colonel Macleod, in charge of Fort Walsh, seems to view me positively of late. But a senior officer cannot become too intimately connected with the rank-and-file, else discipline might suffer.

There are women here but none I have found compare to my poor lost darling Darshani. Mary Macleod, the colonel's wife, is a lovely woman with whom I am on friendly terms. But she, of course, is an "untouchable."

Therefore, I keep largely to myself, and take some moments of joy by strolling the nearby forest and plains with my shotgun in search of game birds.

# Chapter 14

In June 1880, a few months after he had heard of the death of his mother from stomach cancer, Frank Dickens was transferred to Fort Macleod and, despite his spotty record, given additional responsibilities. The fort was situated on the banks of the Oldman River, which flowed eastward from the nearby Rocky Mountains, eventually to add its waters to the Saskatchewan. This was the centre of the homeland of the Blackfoot Confederacy, which included the Siksika, Bloods, Peigans and Sarcee.

Despite the toll of famine and disease, the Blackfoot were still the most powerful force on the Canadian plains. They and others in the northern prairies had resented the arrival of thousands of Sioux refugees under Sitting Bull after the American defeat at Little Big Horn. Too many other people, Sioux and halfbreeds, have been eating our buffalo, one Blackfoot chief complained as his once-proud people sank into destitution. The problem was worsened when in 1879 American troops, hoping to starve the Sioux into returning to their home territory, set huge fires south of the border to prevent the northward migrating buffalo from entering Canada. The presence of the police helped to prevent serious outbreaks of trouble among the hungry Indian nations.

Shortly after his arrival at Macleod, he was ordered to lead a small contingent of police to the nearby Peigan reserve for the annual payments of money due to Peigans and Stonies who were included under Treaty Number Seven. Each chief was to receive $25, chief's councillors would get $15 and there would be $5 for every other man, woman and child. This event, normally routine, was disrupted when a band of 200 American Peigans showed up expecting to be given treatment equal to their brothers on the Canadian side of the medicine line.

The gatherings of the Blackfoot confederacy of tribes were always times of celebration for them. The Canadian Blackfoot and their American visitors feasted together, danced and sang for days as each band arrived. Dickens, however, was disturbed by what he saw.

"These South Peigans live across the line," Dickens told Jerry Potts, the bandy-legged half-Blood Indian, half-Scots scout who kept close contact with his tribal kin and was a highly respected warrior in their eyes.

"I want you to explain to them that American Peigans have not signed the treaty and so are not entitled to the payments."

Dickens resolved to stand firm. He knew all the Blackfoot had suffered since the herds of buffalo did not show up in their lands the year before. He knew, too, that bureaucrats in Ottawa and their agents in the west were demanding that rations to the Indians be reduced. Dickens' colleague Cec Denny had been overwhelmed with pity at the state of the Blackfoot in 1879 and had been disciplined for distributing two thousand pounds of beef a day for three days to the starving tribesmen until angry orders came by telegraph from the east to stop. Dickens vowed he would not make a mistake like that only to be punished by his superiors for excessive generosity. Besides, he thought, the police were suffering from the commanded austerity, too. Although he now had a grander, reclassified title of Inspector, up from Sub-Inspector, his pay and that of all his men had been cut and they were still expected to perform the same duties.

Potts said nothing to Dickens but translated the gist of his comments to the assembled chiefs.

"Tell them I will not begin the distribution until the American Indians have left."

Dickens' declaration caused a heated discussion among the chiefs. All were going to be punished by this policeman for the actions of a few.

"Bear Child." One of the Canadian Peigans used Potts's Blackfoot name. "How can we tell our brothers to leave? Before the white man came, there was no border. We went to their lands and they came to ours whenever there was need. They are our relatives. We help each other and welcome them here, just as they would do to us. Tell the policeman to treat all our people the same."

"What are they saying?" Dickens asked of Potts. Frank stood with hands on his hips, doing his best to look stern.

"They say they all one people," Potts said briefly in English, looking at Dickens.

The inspector looked exasperated. "Well, I have no authority to give to the American Peigans. I have been told to distribute the treaty payments to those bands whose chiefs have signed the treaty. I have been given only so much money. If I give the Canadian Indians less, they will claim that they have been cheated, with some justification. They will demand more, and there is no more. Tell the chiefs to come back when the American Indians have gone."

Dickens turned and walked away, followed by his men.

Potts gestured helplessly to the chiefs. He pursued Dickens back to the police camp.

The standoff continued. Dickens stayed in his camp, keeping mostly to himself. He had been preoccupied with personal matters for months since he had received word of his mother's death. He frequently wondered why fate had banished him to far off lands where he had missed the last years of both his beloved mother and father. Then, word had come that his friend, Dalrymple Clark, only recently married, had fallen severely ill at Fort Walsh from a serious intestinal ailment. From his two-year posting at Walsh, Dickens knew there was something about its location that took a toll on the health of the police, Indians and Metis alike. And now, the government was demanding more work for less pay. Some officers had had enough and were leaving the force, several even deserted and rode south across the border to escape the consequences or to look for gold. He considered resigning, but in his depression could think of no satisfactory alternative. So, camped on Blackfoot lands, within sight of the mountains to the west, he emerged from his tent only when necessary to issue commands, inspect the men or eat meals.

For two days, he refused to budge from his stance. The American Peigans must leave before the payments could begin. Meanwhile, in the Peigan camps some chiefs were upset at the delay and the insistence of the southern intruders that they should share in the bounty. Dickens decided to make distribution to the Stonies, who had no part in the internal politics of the Blackfoot. Envious, the Peigan chiefs saw payments being made to their traditional enemies and then met to decide what could be done. The American Peigans were now sensing rising hostility among their Canadian relatives.

Potts came with a message.

"American Peigan will leave but want you to give them food and tea," Potts said. "They will go home."

Dickens found the solution acceptable and the deal was done. With gifts of beef, flour, tea and tobacco, the southern Peigans were escorted back over the border.

Dickens' superiors at Fort Macleod thought that Dickens had shown some backbone in that affair, but they attributed the successful conclusion to the steadying influence of Potts among the Blackfoot. Leif Crozier, a tough-minded Irishman who was Dickens' commanding officer, found it hard to give Dickens credit for anything. And he believed the Englishman was far less resolute in a dispute over stolen horses that erupted next. That affair would have gone badly if not for the boldness displayed by Sergeant Spicer, in Crozier's view.

Successful horse stealing escapades were a badge of honour for Blackfoot warriors. The bolder and stealthier the theft, the greater the esteem for the thieves by their fellow tribesmen. Even the police had been victims of the larcenous game. A group of American Peigans had stolen some horses at Fort Macleod from right under the noses of police guards, a daring raid that brought much hilarity to the Blackfoot lodges and admiration for the perpetrators.

The episode that involved Dickens began when a group of heavily armed Montana ranchers arrived at Fort Macleod in June 1881, claiming that Canadian Bloods had raided their lands and had run a herd of stolen horses back into Canada.

Dickens was ordered to proceed to the Blood reserve fifteen miles east of Fort Macleod. He took with him Spicer and Constable Callaghan, and some of the complaining ranchers.

The police first stopped at the teepee of Red Crow, head chief of the Bloods. The chief told Dickens he would do his best to help but that many of the wilder young men would pay little heed to his words.

As Dickens and Red Crow spoke, the American ranchers had begun walking through the camp, picking out fourteen horses that they claimed belonged to them. Dickens had emerged from Red Crow's lodge and mounted his horse when Many Spotted Horses, a well-known Blood warrior who had signed the treaty, rode up and confronted him angrily.

"These horses belong to my people," he shouted. "Why do you police take the word of these lying men from the country of the Long Knives? Do our words mean nothing to you? Do you take their word because they have white skins, like you? These men are cheating us and you do nothing. We will have to defend ourselves if you will not."

Dickens tried to avoid the taunts and the threats, staring straight ahead and trying to keep his own nervous horse steady.

Many Spotted Horses maneuvered his horse so that he was again in front of Dickens. His voice had attracted a crowd of young men, some of whom carried rifles and war clubs.

"My friend, Bull Back, lost all his horses last year to that American last winter." He pointed at one of the ranchers. "What did you do then to get them back? Nothing."

The rancher picked out by Many Spotted Horses had been leading one of the horses.

"He's lying," the American said, denying the allegation. Though his response was bold, he was clearly terrified.

The growing crowd of mounted warriors sidled their horses up against the Americans and police, and two or three fired shots in the air. Tension mounted as the yelling and whooping grew louder and more threatening. Then, one of the mounted Bloods reached down and grabbed a rancher by the collar.

The noise and the excitement were too much for one of the ranchers. He broke free from the crowd and raced for a nearby corral, followed by several others. The Americans took cover, drew their Colts and prepared to fight it out. The Bloods looked ready to chase them down.

"Stop," yelled Dickens, trying to move his agitated horse between the fugitives and their pursuers. Few heard his call above the commotion. Dickens ordered Spicer and Callaghan to prepare for action, while the Americans cocked their pistols, ready to fire.

Seeing Dickens between themselves and the ranchers, the Bloods hesitated. Then Spicer, who had learned some Blackfoot, called out that he wished to speak. The unusual spectacle of a white man speaking their language, however poorly, caught the attention of the warriors. Most of the Indians turned to listen.

Spicer spoke slowly and calmly, trying to settle down the angry men on both sides. "If any man had his horse wrongfully taken," the sergeant said,"he should go to the police commissioner and the animal will be returned once the truth is established."

"Killing the Americans will be a serious mistake," he continued. "It will only mean that the Long Knives would cross the medicine line in search of the killers. This would be against the wishes of the police and the Great Mother, who wants to protect her children. The Bloods would become fugitives in their own land, just as Sitting Bull and his people were south of the medicine line. The difference would be that, unlike Sitting Bull, you will have nowhere else to turn for refuge because those who are killed would be Americans."

Spicer's logic succeeded in calming the angry warriors.

Dickens, meanwhile, quietly urged the ranchers to give up the search and to leave the Blood camp for Fort Macleod. "I thought it best to get both men and horses as far away from the reservation as possible," he reported later.

Bloodshed had been averted in that incident, Crozier thought to himself. But the inspector had displayed a distressing lack of authority and determination. If there was a hero in the affair, it was Spicer, not Dickens.

# Chapter 15

Frank commanded the small police detachment at Blackfoot Crossing on the Bow River in January 1882. The Christmas and New Year holidays each year were the one time at the police outposts that all eyes turned to Frank Dickens. This was the son of the man, after all, who had almost reinvented Christmas as it was now celebrated, or at the very least, had been the holiday's prime publicist. Comrades-in-arms who paid Frank scant attention throughout the year were now eager to hear stories about the famous Charles. They urged Frank to give readings of his father's Christmas works, hoping for a ring of authenticity that might be passed along from author to son. The inspector, fuelled by spirits both ethereal and ethanol, did his best to recreate the spell-binding orations of his father.

On New Year's Eve, Frank held up the gold watch bequeathed him by Charles.

"My father would mix up a special bowl of punch. He would blend an assortment of fruit juices — the more exotic the better, carbonated water and a liberal dose of rum into a concoction that would delight the taste buds of a prince. Close to midnight, he would open the main entrance to the house and stay alert as this very watch ticked nearer to midnight. When the year changed, he would bellow out in his loudest voice 'Happy New Year' for the whole neighbourhood to hear. That was a signal for all who heard the joyful acclamation to stop in for some merriment, music, dancing, food and drink."

The men, far from families and loved ones, never seemed to tire of that tale and even the halfbreeds and few Indians invited to the celebrations — most of whom had no idea of who the father was — would smile happily and join in the applause.

As the new year began in 1882, the officers and men had enjoyed an opulent feast of roast buffalo hump, venison and grouse, washed down with the best available wine and brandy. After the meal, the music began. An accordion was produced and the men chose partners among the few available mixed-blood women, or occasionally paired up with other men.

A favourite song was the Buffalo Hunter's Song, written by a homesick Irishman named Welsh. The dancers pranced merrily as one of the men sang out:

Won't you, in your English advancing,
Learn just a few words each day.
Forgive me, my one well-beloved,
If I find a fault in some way.
Oftimes when my poor heart is sighing,
Quite well, do you know "c'est pour vous".
I only am he who may whisper
"Je vous aime, vous, ne que vous",
I love you, yes you, only you.

You soon will see, my sweet adored one
"En anglais" love is not just for mirth.
Not I, a fashionable lover,
I'm just a poor man on earth.
My only fashion is love's method,
A very tender earnest plea,
I beg that you will answer "Yes, dear",
When I say "Prithee marry me."

Their robust feasting and merriment contrasted with the ache of hunger in the bellies of thousands of tribesmen encamped outside the police quarters. The previous year had been the worst ever for starvation among the Blackfoot Confederacy. The buffalo had vanished like morning mist in the preceding years and hundreds of men, women and children had perished from malnutrition and disease.

A severe test of Dickens' ability as an officer came soon after that happy performance. Early January was the time for the government agents and the police to prepare provisions for the rest of the long prairie winter. Spring, before the prairie burst into life and animal migrations began, would be the time of the direst food shortages for both whites and the local Indians.

The Bow River valley was also the winter gathering place for the Blackfoot. The river flowing eastward from the Rockies had eroded deeply into the plain and 50-foot high bluffs along its banks offered shelter from icy winds that swept in from the western mountains and across the treeless plains. The Bow, when not frozen, was fresh, clear and cold, and in contrast to the bare prairie, along its banks there was wood aplenty for fuel and lodgepoles.

The day was sunny but windy at Blackfoot Crossing, and government contracted workers Charles Daly and Bill Barton, hired from the I.G. Baker Company, spent most of it at the farm instructor's slaughtering pen close to the river. They killed selected cattle and hacked up chunks of beef to be stored away for the leaner times. It was hard work and the two men were still feeling the painful aftermath of their effusive New Year celebrations. Their activities always attracted a crowd of on-lookers from the Blackfoot camps who hoped to buy or be given some of the leavings from the slaughter. The white man, the Indians knew, was a wasteful creature, always throwing away parts of the animals they killed. Selling the unwanted remains of animals to the highest Indian bidder was a practice that augmented significantly the modest wages of the contractors.

The brutal times suffered by the Blackfoot and the hard line ordered from Ottawa and acted on by many government agents in their assistance to the native people had increased the interest in the January slaughter this year. With the buffalo gone, the Blackfoot increasingly relied on beef rations from the whites, but as this dependence grew the agents became ever more stingy in negotiations.

Barton, his work coat drenched with blood and smeared with guts, wiped his brow. The winter day was warm, with a Chinook wind blowing in from the west. Barton sweated profusely and his head was pounding as he struggled to cut up the meat. He noticed a Blackfoot warrior and police scout, Dog Child, was among the Indians watching the work.

"Dog Child, help us here and we'll give you some meat," he suggested.

As Dog Child joined in the work, he was approached by Bull Elk, a minor Siksika chief.

"I want to buy the guts of this cow," he told Dog Child. He had hoped that there might be a calf fetus in the cow's womb. Bull Elk examined the paunch, found there was no fetus and then handed Dog Child a dollar. "I'll take a cow's head instead."

Dog Child handed the dollar to Barton, who had been watching the exchange.

"Make sure the head is cut close," Barton told Dog Child. "That means no neck is attached to the head."

When Barton saw the head Dog Child had prepared, he strode red-faced over to Bull Elk. There was too much of the neck on the head for his liking.

"That is not for sale, Bull Elk. I told Dog Child to cut it close and that is not close enough." Bull Elk, who spoke no English, stood uncomprehending.

"You should give his dollar back then," the chastened Dog Child said sheepishly.

Barton stuffed the dollar into Bull Elk's palm and went to Daly, who had been watching events unfold. "Have you sold that head?" Daly asked.

"No," replied Barton, "that one is not for sale."

Bull Elk and one of his wives had meanwhile been picking out a beef heart, lungs and paunch and put them to one side. Then, after looking over the heads, he approached Barton and gave him the dollar back.

The chief pointed out the head he wanted to Daly and told his wife to pack it up. Daly turned to indicate that Bull Elk should choose another head and then he saw the woman leaving with the disputed head.

"Hey," Daly shouted. "You're stealing that!" He ran over to the woman and roughly ripped the head from her grasp, throwing it back on the pile of remains.

Bull Elk was enraged. He felt he had paid for a head and had the right to choose the one he wanted. He rushed over, lifted the heavy head and was near the edge of the slaughter pen when Daly yelled in anger.

"Bring that back, damn you!" Daly raced across the pen, wrestled the head from Bull Elk and returned it to the pile. He was no sooner there when Bull Elk grabbed his arm from behind, twisting it behind the contractor's back.

"Keep away, Bull Elk. I don't want to fight," Daly shouted, turning and pushing the chief away. The Indian stumbled and fell in the muddy gore. Barton tossed the dollar onto the fallen man. Bull Elk rose and approached again but now Dog Child and other Blackfoot dashed in to separate the chief from the two contractors.

Bull Elk and his wife left. The chief felt humiliated and cheated by Daly and Barton. He boiled with anger and talked openly of revenge.

Charles Lafrance, a Metis employed by the government, had been cutting timber on the north side of the frozen Bow River. As he crossed the ice to his cabin, he saw Bull Elk with two wives in tow coming in his direction. Bull Elk did not even turn his head as Lafrance passed but stared straight ahead, scowling. One of the wives pulled out a knife and drew it across her throat in a threatening gesture. She spoke a few words. Lafrance had some limited knowledge of Blackfoot and understood the woman to say that a white man was going to die.

Then Lafrance saw Daly and asked why Bull Elk was so angry. Daly explained.

"This is very dangerous," said Lafrance. "The Blackfoot are desperate now. Bull Elk's wife said he intends you harm. Take care. You and Barton must go to the house and get out of sight before Bull Elk comes back to the corral. Give him time to calm down."

A few minutes later, Lafrance, government agent William Scott and Dr. Lauder were walking to Barton's house. As they walked in the twilight, Lafrance spotted Bull Elk about 150 yards away. He had his musket raised to his shoulder.

"Down, Scott!" Lafrance yelled. Instantly, the sound of a shot reverberated among the cluster of log buildings, and a whistling musket-ball struck a log about ten feet from the ration-house.

Bull Elk raised his single-shot gun, loaded and fired again. In the mid-winter gloom the men could not be sure what the Blackfoot was firing at. The second shot hit the ration-house walls.

The men did know they were near the line of fire. Lafrance and Scott ran to the nearby mess-house and grabbed their rifles, loading as they ran back.

Barton and Daly had been struggling with a load of cattle hides to the ration-house where they planned to hang them outside for curing. They were walking between two houses when the first bullet spun by Barton's right leg and hit the log. Both men dashed off to get their guns, and Daly headed over to the police post.

After the second shot rang out, Lafrance edged out and walked cautiously toward the slaughter pen. Peering into the twilight, he spotted a young Blackfoot warrior gripping Bull Elk by the arm and trying to lead the older man away.

Lafrance saw two other men. Heavy Shield, a head chief of the Blackfoot, and Running Rabbit, a minor chief who had been standing between Bull Elk's position and the log hit by the first bullet.

Lafrance hailed them. "What was Bull Elk doing? Why did he shoot in the camp? Was he trying to hit Barton?"

"Bull Elk was not shooting at anyone," said Heavy Shield. "I saw those two government men. The bullets did not go near them. I have hunted with Bull Elk and been at war with him. If he wanted to kill them, he would not have missed."

Lafrance thought Heavy Shield was protesting too much.

Daly had burst excitedly into the police building, looking for Dickens. He waved his rifle in the air.

"Bull Elk tried to kill us," he shouted. "You must arrest him, now, damn it, before he escapes in the darkness."

"What's this all about?" Dickens demanded.

"He wants to kill us, captain. If you don't arrest and punish him now, we'll all be in danger, because others may try to shoot and kill us."

Dickens listened to Daly's complaint and the second-hand description of Lafrance's encounter with Bull Elk's wife. Yes, he concluded, Bull Elk must be arrested. His behaviour was threatening, if not murderous, and could not be tolerated.

"Sergeant, get two constables and meet me outside," he told Joseph Howe.

Within minutes, Dickens, Howe, Constables Wilson and Ashe were on their way to the Blackfoot camp. The January evening air had now turned cold and damp, chilling to the bone. As they neared the camp, Howe spotted an Indian who carried a gun and sack running across the path and up a small hillock. The man was warmly dressed and apparently settling in for a long spell outside. Howe walked cautiously toward the hill. Bull Elk's rifle pointed at him, ready to fire.

"Stop! He will shoot you!" someone shouted in Blackfoot.

It was young Eagleshoe, the warrior who had guided Bull Elk away from the cabins earlier. "Wait here. I will talk to my mother's brother," he said in English.

Eagleshoe walked up the rise to Bull Elk's refuge and they spoke for a few minutes. The chief lowered his weapon. Then Eagleshoe emerged with his kinsman.

"My uncle's anger has softened and he will not fight now," the young man said. "But he wants the police to be fair. He is hungry and only wants to feed his family."

Howe marched up to the edgy chief and grabbed him by one arm. Constable Wilson, took Bull Elk's other arm and the four policemen began crossing the river ice, returning to their post.

A group of about thirty young warriors arrived from the Blackfoot camp, angry and eager for a fight.

"What are you afraid of?" some of them taunted the growing crowd. "Don't let them take Bull Elk. They are only four. We are many!"

Harassment by the crowd grew as the policemen struggled across the windswept river ice, dragging their increasingly resisting prisoner. Some older women arrived with knives and axes, others with lit torches, and a few of the young men carried carbines.

Howe's right arm, carrying Bull Elk's gun, was yanked at the same time as one of the crowd stuck out a foot and tripped him. He stumbled and a woman ran at him and grabbed the gun away. The rifle disappeared quickly into the crowd. Constable Ashe, slipped on the ice and fell. While he was down he was kicked in the ribs, but rose quickly despite the pain, fearing a worse beating if he stayed down. A woman cursed at Wilson and swung a hatchet at his arm, but missed.

Dickens, meanwhile, had been walking backwards behind the others, protecting them from harassment from the rear. He held a six-shot Enfield revolver in hand, and pointed it at the closest members of the trailing mob, threatening those who rushed toward the policemen.

"Inspector, they are loading carbines!" Howe exclaimed, hearing the clicks of guns readied for action.

A sharp explosion followed and Howe heard a bullet whistle over his head. This was too much. He drew his revolver and fired three times in the air hoping the other Mounties would come to the aid of the four men. Soon, a dozen officers arrived on the run and pushed back the crowd. They were now able to manhandle Bull Elk to the police post.

Dickens was wheezing and coughing from the exertion of getting his charge back to the headquarters. He called for an interpreter and prepared to take statements.

"Bring me Daly, Barton, Scott, Lafrance and anyone else who witnessed the shooting," he ordered Howe. "Wilson, lock the prisoner up. Make sure he doesn't go anywhere."

The constable pushed Bull Elk into a small cell, and shackled the unwilling prisoner's feet. Bull Elk began chanting a song of pain and loss.

Outside, a group of policemen tried to keep the growing crowd away from the building, to little avail. The people were ominously quiet but sullen and angry, and kept pressing forward against the police, confining them to an ever-smaller circle around the building. A few armed warriors broke away to surround the stables and cut the police off from their water supply and storehouse. The redcoats were going nowhere without the consent of the Blackfoot.

Dickens sat at his desk and readied himself to take statements. The mob outside made it difficult to concentrate on the task at hand. His hand trembled and it was great difficulty that he kept his stuttering under control. Even when the crowd was quiet, there was a low mumble outside the walls. A warrior broke into a war song, joined by others. A shot was fired in the air and the song rose like a wave, before settling down to a babble of excited voices.

This was now Dickens' third troublesome confrontation with the Blackfoot and this time he feared that a serious outbreak was inevitable. They were a proud and arrogant people, Dickens knew only too well. The members of the Confederacy were much to be admired, and had been feared by their enemies. But they had been humbled by year after year of starvation and disease, compelled to become beggars in their own land, against their will dependent upon the unwanted white man. Some of their young men believed the way to restore their pride and self-sufficiency was to take the path of war against enemies, including the whites.

Howe had returned with the three white men, Lafrance, and Dog Child, Heavy Shield and Running Rabbit. Dickens began taking notes.

Daly accused Bull Elk of stealing the cow's head and threatening to fight him. He said he saw the chief shoot at him. This was translated into Blackfoot.

Bull Elk had been brought from the cell and placed in a chair facing Dickens' desk. Angry, he rose and spoke of how he had given money in exchange for the head. It was a fair agreement. He was confused why the white man said he had not paid for the beef. It was not his fault that the white men refused to accept his money. He had no intention to steal but Daly had gone back on his word and humiliated him before his people.

Dickens interrupted. "Bull Elk, you must just ask questions of Daly now. You will have a chance to give your version of events later.

The inspector glanced at the windows, where angry faces filled the panes.

Bull Elk glared with contempt at Daly. "Did you see me give Barton a dollar?" he demanded.

"I did not see you give Barton any money," Daly replied curtly.

Barton admitted Bull Elk had given him money but he claimed it was not for the head that the chief took. He had not seen who fired the shots.

Bull Elk fixed his eyes on Barton. "I gave you a dollar, didn't I? Did we not make an agreement?"

"The dollar was not for the head. It was for the organs," Barton asserted, looking straight at Dickens.

"The details of your dispute over the cattle parts are not my main concern," said Dickens. "The larger question is whether Bull Elk tried to kill Daly and Barton."

Lafrance then told of the threat made by Bull Elk's wife, and seeing Bull Elk with gun in hand at the first shot. Both he and Scott had witnessed the second shot but neither could be sure of the target.

Dickens called on Bull Elk to give his version. He warned the Blackfoot chief that he was accused of a serious offence in the white man's world and that anything he said might be used against him at a criminal trial.

"I fired two shots," Bull Elk admitted. "I did not fire at these two men. I was walking away from the camp. I had not loaded my gun for the first shot. Perhaps one of my sons had loaded the gun before I got there."

The three Blackfoot witnesses testified for Bull Elk. Dog Child gave his version of events at the corral. Heavy Shield repeated that Bull Elk was a good shot who would not have missed. "If Bull Elk had fired at these men, you would have two fewer witnesses here tonight."

# Chapter 16

Dickens sat back in his chair, silent. His face was flushed and he was clearly agitated. He faced a grave responsibility. Whatever he said now could put the entire post in jeopardy. The crowd outside had grown to hundreds, many carrying weapons. A wrong move and the result could be many deaths. The road was blocked and the police stables taken over. Escape was impossible and it was unlikely the prisoner could be removed from Blackfoot Crossing. Darkness was complete now and his men could be picked off in the winter night. No one would ever know who the culprits were. But he had a duty as an officer of the Queen. He inhaled deeply and measured his words out precisely. Despite his efforts, the cursed stammer had returned. The Blackfoot present sneered, taking it as a sign of fear.

"I b-believe a charge of attempted m-murder is warranted. I wish to take the p-prisoner to t-trial at Macleod."

Running Rabbit leapt to the door and yelled to the mob. Angry cries erupted immediately, rising to a crescendo. Warriors chanted battle songs and fired rifles in the air, accompanied by fierce drumming. The police and whites inside the building could hear ugly threats of death and destruction. Someone threw a firebrand against the walls of the barracks but a quick officer stamped out the flames.

Word had now gone to all the Blackfoot camps and about 700 warriors swarmed about the buildings. Many carried Winchester repeating rifles obtained from American traders, meaning they were better armed than many of the police with their single-shot carbines. Some Blackfoot had daubed their faces with war paint. The high-pitched din soared to a black winter sky and shook the log buildings. A hundred men hurled insults at a frightened, lonely sentry stationed at the stable, and another eighty threatened a second officer at the storeroom. A few warriors on horseback bumped the police officers on the ground with their horses, trying to provoke or intimidate them. A breakdown in police discipline, a drawn and fired gun, could mean annihilation.

Billy Gladstone, the interpreter and an old Blackfoot hand, leaned toward Dickens and spoke loudly into his ear, trying to be heard over the cacophony.

"I have never seen these people so enraged, inspector. If you have never known fear in your life, be afraid now. Remember what they've gone through. Since their treaty five years ago, the buffalo are gone and they have been reduced to hunting prairie dogs and squirrels for food, or depending on the white man's handouts. They are disgraced in their own eyes. They seek a return to past glory."

What could be done? Dickens wondered. He beckoned Lafrance over. "Charles, bring me Crowfoot as quickly as possible."

Crowfoot, paramount chief of the Blackfoot Confederacy, arrived soon after with Lafrance. He had already been on his way after hearing about the dispute and the shooting. Always charismatic and in control, he led a retinue of lesser chiefs into the building. Around his neck he had put on his silver treaty medallion, a gift from Queen Victoria. He stared without speaking at Dickens until the police inspector offered him a chair.

Crowfoot turned to face the interpreter, Gladstone, and spoke forcefully but slowly.

"Inspector, I have come to honour the pledge our people made to your predecessor, Stamix Okotan, the one you call James Macleod. In the times that he was here, our people lived in friendship with the whites. He and I promised, together, that we would walk a long mile to settle the disputes that arose between us. We trusted you then and had faith that the redcoats would defend us against bad men who sought to exploit us.

"Now we find that you are coming to the defence of these bad men. Some of the white men living among you treat my people cruelly and with insults, as they would dogs. Bulk Elk is an honest man who was involved in a dispute. I know that you too are an honest man. I cannot speak for the men Daly and Barton, but perhaps they, like Bull Elk, lost their heads on this day. I do not defend Bull Elk's angry outburst but I think this quarrel can be resolved between us. Like Heavy Shield, I too know this man well. If he had meant to harm the whites, you would have bigger troubles to settle."

"Chief Crowfoot, no one respects your words more that I," replied Dickens, calmer now that the paramount chief was present. "There is a complaint and a strong body of evidence to suggest Bull Elk must go to trial. I must take him with me to Fort Macleod. You believed in our justice before. If this man is innocent, he will be released. That is my pledge."

Crowfoot pointed at Daly and Barton, who stood nervously to the side, away from the windows. "These men do not love the truth. They see only what their half-blind eyes have told them. They do not know the contents of Bull Elk's heart. They do not wish to lose face among your own people. I ask you, Inspector, leave Bull Elk here. He is calm now and will not cause you trouble again. I will take him into my lodge to ensure his good behaviour. If you do otherwise, I cannot say what will happen. My people are desperate, and desperation is the sire of rage. And I am getting older, my words do not ring as true in the ears of the young as they once did."

Dickens scanned Crowfoot's face. There was a determination stamped there that impressed him. The chief spoke wisely and with sympathy, but the police had a duty to perform.

"Will you allow my men to take Bull Elk to Macleod?" Dickens demanded.

A smile flickered over Crowfoot's broad face. His eyes twinkled as he squinted at Dickens.

"You are bold, inspector. But look outside. My people have your stable surrounded. How will you get by them to saddle your horses and get your provisions? Do you think you will not be followed? It is still a long way to Fort Macleod, with many coulees and stands of trees to pass. It is dark now and the winter cold closes on us. Are you a man who takes risks, inspector?"

"So, you do not mean us to go." Dickens wheeled about in his chair. He looked at the plaintiffs, now sullen and downcast. Bull Elk stared at the floor. Dickens studied the map behind his desk. The trail was good and direct, over favourable territory, but the fort was still eighty miles south. He called Howe over, who bent down as Dickens whispered to him. Howe nodded.

"Inspector?" Crowfoot said. Dickens turned to hear. "I know that Stamix Okotan believed in his duty and that is your creed as well. Turn Bull Elk over to me. I will be responsible for him and bring him with me when the magistrate comes here to hear his case."

No chief on the northern plains had a greater reputation for keeping his word and personal honour than Crowfoot. Dickens believed he could trust this man. Besides, there was little option. Getting the prisoner to Macleod seemed impossible and foolhardy. It would provoke the Blackfoot militants and he would lose the co-operation of Crowfoot and his moderate followers. He would accept Crowfoot's offer, despite his fear that some might challenge his decision as a sign of weakness.

"I believe you, Crowfoot," Dickens said quietly. "You may take charge of the prisoner but you must promise to produce him when the magistrate comes by. He must not come back to the corral when the contractors are cutting meat, and I do not want to see him with a weapon in his hands."

"You have my word." The two men rose and clasped hands.

Wilson unshackled the exultant Bull Elk, and Crowfoot led him from the building.

As the two chiefs emerged from the building, many of the hundreds of warriors whooped in victory. The excitement grew and they fired their guns skyward. The demonstrations continued for hours. There had been little reason for the Blackfoot to celebrate recently. Now they would take advantage of this modest victory.

Few of the whites slept that night. The shaken Dickens finally rose, dressed and went to his office to file his report on the day's events, to be sent to his superior officer, Leif Crozier at Fort Macleod.

"I beg to point out that there was no time to put the house in a state of defence or to make any preparations whatever," Dickens wrote. He paused thoughtfully before adding the next line. He knew there would be second-guessers.

"If my conduct in the matter is considered blameable, I respectfully beg for full enquiry."

Crozier was Dickens's commanding officer at MacLeod and had come to know Frank well over the years in the southern Prairies. Crozier was a tall, vigorous, dark-haired man of military bearing, with a reputation for courage, daring and resolution. He was born in Ireland but raised in Canada and had an underlying contempt for some of the softer officers who had come to the Canadian West from Britain. Frank was one he quietly despised.

Crozier growled in disgust when he read Dickens's report on the events at the Crossing. He was appalled at the inspector's lack of preparedness, his weak resolve and his willingness to compromise. No one should be permitted to stare down the police in that manner, he thought. It would bring disrepute upon the force and make it more difficult to enforce the law.

Compromise was not a concept that came easily to Crozier's mind. He had never applied it, and he saw no reason to now. He believed in the letter of the law and in action and he reveled in that reputation. He had made the first arrest of whiskey traders when the force arrived in the far west after the long trek of 1874. When the prime minister, John A. Macdonald, grew impatient at Superintendent James Walsh's close friendship with Sitting Bull, a relationship that Canadian authorities felt had encouraged the Sioux chief to overstay his welcome in Canada, it was Crozier who was named to replace Walsh. Crozier had blocked Sitting Bull's attempted forced entry into the Wood Mountain police post after a fugitive Blood had fled there for sanctuary from Sioux enemies. The muscular policeman grabbed the formidable chief and unceremoniously manhandled him outside in full view of startled Sioux warriors.

Still, Crozier saw a positive side to Dickens' shortcomings. This incident could be used to reinforce a point the police had been trying to make with the sluggish politicians and bureaucrats who held the fate of the force in their hands. Then, he would try to salvage a solution that to his mind would be acceptable.

Pen in hand, Crozier wrote a letter copied to the Commissioner of the police and the Deputy Minister of the Interior:

"The detachment of an officer and fifteen men at Blackfoot Crossing is as many men as I could possibly spare from this post. Mr. Dickens' despatch and other documents referred to will give you a very good idea of the conduct of the Indians as well as the inadequacy of the force in this section. Unless the force in this district is largely increased, I cannot answer for the consequences.

"It seems to me that under the circumstances, Mr. Dickens acted discreetly; at the same time, it appears plain that he had not force to carry out his original intention."

Crozier had his private view of Dickens' capacity to resolve the Bull Elk affair, but he was not about to allow his superiors any comfort.

He sealed the envelopes and called in the duty officer. "I want the twenty most senior officers and men to collect their gear and saddle up, now. We're going to Blackfoot Crossing."

Crozier was unstoppable. He and the twenty men left in the dark, riding across the snow-covered, windy high prairie. By midnight, they had reached the frozen Little Bow River. Urging their horses on, they rode above the coulee of the Snake Valley to the east, skirted Buffalo

Hill on their left. There they stopped for a quick breakfast and by sunrise Blackfoot Crossing was in sight.

Dickens looked up in surprise as Crozier and his troop rode into the little settlement. Crozier ordered most of his men to get a few hours rest, and instructed Dickens to prepare for action.

"The Blackfoot are greatly excited," Dickens observed. "They may be quiet now but they are only waiting for an attempt to take Bull Elk from them and they will certainly resist."

"Well, then, we must prepare for war," Crozier replied. "Have your men collect all the bags of flour, oats and other supplies and pile them against the walls and windows of your headquarters. Get in an ample water supply, both for drinking and for fighting fires in case the Indians try to set fire to the building. Cut loopholes in the walls for firing your guns. Cut holes in the interior walls too, so the men can pass ammunition as required. Bring the horses inside and take down the corral. It's an obstruction that might prevent a clear view of any attackers.

"When my men have had a short rest, I want them to put up bastions at the northwest and southeast corners. You have timber available for that? I'm concerned that any attackers might take cover at the riverbank or in that old earth cellar, but there's not much we can about that right now. And bring in the government agents and contractors, too. If there's a fight they will be at risk, and they'll add more hands to our force. So, that's how we prepare for action, Dickie." He said the last with a smile.

The energy and efficiency of the policemen was impressive. By noon most of the preparations were complete.

"Now, I'm paying a visit to our friend Bull Elk."

Crozier took interpreter Gladstone and several senior officers with him and rode off to the Blackfoot camp.

The swiftness of Crozier's action took Bull Elk by surprise. The superintendent strode to Crowfoot's lodge, seized Bull Elk before he could rally help and the policeman and prisoner rode back to the police headquarters. The arrested chief did not resist, and Crozier immediately began a preliminary examination.

That afternoon Crowfoot arrived at the police post. He was astonished at the preparations that had been made.

"You have finished questioning Bull Elk for today," the Blackfoot chief said. "Can he return to our camp now?"

"Positively not," Crozier responded. "He will stay in custody with us until we have decided if he should go to trial."

Some of the chief's followers muttered angrily at Crozier's answer.

"But I have made an agreement with Inspector Dickens," said Crowfoot, dismayed. "Do you intend to fight us?" the head chief asked.

"Certainly not, unless you commence," Crozier replied. The policeman's mind was set. He was prepared to resort to "extreme measures" if any attempt was made to stop him from taking the prisoner to Macleod.

"Crowfoot, we came to this country to maintain law and order. If a man breaks the law, tries to kill another, he must be arrested and punished. This applies to both my people and yours. You are a great chief of your nation. Do you intend to assist us with the law? Or will you encourage your people to resist? If I find sufficient evidence against Bull Elk to warrant me in taking this prisoner to Fort Macleod, I intend to do so. If some of your people try to prevent me, they will bear the consequences. You know me as a man of my word. When I announce my intention of taking Bull Elk with me, I expect you to speak to your people, saying that I have done right."

Crowfoot marvelled at Crozier's determination. He did not contest the policeman's words but explained how his people felt.

"Many times, my people have been cheated by some of the whites. Sometimes, when they need help and ask for it, it is denied. To us, generosity is a virtue. There have been many hard years for my people since you first came to our land, and many of the whites, who have so much of their own from this country, give as little as they can. I will speak to my people, but if your people do not change, I might as well tell the rivers to stop flowing in the spring."

The next day, Crozier completed his examination. He packed up with his men and rode off with Bull Elk to Fort Macleod. There was no resistance from the Blackfoot.

"Crowfoot did speak to them in his usual vigorous manner, endorsing perfectly what I had done, and had decided upon doing," Crozier wrote in his final report to his superiors. "The reinforcements that had arrived from Fort Macleod in so short a time had astonished and awed them; for these reasons, the chiefs and people were willing to listen to reason, and did so."

Bull Elk was found guilty of attempted murder but in light of circumstances of the case, his sentence was lenient. He served fourteen days in the guardroom at Fort Macleod before being released.

Crozier had made his point to the decision-makers in the east. Soon, thirty more officers and men were transferred to Fort Macleod.

# Chapter 17

Leif Crozier strode across the muddy parade square at Fort Carlton, situated on the south bank of the North Saskatchewan River. It was a fine spring day in 1883. He saluted a junior officer in passing as he entered the police headquarters, stroked his mustache and straightened his uniform. He had been summoned by Commissioner Acheson Gosford Irvine. Crozier, besides being audacious, was ambitious. A meeting called by Old Sorrel Top, as the commissioner was affectionately known to his troops, would be of the utmost importance. After all, Irvine would not be the head of the North West Mounted Police forever and his favourable recommendation on a successor would likely count in the highest circles of government.

"Superintendent Crozier, sir," Irvine's aide announced.

Irvine had been gazing at a map of the country to the northwest. A wiry man with reddish-brown hair and a ruddy face with piercing blue eyes, he also possessed a substantial greying beard.

"Come in, Crozier," said Irvine. There was warmth in his voice. "I have an urgent matter we need to discuss, and would like your advice. Please, sit."

Crozier felt relaxed in Irvine's presence. There was no pretense to the commissioner. Indeed, the biggest criticism of Irvine by his more formal superiors was that he was too good-natured and friendly to his men, and would not be able to command their obedience when needed. The word used by his enemies was "soft." Irvine, though affable, extended his friendship less generously to those few officers he did not like.

"Big Bear's band has been reported heading north toward the Fort Pitt area, Leif," Irvine began. "We have a small police contingent at the trading post but I want to strengthen the garrison there, perhaps to two dozen officers and men. I want an experienced man to head them. As you know, we have a desperate shortage of qualified officers. So many have left because of this government's miserly attitude toward its devoted staff. Scores of good men left when the government reduced the men's pay. Quite frankly, many men of character and ability are quite able to do better in other occupations."

"You want me to go to Pitt, sir?" inquired Crozier. He had waited impatiently for the opportunity to ask.

"Good Lord, no, man. You are too valuable here. I need a strong hand in this area to deal with the halfbreeds. There's trouble brewing in that class, of that I'm certain. No, sir, I want your suggestions."

The superintendent looked relieved. Crozier had been a devoted officer for many years but consignment to isolated Fort Pitt was not on his list of stepping stones to the top of the force. "What about Cec Denny?" he offered.

"Left the force," said Irvine. "He was appalled at the government's lack of generosity toward the Blackfoot. With good reason, I'd grant. Those people have been very patient under appalling conditions." Irvine paused, then lowered his voice. "Also, there's talk of some involvement with an Indian woman, although I myself put little credence in that. He is too much the gentleman."

"And Jimmy Walsh?"

Irvine snorted. "That attention-seeker? Much too friendly toward Sitting Bull and his Sioux. 'Sitting Bull's boss,' the American newspapers called him. Sitting Bull's toadie, I'd have it. He's the reason the Sioux took so damnably long to go back across the line. No, sir, he's on his way out anyway. I'd warrant he'll be gone by the end of the year."

Irvine stood, turned and gazed at the map, at the ceiling, then slyly ventured a name. He deliberately avoided looking at Crozier. "What about Dickens?"

"Dickie?" Crozier's eyebrows shot up. That choice had never occurred to him. He studied the commissioner's face. Was this a joke?

"I'm serious," said Irvine, smiling as he read Crozier's thoughts. "I have concerns, of course, but let me explain."

"He's been of no assistance to me," said Crozier. "He's been too easy on the Indians, to my mind. Too easily pushed about. Indecisive. Lacks conviction."

"I know that full well. But he has experience, he has survived onerous conditions when others have left the force, and he knows Big Bear. Dickens was at Sounding Lake when that scoundrel refused treaty and led some of the Cree away. We have a dire need of officers with experience. My chief concern is the stability of his mind. In the past I've been of the view that his brain has been affected by his experiences and he is unfit for the force. I've seen him muttering to himself as he walks along."

Crozier was loathe to remark on Dickens's mental condition. He himself had experienced a breakdown several years before, when he disappeared alone on the prairie, to be found wandering and babbling incoherently several days later by a scout sent out to search for him. Irvine had forgotten that episode.

"I'll grant you he's an odd duck. Moody. Not a sociable sort. Few friends. But he's improved of late. Escaped some near misses with the Blackfoot," Crozier said. This was a pointed reference to some of Dickens's past failures.

"Yes, I know of those. Seems he is quite proficient in retreat. The question is, can he advance?" Irvine smiled, tugging at strands of his beard.

Crozier chuckled. "You said you would.explain, sir."

"Here's my reasoning: The government in Ottawa is very nervous that Big Bear will get into some confrontation with the Americans and that Canada will be held responsible. We don't want American troops pursuing our Indians across the boundary because, once here, they may find they quite like it and decide not to go back. Already some of Big Bear's followers have been captured and escorted back across the line when they were found hunting in the territory of American Indians. The government wants him kept away as far as possible from the border. My strategy is that we will station our strongest officers in posts closest to the line. If Big Bear is harassed everywhere he goes in the south, perhaps he will find the northern plains more to his liking. And if he sees in Dickens someone who is sympathetic on occasion, he might feel inclined to stay. Above all, we don't want trouble with the Americans. All we need from Dickens are reports on the where-abouts of Big Bear and whether his band will pick reserve lands in the Fort Pitt area.

"Another consideration," Irvine continued, "is that Ottawa wants to leave the farmable areas south of the Canadian Pacific rail line open to settlers. That means no troublesome, roaming Indians in those districts. So we want them in the north. The decision has been made already to close Fort Walsh so the Indians won't be attracted to settle in the hills near the border."

The pair chatted amiably for a few minutes about other matters, then Crozier asked permission to go..

"I see you've thought this out," said Crozier. "May I go, sir?"Abruptly, he turned back to the commissioner.

"One thing, sir. Permit me to break the news to Dickens."

Crozier smirked as he returned to his room. He had known Dickens from the early days of the force. Both had been posted to Fort Macleod on the Old Man River, in the heart of Blackfoot territory, and then they served together at Fort Walsh in the Cypress Hills, sacred and neutral ground for all the plains tribes. Those times were tense.

Soon after his meeting with Irvine, Crozier called in Dickens. He explained what was expected: That Big Bear's movements in the Fort

Pitt area needed to be watched and tracked scrupulously. His contacts with the Metis and with other Cree chiefs were to be recorded. If Big Bear ever considered moving from the district, he should be discouraged from doing so with all the persuasive power possible. If persuasion was not enough, then by a show of force. If Dickens found himself grossly outnumbered, he was to call for assistance.

"This is the largest garrison you will have commanded so far," Crozier said. "It's because I put in a good word for you, Dickie."

Dickens seemed pleased. He was convinced his improved behaviour had come to the notice of his superiors and he would now be considered for future promotion.

"Thank you, sir." Dickens saluted and turned to leave.

"One more thing," Crozier said. "On a personal note, Dickie. Could you see your way to lending me some money? I've run into some unexpected expenses and need to borrow about $120. I'll repay you, naturally, with full interest."

"Of course," said Dickens, and left.

By July 1883, Frank Dickens had been dispatched with a complement of 14 policemen to escort Big Bear and about five hundred and fifty followers to the Fort Pitt area. Like other western Indians, the band was desperately short of food and Dickens had authority to share food with the Cree enroute. Big Bear remembered the sad-looking, quiet officer from his first encounter with him five summers before The chief expressed some gratitude for the gifts and resolved to stay in the Pitt area for some months even though he had not yet picked out a reserve. Dickens tried to make clear that Big Bear's people would be fed if they were willing to accept the rules set by the government agents. "Those who work will receive quite enough to eat," he told the chief and his councillors.

By mid-1884, Dickens had a full complement of 24 officers under his command in the Fort Pitt area, including a sub-detachment of six men at nearby Frog Lake under Corporal Ralph Sleigh.

# Chapter 18

*I must say I am a loss for words. I am to be posted to Fort Pitt in the north-ern part of the territory, situated on the upper branch of the Saskatchewan River, and put in charge of a battalion of twenty-four policeman. From this honour I must conclude that it has come to the attention of the superior offi-cers that I have become much steadier in my personal habits. Whether that is due to alterations of character, or simply owing to the fact that I feel older and more fatigued as I advance in age, I do not know. However, it is a respon-sible posting and I should not complain if this is to be my career. I am hopeful that it is a good omen that this is the second Fort Pitt of my acquaintance, the first being near to the family home in Kent.*

*On the other hand, as it is more remote and likely considerably colder in that part of the world than in the southern prairie where even in winter occasional warming winds sweep in from the western mountains, it might be yet another burden to me. God must be punishing me for some unshriven sin for first having me sent to hot and humid India, and then banishing me to the frigid hell of winter in western Canada.*

*The news was broken to me by Crozier, who announced it with a broad smile. Indeed, he occasionally broke out into a discomfiting chuckle. I find him hard to read. There is no question that he is a brave man, perhaps the* boldest of our lot, but I can't help thinking that one day his gallantry will get him into difficulty, as yet unforeseen. At any rate, he was friendly to me, and I can't think of a better wagon to hitch myself to as he inevitably rises in the ranks of the North West Mounted Police.

I find him a complex man, one to fear if you are on his wrong side. He can be a bully and made me appear weak in the events at Blackfoot Crossing. He has an authoritarian streak like my father; someone not to be disobeyed. At times, I wonder if there is something within me that compels me to stick it out with the police — in short, I fear the consequences of leaving. Still, it is an advancement and I shan't grumble.

"This is the largest garrison you have commanded thus far," Crozier said. "It's because I put in a good word for you, Dickie." As much as I dislike his casual reference to my name, I could not help but feel pleased.

At Pitt, my job will be to watch the movements of Big Bear and his band of Plains Cree, which the authorities believe to be the most troublesome of the native peoples. "I expect you to monitor his activities scrupulously," Crozier told me. "Especially any contacts he might have with the Metis and other Cree chiefs."

Also, I will be expected to jolly along this charismatic chieftain until he decides where he would like his band to settle down for keeps. I met the man at Sounding Lake several years ago, and though he is not a noble-looking sort of fellow like Poundmaker, he is believed to have mystic powers and is able to sway his followers. If Big Bear shows signs of moving on, I must do all in my power to discourage his departure. If persuasion is not enough, and my force is grossly outnumbered, I am expected to call for assistance. Having experienced Crozier's impetuous, albeit successful, behaviour before, I have no doubt he would be on the move with alacrity if we wired for help.

A misgiving I have about the post is that Sam Steele, another of our intrepid officers, with a sound military mind, took one look at the fort and declared it "vulnerable, if not indefensible." No doubt the best policy will be to ensure the peace is kept, and that will be my goal. Fortunately, although Big Bear has a crop of troublemakers in his own band, the Cree people of the forested areas north of the Saskatchewan, known to some as the Wood Cree, are a generally peaceable lot and may be a moderating influence on their fellow tribesmen.

As I undertake this mission, I can't help but think that my dear departed mother and blessed Aunt Georgy would smile at my success.

Crozier made an odd request of me after I thanked him and saluted. He begged me to lend him $120 to cover some unexpected expenses he had incurred. He promised to repay with interest. Somehow he knew that I had put away some of my salary each month, hoping to save enough to escape this country and return home, or at least to the cities of the east. Under the circumstances, and seeing as he had put in a word for me, I felt obliged to meet his request.

# Chapter 19

Sam Steele was right. The name "Fort Pitt" was grossly exaggerated. The reality was that like many western "forts" it was merely a trading post of the Hudson's Bay Company, recently converted into a police depot. Pitt had been built on a scenic but flat site on the north side of a sweeping bend in the North Saskatchewan River, surrounded by low rolling hills. In military terms, those pleasant attributes only meant that it was highly exposed to any attacks. The sole source of water was the river, four hundred feet away. A low palisade of spruce logs, intended mainly to keep roving domestic animals out of the gardens or drunken visitors out of the fort, enclosed a half-dozen square-timbered and mud-caulked buildings. This modest defence was almost useless against any enemies with serious intentions, and the logs were bug-infested and rotting, easily moved where they were in contact with the muddy soil of the flat. The drafty, chilly buildings were the residences, storehouses and offices of twenty-four policemen, and another thirty to forty civilians, principally employed by the company. Some who were not impressed by their posting referred to it as "Fort Arm Pitt". Visiting Indian bands would set up their camps outside the walls when they brought in furs for trade.

The post was first built in 1829. It had been in prime buffalo hunting country when the herds were large and plentiful. Fort Pitt became an important gathering and distribution stop as travellers moved up and down the river between Fort Carlton to the southeast and posts west along the North Saskatchewan, including Fort Edmonton in later years. The Indians and Metis would bring in thousands of buffalo robes and furs of wolf, fox, muskrat and beaver. In exchange, they would get guns and ammunition, blankets, sugar, tea and flour. The post was also a collection depot for thousands of pounds of pemmican, the staple of western traders and hunters made from pounded meat, berries and fat; dried meat, grease and cured buffalo tongues. Anyone travelling the river would stop to re-equip, share news and renew old acquaintances.

Only once had its vulnerability been tested, a few decades before Dickens' arrival, when a band of marauding Blackfoot ransacked the fort. But in recent years there had been little trouble. Pitt was once in neutral territory between the warring Blackfoot and Cree, in fact had been chosen because of that, but now the Blackfoot seldom ventured this far northeast. Smallpox had ravaged the Blackfoot tribes fifty years before, when it was believed two out of three of the once numerous and feared people had perished. The Cree, seizing an opportunity, had moved into territory now vacated by their declining enemy. Not that the Cree escaped the dreaded epidemics. Mounds in the hills across the river concealed remains of about one hundred Cree who had died from smallpox in 1870, as well as others that starved because they were too weakened from disease to summon the strength to hunt for food.

The police had not come to Pitt until 1876 and even then it was regarded as a post of minor significance. Big Bear's band, the last of the buffalo hunters and the most resistant to white encroachments, arrived in the area in the summer of 1883. When the chief declared his intention to take up a reserve nearby, the senior police command took a serious interest in the fort. By now, the buffalo, the staple of the tribes, had virtually disappeared from the northern plains. The once lucrative trade in buffalo hides at Pitt had ceased and the furs coming to the fort were of lesser animals. Big Bear had come under increasing pressure from the government to pick a reserve site west of Frog Lake, but he didn't like the land the government agents chose for him. Big Bear's reluctance to give up the free life of the prairie nomad was seen by the authorities as intransigence. No matter what he said, they suspected he was up to no good. Still, he stayed in the area. It was the closest he had come to settling on a reserve.

The south bank of the North Saskatchewan featured low hills, grassland with occasional groves of deciduous trees in the hollows and along the stream banks. The River Cree who lived here received their name because they roamed the prairie between the north and south branches of the Saskatchewan, that dominating stream that drained all the plains north of the Missouri Coteau and between the western mountains and Hudson Bay. These skilled prairie hunters had for uncounted generations followed the northward and southward migrations of the buffalo herds, as far south as the Judith Basin in Montana, well across the white man's medicine line.

Big Bear had come to be regarded as the pre-eminent chief among these proud hunters and warriors, although lately he and other chiefs had lost prestige among the younger men because the elders urged caution in dealing with the whites. As hunger and illnesses mounted among Big Bear's followers, the old chief was losing much of his influence. Some of his own family even lost confidence. His son Imasees went south of the American border with fifty followers in the spring of 1883 in search of the scarce buffalo, only to be turned back by a troop of soldiers who took their horses, seized or destroyed their possessions and burned their wagons. Now they seemed to have little choice but to give in to the demands of the government that they choose a permanent settlement.

The north side of the wide river, where the forests grew thicker and spruce increasingly mingled with cottonwood and poplar, was the hunting territory and home of the Wood Cree. These people trapped and fished for a living, depending heavily upon the fur trading company. They lived peaceably with their white and Metis neigh-bours, although some resented the power of the government men and the indignities sometimes forced on them by some whites who were disagreeably abusive and paternalistic. They, too, had fallen on hard times and watched with suspicion as increasing numbers of settlers arrived from the east to take up land. They wondered about the future of the fur company and what would happen as the newcomers upset the balance.

# Chapter 20

Besides the determination of the authorities in Ottawa to cajole, entice or force the native people of the plains to take a reserve, they also wanted to turn the Cree and other peoples into farmers or ranchers. Some of the chiefs actually urged their followers to try this drastic adoption of a quite different way of life but success was rare, and the tribesmen reverted to the ways they had lived for countless generations. But the mainstay of the old way were the herds of bison, and these had been decimated. Many of the government agents and farm instructors tied the provision of emergency food to settling down on reserves. This led to hostility toward the agents. .

These government agents were a varied lot. Some had matured in the west and knew it intimately — sometimes too well, because they bore with them prejudices developed over a lifetime of familiarity. Others were principled men, who acted honestly but chafed under the parsimonious orders forced on them by an absentee government. Too many were corrupt, and took the opportunity of lining their pockets with a share of the aid they were supposed to use for local Indian bands.

Many were frustrated at what they regarded as the lethargy of the Indians, who were expected to give up the skills they had used from time immemorial and were now, in the government's eyes, to become farmers, coaxing unfamiliar plants from rocky or drought-ridden soil. When the crops failed, the neophyte farmers were chastised as lazy and ignorant. The government sent farm instructors to help with the transition from hunting to agriculture but often these men were the most reviled of all by the native people. The farm instructors' credo was no work, no food, and if the Indians did not match up, and the plants did not grow, then they were not working sufficiently hard and deserved to suffer the consequences. When some agents caved into humanitarian instincts and fed destitute bands of Indians, they could anticipate harsh reprimands from Lawrence Vankoughnet, the Indian Commissioner in Ottawa, nearly two thousand miles away.

The Metis, the mixed-race people who sprung from the unions of mainly French and Orkney fur traders with native women, occupied a middle place. They saw themselves as another race, and as such had tense relationships with both the whites and the Indians. Many farmed, but the roots of the Metis lay in the fur trade. When their employer and supplier, the Hudson's Bay Company, sold its vast territorial rights in the west to the Canadian government in 1870 for 300,000 pounds sterling, both the Metis and the Indians were surprised that the land could be sold at all, and astonished and angry that they should see none of the benefits. The sale had been made in a land across the sea where none of the Indians or Metis had ever been, the homeland of the great Queen. Many company men, too, were enraged by the transaction, fearing changes that would be the death of centuries of the fur trade and the loss of their livelihoods. Before, despite occasional disputes between the company, the Metis and the Indians, the ultimate goal of all was much the same — bring in the furs and receive coveted trade goods in return. Now, settlers were arriving from the east, planting crops over land that had been freely travelled and that were seen as hunting and trapping territory for the aboriginal people. The farm instructors, Indian agents and police came too, to badger the nomadic hunters into settling down in one place and to relinquish past freedoms, all in the name of "peace, order and good government."

In 1884, resentment among the Cree at the treatment they received from government agents across the northern prairies led to increased restlessness. That summer, a Thirst Dance, where young men proved their worth as warriors through personal sacrifice and self-inflicted torture, had been held on Poundmaker's reserve at Cut Knife Creek, west of Battleford. Cree bands, including Big Bear's, from across the plains had gathered for this rite of passage. What might have been a routine celebration deteriorated into a dangerous confrontation when a Cree warrior, Kahweechetwaymot, approached local farm instructor John Craig for food for his sick child. Craig refused and told the angry warrior to go away, whereupon Kahweechetwaymot returned with his brother and beat Craig with an axe handle.

History repeated. Again, Leif Crozier arrived on the reserve land with twenty-five police, methodically prepared his defences and went to arrest the offender, with the intention of taking him to Battleford for trial. The Cree chiefs agreed to turn over Kahweechetwaymot but only if the trial was held on the reserve. Crozier was adamant that he must be taken to the prison in Battleford but Poundmaker said the young men would never allow the accused man to be arrested and jailed. Exchanges grew tense and heated, and the usually restrained and dignified Poundmaker lost his composure.

Waving an apukamakin, a war club with three knife blades, he taunted Crozier.

"You want to take him? Take me first, if you dare," the chief said, tapping his chest. When another officer insulted Poundmaker, he rushed at the police lines, stopping only when Constable Prior levelled his carbine directly into Poundmaker's face.

The police interpreter, Louis Larande, and one policeman were surrounded, stripped of their weapons and briefly made prisoners.

Young warriors whooped, jeered and rode their horses around the outnumbered police lines, some urging their companions to fire. But in a stroke of luck for the police, the Cree were divided. Big Bear's son Imasees, one of the hawks of his band, and his friend, the war chief Wandering Spirit, were eager for blood, but other chiefs tried to calm the frenzy. "Let the redcoats fire first," some chiefs shouted.

Discipline held, and no shots were fired. Had gunfire broken out, an immediate uprising could have resulted that would likely have been supported by most of the Cree bands on the plains. A confrontation then would have been bloody, costly to both sides and an unstoppable juggernaut.

Frank Dickens, remaining at his post at Fort Pitt, had played no role in that drama, but it was clear to everyone that there would be more unrest. And Crozier's actions again confirmed Frank's opinion of him as a bold but rash officer.

On the frontier, Thomas Trueman Quinn was the antithesis of Francis Dickens. Born by the Red River of the North of Irish and Sioux halfbreed parents, Quinn had spent nearly his entire life in the west, the exception being service in his early twenties with Union forces during the American Civil War. He was tall, strong and handsome, a self-reliant man with an affable personality and an easy manner. He spoke several languages, including French as well as English, and Ojibwa, Assiniboine, Cree and notably Lakota, so that the Cree knew him as Sioux-Speaker. His Sioux connections, it was rumoured, had preserved his life in the United States. As a lad, Quinn worked with his white father in a trading post. With the Santee Sioux uprising in Minnesota in the 1860s, Quinn's father was killed in an attack on the post, but the boy was spared when a Sioux relative hid him under a pile of blankets. His life saved, Quinn joined a Wisconsin regiment for Civil War service and then fought in Indian wars before crossing the border into Canadian territory. There he remained, making a name for himself in government circles as a stubborn and efficient agent who dealt firmly with the natives and knew their ways. The same characteristics that built his reputation in the Canadian bureaucracy also made enemies among the native people.

Quinn had married a Cree woman, a distant relative of Big Bear, and they had a young girl child. But if the Cree expected that kinship would make the government agent more sympathetic to their worsening plight, they were mistaken. When they saw how fiercely he guarded the government rations, some began to call him Dog Agent or The Bully.

Quinn and Dickens struck up an unlikely friendship in their personal isolation. It could be lonely on the frontier without companionship. As a commanding officer, Dickens had to maintain an arms-length relationship with his men. Quinn's position as a government agent left him outside the Hudson's Bay Company circles that dominated the social life at Fort Pitt. The interests of the government and the company remained at odds. Most company men were not happy to see new settlers arrive, a development that they believed would upset centuries of lucrative business with the local native people. The Indians saw the company men, who supplied them with goods and were only interested in trade, as more compatible with their own way of life than were the newly arriving settlers who coveted and took up the best land, all with the blessing of the mysterious and remote Canadian government.

In October 1884, with the first winds of winter rustling through the trees, another angry exchange occurred. Tom Quinn had a bitter conflict with the Cree chiefs Little Poplar and Big Bear over government rations. Orders had come from Ottawa to restrict the food and other goods given out to the Indians. Budgets had been heavily slashed by the government at a time when the need for assistance was mounting. Treaty money was being distributed that month to the bands at Fort Pitt, but the chiefs had a more immediate need — meat for their people. Little Poplar, an enigmatic man whose public utterances ranged from the ramblings of a inarticulate buffoon to the orations of an eloquent demagogue, demanded three times to know if Quinn would give out some government beef. Each time, Quinn said no.

Little Poplar raised his hands and shouted: "Does this evil and selfish man know only the word 'No'? Let him keep his money." With that, the irate chief spread his arms and quickly herded the other chiefs out the door of the government building.

Outside, men fired guns in the air and others beat drums, chanted and performed war dances, but by nightfall all was quiet but for the ominous voices, a rolling grumble, that could be heard in the Cree camps.

The police were always present in force at the annual distribution of treaty money. Dickens and his men had been edgy, ready for action in case trouble broke out. Quinn told them to stand down.

"It's just play-acting, Frank, don't you see?" Quinn said with a smile. "I know them. They'll come around."

Early the following day, the chiefs returned to meet with Quinn. Big Bear, who had been silent the day before, spoke vigorously this time, reciting a lengthy list of broken promises made by the government. Finally, he approached Dickens who had been watching the scene unfold.

"You are a man whom God made to be a chief. We like you; your heart is good. But that man's heart is stone." He pointed at Quinn. "The Queen's man told us when the treaty was made that we would have meat at every payment. Where is this meat? Is this man, The Bully, cheating us, keeping it for himself, hiding it away as a dog hides a bone?"

"I am here only to keep the peace, Big Bear," replied Dickens. "Mr. Quinn, the Sioux Speaker, as you sometimes call him, is the government man who distributes what is due under the treaty."

Big Bear continued his allegation of corruption, insulting Quinn, cursing him and threatening, but the agent sat quietly with a smug grin. He would not be provoked nor induced to change his stance through these antics. No one among the white men knew the Indian mind as he did, of that he was certain.

The war dancing continued for two days, and the police stayed clear of the Cree encampment, with their guns close to hand in case trouble broke out. Finally, Angus McKay, then the senior Hudson's

Bay man at Fort Pitt, ordered a company steer to be butchered and the meat delivered to the Cree.

"We thank you," Big Bear told McKay. "But we are not fooled. We know this meat comes from the company and not from the government men who are obliged to give us provisions for the winter."

Now Quinn announced he would return to his post at Frog Lake. He was fed up waiting for the chiefs to come to him for their payment. He saddled up, bundled himself against the morning October chill and rode out. Some chiefs followed, persuading him to return and make the settlement. They were desperate and saw that Quinn would not be shaken by threats. Quinn relented and handed out the treaty money. But he felt he had won a victory, stayed the course of the orders from the east, and he did not feel the need to conceal his satisfaction at what he felt to be victory.

# Chapter 21

With the payments crisis apparently over, Dickens saw an opportunity to venture out into the wooded prairie land north of the fort for some sport, alone but for his loyal Irish retriever, Connemara, and his shotgun. He enjoyed the solitude, the freedom from the pressure of duties, the time by himself for reflection, the company of his dog, and the gifts of nature. The late October day was fine and there would be only a few more like it before the snows of another winter began and the ground froze.

Clouds of a chilly early morning had given way to Indian summer sunshine when the dog raced ahead and pointed toward a clump of brush halfway down a watercourse that cut through the rolling grassland. The hunter, his breath condensing in the cold air, dismounted from his horse and hastened on foot to catch up with his companion. He could hear faint chirping noises in the thicket.

"At them, old fellow," Dickens urged, and the dog took two steps forward into the brush. There was a sudden, startling beating of wings and a covey of spruce grouse took flight, rising in panic from the advance of the threatening enemy.

Dickens raised his shotgun and fired. The sound of the blast echoed off the slopes of the coulee. Two of the grouse flew a few feet into the air, then plummeted abruptly to the tall, drying grass, the rest of the rest flock making good its escape.

"Good boy, Con. Fetch." The dog raced forward, gently picking up each of the fallen birds and bringing them to the feet of his master. Dickens stooped and picked up the grouse to examine them. They were fall-plump, red spots in the feathers where the pellets had entered. He placed the two birds in a sack he carried with him, then noticed the fluttering of wings in the grass about forty feet away. It was another bird, this one with a broken wing, tortured, vulnerable, and in shock. He picked up the suffering grouse by the head and with a quick, jerking motion snapped its neck. Dickens made sure it was dead, then added it to the others.

From behind, he heard his horse whinny. Con had returned to his side, uttering a low growl. Someone was approaching, a swishing sound in the tall, ripened prairie grass. As a precaution, he held his shotgun across his chest. Although there were no enemies he knew of in the area, he recalled the fate of Constable Graburn, killed in an ambush by an unknown person who had never been apprehended.

He was relieved to see it was Francois Dufresne, a halfbreed scout and occasional cook for the police. Dufresne's horse was moving at a leisurely pace.

"Captain," the Metis said. "I heard the shot. You have success today?"

He rode to the place where Dickens stood, and dismounted.

"Corporal Cowan sent me. The new company factor, Monsieur McLean, has arrived. The corporal thought you'd want to come back to meet him."

"Very good, Dufresne. I'll ride along with you."

Dickens reached in the bag. "Three good-sized grouse today. Cook them up and you can have one, Dufresne."

As the two riders trotted back to Fort Pitt, Dickens was seized with an interest in this man who was about his own age but whose history was so disconnected from his own.

"When did you come to this country, Francois?"

"About twelve year ago," the other said in a sing-song accent. "I come from the Riviere Rouge, with others of my family. Mos' went to Batoche, south of here. I move along to the fort."

"Why did you leave Manitoba?"

The Metis paused before answering. He did not want to expose his feelings too much to this inquiring policeman.

"I want freedom to live my own ways, to hunt the buffalo, to go where I want, to have my own place. I don't want others to tell me what I can do. *Comprends?*" Dufresne felt comfortable enough with the inspector to use the familiar form.

"And was this not possible in Manitoba?"

"Possible before the Canadians came to our country, captain. When government took the land from the Hudson's Bay Company, that change. The two made an *entente* without talking to us. We had no say. We still have no say. We do not count in their eyes."

"Yes," said Dickens. "I've heard that complaint before. But surely the Red River settlement was a more comfortable place to be? You could live well on a farmstead, raise some animals, make some money."

"Many whites do not understand our soul, captain," Dufresne said. "When the government sent surveyors, they broke up our settlements. The land must be divide their way, they said. We live as families and neighbours for many generations, with each of our lands reaching down to the river. Every family had a place to get water, to fish and wash. The surveyors did not respect our ways. Our titles were ignored. Then many of our people, foolishly, I think, but they did not know better, sold the certificates for their land to those thieves, those sharp dealers, that come along with the settlers. I call them bone-pickers. What do you call them?"

"Speculators?"

"Oui, that's the word. So we pack up and lef', thousands of us, to look for a new life of freedom. But the buffalo that we hunted, a big part of our lives, are all gone now. And the scrip they gave us, they said we could choose places to live anywhere in the west. But now, when we want title to our land again, we are again ignored by the government. We are worse off than the Indians. They get lands and treaties, for sure. We get nothing. Do you know these government people in Ottawa? What is their problem, eh?"

"I understand," Dickens remarked. "I have had my own problems with them."

"Do you feel the way many others feel?" Dickens prodded. He paused: "Some talk of rebellion."

"I don' want to live in the past, captain. My family will adapt. The days of hunting for a good living are gone. I just want my rights to my land, my culture, and I will work for wages as life changes. I will not fight. But others believe they can go back to the past, who think they can order their lives and the lives of others and the buffalo will come back like Jesus. These are angry men. They will do what desperate men do. I believe the government men in the east do not understand. What else can this mean but trouble?"

A wandering photographer had arrived at the fort. He persuaded some of the notables of Fort Pitt and Frog Lake society to pose before his camera. Quinn seemed faintly annoyed at the prospect, but Dickens and most others, including Big Bear and other Cree leaders, readily agreed. The inspector had his men decked out in full dress uniform on the parade ground in front of the store room and police barracks. Dickens, with sword in hand and with the other policemen carrying rifles, engaged in marching drills.

Then Dickens worked on the reluctant Quinn to join in the fun.

"Come, Tom. If only for posterity. People in the east might like to know what our lonely fort on the Saskatchewan looks like."

"I've never liked being caught in the camera's eye," Quinn grumbled. "It's bad luck, to my mind. I had comrades photographed in the war. Within days, they were all dead."

"I understand your reluctance, then. But my experience is more positive. My father never saw a photographic apparatus he didn't like, and now his unforgettable portraits are shared widely with the public. We're not living in wartime. This is not the War Between the States, Tom."

Quinn looked doubtful, but allowed himself to be persuaded. "All right, then."

Dickens changed into the casual hunting togs he preferred and looped his arm in Quinn's, dragging him to the place before the store-house where the photographer had set up. Angus McKay, clad in his best summer gear, a dandified Stanley Simpson with his three-piece suit topped by a sombrero, and a third company man in work-day clothes were already there.

"Come, Connemara," Dickens called to his retriever, and the dog settled into the scene as well.

Quinn, towering above his friend Dickens, shoved his hands in his pockets.

"Could you stoop just a little, Mr. Quinn?" the photographer said with a smile. "You are so much taller than the others."

Quinn scowled at the camera just as the flash captured their images.

Near the end of October, Dickens reported to his commanding officers in Battleford. Several hunting parties had gone out from Big Bear's camp, he said, and Little Poplar had enticed some young men from the reserves around Battleford to go south to hunt with him. Most of the Cree expected Little Poplar to return to stay the winter with Big Bear. He pointed out that many of the Cree men had gone to work for food, cutting six hundred cords of wood for the company and police. Fifteen warriors in the area of Fort Pitt had Winchester rifles but were short of ammunition, while another twenty had older smoothbore muskets.

"Unless the rations are stopped I do not anticipate trouble. Should however the sub-Indian agent (Mr. Quinn) receive orders to discontinue the issue of rations the Indians might and would probably try to help themselves from the store, in which case there might be a collision between them and ourselves."

Dickens never knew if his remarks were passed along to senior government agents. In any event, the hard line orders in the distribution of provisions did not change.

Frank Dickens admired Tom Quinn's efficiency and creativity, his sense of humour and conviviality. He was less enthusiastic about the Minnesotan's attitude toward the people who relied on him. The agent's treatment of the increasingly indigent Cree brought to mind the hard paternalism of his own father in dealing with his errant sons.

The inspector was always delighted to see Quinn when he rode in from Frog Lake. The frontiersman was vibrant, friendly, unexpectedly literate and brought a wealth of tall tales and experience that Dickens found enjoyable and instructive. When not burdened with his work, Quinn was good-natured and easy-going. The two men also shared a taste for good French brandy, and would share a few drinks on those rare occasions when a bottle was available.

One evening in late February, Dickens and Quinn sat in the inspector's quarters, savouring a drink. There was a blazing hearth to ward off the winter chill and the oil lamps flickered. The inspector offered Quinn some tobacco for his pipe and lit up his own. It was the perfect setting for relaxed, informal talk. But Dickens wanted to get beyond the superficial and probe Quinn's private thoughts about the underlying discontent in the northwest.

Quinn had brought some good news. Metis teamster Peter Ballantyne reported that Big Bear had told him that his band would take a reserve on good land thirty-five miles from Frog Lake, on the banks of the Saskatchewan. Finally, Dickens thought, the most recalcitrant of the buffalo hunters would be settling down and the government's objective, the settlement of all the western Indians, would be achieved.

"You are not my first visitor from Frog Lake this week, Tom," Dickens began. "Big Bear was here with your wife's kinsman Lone Man and some of his councillors. They were complaining about you, as usual. McLean sent them homeward with the freighters and the promise of some provisions — flour, sugar and tea — if they helped with the wagons."

"Ha! I can imagine their complaints," Quinn laughed. "I told Big Bear that until he had chosen a reserve for his band, his people would have to work for any supplies from the government store. I will not tolerate Cree layabouts sitting about doing nothing when there is a need for firewood and lumber. They can cut wood and then they will receive the goods they need. No handouts. That's my view, and those are my orders from Ottawa. Well, at least this time they helped with the wagons and earned their keep."

Dickens sipped his brandy. "They are a pretty wretched looking lot. I recall when I first came into this country, they were masters of all they surveyed, except when contested by the Blackfoot and Sioux, of course. It's not easy to watch their downfall. They indeed seem to be heading toward extinction."

"Look, Frank, the blood of the Sioux flows in my veins and I am married to a strong Cree woman, but I am a realist. They must adjust to our ways and to the future of this country. That means hard work or no living. The fittest will survive — isn't that the catchphrase of our modern scientists?"

Quinn drained his glass and Dickens poured another for him. Quinn continued: "I must tell you that Big Bear is losing his authority over his band. Some members are drifting away, joining other bands, others are challenging his control. One of the rivals is his son, Imasees, a trouble-seeker of the first degree. His name — some translate it as Bad Child or Little Bad Man — is well and truly chosen. He's allied with the band's war chief, Wandering Spirit. It's all I can do to keep them on the straight and narrow. And Big Bear seems to be losing interest in being a leader.

"'Course, I give no credit to some of the white folks. They are no help and go looking for trouble. Especially that farm instructor, Delaney. The man can't keep his hands off the Indian women. If it were one, I'd understand. I have a Cree wife myself, and a fine woman she is. But he's always doggin' them, taking risks. I keep telling him to leave them be, that he is only courtin' disaster. I pity his long-suffering wife, she's new to this country. Not a pleasant-looking woman, God knows. I don't know why Delaney married and brought her here, other than to cook and wash. It certainly hasn't curbed his preference for young native girls. Why only two days ago, I had to intervene with an irate father whose daughter was promised to one of Big Bear's councillors until Delaney came on the scene and to put it politely, spoiled her. Still, Mrs. Delaney continues the dutiful wife, turning a blind eye to her husband's meanderings. The Indians also suspect Delaney is keeping some of the best equipment sent by the government for himself, leaving them with goods of lesser quality. Sadly, they may be right. I must have a word with him about that, on the sly, like."

Dickens shook his head. He had focused on the word "promised". How he hated that word! Instead of revealing his private thoughts, he commented briefly. "Very difficult."

Quinn went on. The brandy was making him feel at ease, talkative. "Then there's Father Fafard, the French priest. A few years ago he took in an orphaned Indian boy, Round-the-Sky. A handsome lad. Used him as a servant, doing menial tasks. And worse, if rumour can be believed. He certainly kept the boy fed and clothed, but also used him for unspeakable acts. Ruined the poor boy for marriage. No Cree woman wants him, and he's not an attractive son-in-law for their fathers."

Dickens gasped. His hand shook as his poured himself another shot.

"Is there any proof of this? Any accusations made? We could take action."

"No. The Cree won't talk of it to white folks or 'breeds, especially. But they talk among themselves, which is how I heard it. Jokes, like. 'Don't go into your lodge alone with the black robe. The man carries no weapons, but he has a big lance.'"

Quinn sipped his drink, and carried on:

"You know, Frank, despite all this I don't anticipate any serious trouble. Look at all the times when there have been confrontations on this side of the border, with little result. No, I think the Cree are too craven and dependent to take matters into their own hands. They are not the Sioux, or Comanches, or even their cousins, the Cheyenne. There are no buffalo left. What will they do for food? What choice do they have? They need us. Oh, sure, there's some pie-in-the-sky notion Imasees and some of the Metis have that they will take back the land and sell it to my American compatriots for a stack of money. But that's not in the cards. My former countrymen are too wrapped up in their own Indian troubles to want more of the same. I should warn you, though. Your officers are seen by many of the Cree as protectors of the people they hate. They must be on their guard at all times. Beware of treachery."

Dickens thought Quinn was being too harsh.

"I'm too much my father's son not to hold some sympathy for people in distress, Tom, particularly as it concerns their livelihood," the inspector said. "My father spoke out against the workhouses, and the Poor Laws in England that gave those evil establishments legitimacy and forced the poor to work for their relief. These people have witnessed rapid change in their lifetimes, too, even more than our fathers did. They are struggling with the shakeup of their world, and often they are unable to come to grips with it. The result is anger, resentment, violence, drunkenness, the same vices displayed by our own fathers and grandfathers when they were dealing with change they could not understand. Look at the divisions engendered in our own American and European societies over the last fifty years."

Quinn stared into the flames. He was moody and agitated, Dickens noted. Several times he appeared about to speak but held his tongue, swallowing his drink in great gulps. After a few minutes he could no longer control his thoughts.

"Frank, I used the word craven before. They are cowards. My life is proof of that. My father was murdered in cold blood by the Santee Sioux. I saw his assassination before my eyes. Three men shot him down, an unarmed man who was always fair to them in his trading. I often curse that part of my mother's lineage."

The night of Tom Quinn's visit, Charles Dickens haunted Frank's dreams. Quinn's caustic opinions of the Cree had left an impression on the policeman's subconscious. Charles could be cruelly savage, too, when chastising his seven sons.

"Confound it," Charles was addressing his boys, lined up before him in his study, all with their eyes downcast. "Never have I encountered such a tribe of vagabonds, idlers and wastrels."

In his vision, Frank was a grown man with a full reddish beard. His brothers — Charley, Wally, Henry, Sydney, Alfred and young Edward — were still lads. Embarrassed by their father's stern lecturing, each of them stared at the floor, ashamed, and at their muddy boots and soiled and torn breeches. Frank was in full dress uniform of the North West Mounted Police, but he was not standing proudly erect as the force maxims demanded. His shoulders slumped forward and his eyes wandered in panic. He feared to lift them only to meet the blazing eyes of his angry father.

"What must I do to teach you the value of a shilling? In my day, every penny earned had to be saved for the family, to keep us from the gutter, from the days of want and nights of despair in the debtor's prison." Charles shivered visibly as painful memories flooded back.

"It's not enough that I must work day and night to cover the bills of the senior members of the family. Now I must also contend with a tribe of indolent, spendthrift boys, each and every one of you devoid of any spark of ambition."

Frank's eyelids fluttered as the dream raced on through his troubled mind.

He awoke with a start. He regretted not being able to please his father more while the old man was still alive. Charles had been dead nearly fifteen years now, but his impatient intolerance of his sons still bore heavily on Frank and all the other surviving Dickens lads. I failed Father, Frank thought in his darker moments. I should have been more diligent in pursuing my opportunities.

# Chapter 22

Soon after the photographer's visit, William McLean replaced Angus McKay as the Hudson's Bay Company factor at Fort Pitt. The new man had long service in the West, and he arrived with his wife Elizabeth and a large family in tow. McLean's reputation was impressive and he had won the respect of the native people wherever he had been posted. Dickens and Quinn welcomed a man with such credentials to the area and hoped McLean would bring some stability to the unsteady relations with the local Cree.

Dickens thought the McLean family to be strikingly similar to the family he grew up in. Most of the McLean children were boys but there were three young women, sure to be popular among the young men under his command. Amelia was eighteen, Eliza sixteen and Kitty fourteen. William was a decisive man of boundless energy and strong opinions, much like Charles Dickens, Frank thought. Mrs. McLean was quiet and content to remain out of view. Frank assumed he would get along well with the newcomers.

McLean, for his part, viewed the police with a critical eye, regarding them as the adjunct of a malfunctioning government led by men who knew little about the West, rarely ventured there, and seldom took the pains to acquaint themselves with the true state of the native people. His tolerance for incompetence was limited. In his mind, the officials in the bureaucracy were at best a mixed lot. He characterized them as an arrogant crowd who were too ignorant to recognize the depths of their ignorance. Still, McLean did not feel contempt for the police. He knew the West was changing and had no reason to doubt the courage of men like Dickens. But from his own contacts at high levels, including his wife's brother, Major Bedson, he was also aware that the field operatives ultimately answered to imperious bureaucrats in Ottawa.

McLean had been previously stationed at Fort Qu'Appelle in the southeast of the territories and at Ile a la Crosse in the northeast. He was an impressive-looking man, a tall, broad-shouldered Scot in his late forties whose hair and beard were turning white. He had gained wide respect among the local Cree and Chipewyan people as a fair trader with a streak of personal generosity that was assumed to be uncommon among white men. He was astute and knowledgeable, too, about the places where he was posted and the concerns of the people who lived there. His children, particularly his older daughters, were in some ways even more impressive. They had grown up among the native people and took pains to learn their languages. Unlike many newcomers, they did not fear or despise the Cree, nor did they mistreat them. McLean was aware who buttered his bread. If the Indians stopped coming to his post to trade, his career would suffer. So, of necessity and of temperament, he gave them ample respect and ensured that no client went away unhappy.

When McLean first came to Pitt, he did not know what to make of Dickens. He was surprised at the amiable relationship between Tom Quinn and Dickens, because he saw them as utterly different personalities. Quinn held firm and rigorously applied the rules issued him by the Indian department of government, but Dickens, while his manner was often officious, would sometimes bend to the will of others when hard pressed. Dickens, as all the long-standing officers of the North West Mounted Police, had acquired a reputation over time. Frank's was that he was indecisive, drank too heavily and frequently lapsed into moods of depression. He could be belligerent and defensive when his actions were questioned by others, especially senior officers or bureaucrats. Dickens had few personal friends in the Fort Pitt area. He seemed close only to Quinn and the devoted Irish retriever that followed him everywhere. When the weather was fine and duties were light, Dickens would venture into the prairie or the fringing woods along the streams to hunt, delighting in the company of his loyal and courageous dog. He never asked anyone else to go along. His time alone was highly valued.

The Hudson's Bay man held strong opinions about the innate tensions that existed between his employer and the police. The police, after all, had been sent west — in part to establish the Canadian claim to the western plains and to control the whiskey trade — but also to prepare the way for settlement. That would ultimately spell the decreasing influence of the fur trade that the company's fortunes had been built on over two centuries and more. Settlers, claiming the best land and breaking up the prairie to grow crops, would displace the Indians and Metis who were at once both the prime clients and independent suppliers for the company.

McLean was willing, however, to make his own judgment of the inspector. He knew that some in the West whose reputations seemed larger than life in fact had feet of clay. The opposite, he hoped, might also be true.

The first connections between McLean and Dickens, if not close, were cordial. At Christmas 1884, McLean frankly enjoyed Dickens' change in character. The policeman became less inward directed, more charitable and high spirited, even jovial. Dickens, for his part, enjoyed the presence of the large McLean family, a relationship he now lacked in his own life. There were nine McLean children, just as there had been nine in his family, excluding his infant sister who survived only a few months. Frank would think back to his own childhood, when his father grumbled about children being underfoot at all times. But at Christmas, Charles had always become a much more indulgent and tolerant parent. And the presence of children in the Canadian northwest, just as in Britain, seemed to be a necessary ingredient for enjoyment of the season.

The McLean girls were in special demand when the local musicians assembled and began to play dance tunes with fiddle, squeezebox, banjo and mandolin. Amelia sat down to play the family's prized possession, an organ, but she could not be left long in peace, for Fort Pitt had a shortage of available dancing partners and she had to be pressed into service. Women, whether white, Metis or Indian, were a decisive minority at Pitt, and available women were even scarcer, so all were required to take up the dance. The young McLean girls were especially popular with the police officers and were not permitted by the dashing uniformed men to sit for a moment.

Amelia had caught the eye of Ralph Sleigh and he was the first to urge her away from the keyboard of the organ and on to the floor.

As they took in a waltz, Amelia thought to tease him.

"My sisters tell me you are something of a dandy, corporal. Is this so?"

Sleigh swung her about more vigorously than before.

"I find nothing in the police maxims contrary to the notion of being smartly turned out, whether it be in uniform or civilian dress, Miss Amelia."

She looked to see the expression on the corporal's face, and was relieved to see he was smiling.

"Can you persuade your Sergeant Martin to dance? My sisters would be delighted."

"I'm certain you would be more persuasive than I in that regard, Miss Amelia, but I'll plant the prospect in his head. He is a quiet, reserved man, but friendly enough. Are they enchanted also by Corporal Cowan? I could put in a word with him too, if you'd like."

Amelia grimaced. Sleigh chuckled. Cowan was not a favourite with the ladies. Too brusque and coarse in his manners.

"You are a tease as well as a dandy, corporal," was all Amelia said in response.

Because there was a less than plentiful supply of available women for dancing, the custom was that some of the men would dance with one another. All wanted to dance, for certain, and the imbalance of the sexes was to be no bar to a good round of lively reels, polkas, lancers and schottisches on the floor. Some of the policemen, like husky 'Grizzly' Leduc, had to be persuaded when it was their turn to play the woman's part in the dance, but this reluctance diminished after a few bottles of Perry Davis Pain Killer had been surreptitiously emptied into the Christmas punch. Even Frank Dickens was persuaded to give up his self-imposed shyness to tread the rough-hewn floors with Mrs. McLean and Mrs. Simpson.

After the dancing, food was brought out. Rarely was such luxury seen at the fort. Roasted geese and hips of beef and venison were the centrepieces on the table. Tantalizing side dishes of smoked goldeye from the lakes of Manitoba, as well as pickerel and pike caught in the lakes to the north, were arranged among the bigger platters. There were rare oranges and apples, shipped by cart from Fort Benton on the Missouri, and Christmas puddings featuring the fruit of the country, dried saskatoon berries replacing raisins, and raspberries and blueberries standing in for other fruit hard to obtain, all soaked in liquors sneaked from the police medicinal stores or confiscated from unlucky whisky traders. Naturally, the captured liquor had to be sampled first to ensure it would not overwhelm the taste of the puddings. Relishes and sauces brought across the sea were scattered on the tables — pickled walnuts, bread-and-butter pickles, date chutney, along with cranberries and lingonberries collected in the bogs of the north. Bannock and breads, baked by the police cooks and the local Metis women added to the feast. No one would go hungry today.

After all had eaten their fill, Dickens was pressed into his expected duty, to read some lines from *A Christmas Carol*. In good humour and fortified by a glass or two of punch, he also read a piece from *The Chimes*, and his men hooted and hollered when he referred to buxom Mrs. Chickenstalker. Dickens, who usually winced when he heard the name, this time only paused and smiled, waiting for the shouting to settle down.

After the reading, McLean approached Dickens.

"How wonderful it must have been to grow up with such a father," McLean exclaimed. "His passion and humour, the life simply springs from each page. You are so fortunate to have grown up in such a delightful household."

"There were many good times," Frank admitted, his eyes flitting nervously about the room. He said nothing more, but excused himself from McLean's company.

McLean first thought Dickens was being unfriendly, but then sensed that there was a sadness in the policeman that he would rather not discuss — experiences that had affected him deeply that could not be revealed further.

The more McLean thought about Frank Dickens's odd reaction to his friendly comments at Christmas, the more McLean came to find fault with the policeman. Watching Dickens more closely over the following weeks, he found the inspector to be sluggish, remarkably unobservant and slow to take charge when action was needed.

As winter dragged on, McLean came to believe that negative things he had heard about Frank were close to the mark. The two had small but evident clashes of opinion. The company man began to think of Dickens as a *parvenu*, an upstart. The inspector had been in the West for eleven years but he seemed to have little knowledge about the realities of the country and little inclination to learn. If Dickens had any appreciation of the danger, the isolation, of the whites in the West, he did not show it, McLean felt.

McLean's assessment of Dickens grew bleaker when he had a chance encounter with the inspector's old acquaintance, William Casey, the onetime member of the police force who had run the billiard hall at Fort Walsh. Casey, never one to hold back from lavish description, told McLean about Nigger Annie's laundry, the emporium for liquor and reputed brothel. "The men would go there to be starched and pressed, if ye take me meanin'."

Casey brayed like a donkey.

"Did you know Dickens?" asked McLean. He seemed unamused.

"Why ev'rybody knew Dickens, to be sure. A great boozer he was, too. Ev'ryone thought Dickie must have the cleanest outfits of the whole town, he went that often. Once in a while on his way back, he'd slip and fall in the mud, n' have to go back to get cleaned up ag'in. Senior officers were not amused, y'know.

"Mind, he might have had good reasons fer it."

"How so?"

"Well, " said Casey. "Poor lad was goin' through a bit of a hard time. His mother very sick, y'know, and he worried a lot about the old lady. B'lieve she died sometime in the first year he was there and it tore him up. Seem to recall Dickie said he was in India when his old Pa died and now was on the other side of the world when his mother passed on. Felt a bit sorry for the lad, meself. I mighta hit the old jug a bit hard too, if I were him."

"Did his drinking affect his performance as an officer?"

Casey smirked. "Well, y'know, there's a lot that say he weren't much of an officer to begin with, so can't see that the boo' would hurt much."

What was not immediately obvious to McLean was that Dickens missed much of what was being said around him. Dickens's advancing deafness, which would improve for a time, then worsen, accounted for much of what McLean took to be stubbornness and an unwilling-ness to listen to contrary views.

To McLean, the policeman seemed out of place, like the younger son of a prominent Londoner suddenly transported to a new world, which of course Dickens was. McLean was intolerant of what he saw as the insufferable pomposity of the sons of gentlemen who had migrated to America. He disliked the stuffy, preachy tone of Dickens' voice, which reminded him of a young cleric fond of delivering wordy and unworldly sermons that had shallow roots in life's experience. Some cynics referred to men like Dickens as "decayed gentlemen," and in McLean's view there were too many of that unworthy class populating the ranks of the police. The word "feckless" came to mind. Weak and impotent, that was how he viewed Dickens. And he feared that if it came to confrontation with a determined adversary, all under Dickens's power would suffer for that weakness. He decided that if need be, he would challenge the policeman's authority.

McLean was a shrewd man who kept his ear to the ground, and so was better informed than most whites about the turmoil in the Cree camps and the overtures that the Riel faction of the Metis were making to the Indians. One day in mid-February, McLean approached both Dickens and Tom Quinn to note that no one from Big Bear's camp had come to the post to trade for about a month. Dickens looked blankly at McLean.

"I believe that is an indication of unfriendliness toward us," McLean opined. "It's unusual for the Cree not to bring in their goods for trade in exchange for supplies, especially at this time of year. Furthermore, few of them joined us in our celebrations at New Year. In my experience, they love those festivities and I take that as another sign. The weather has been mild enough for travel this winter, and it's not like they have much to do."

"Don't be concerned, Mr. McLean," replied Quinn. "Big Bear's people are no more upset than they were last fall and, other than the usual dose of bluster, nothing serious developed then."

"Still, I believe caution should be the order of the day. Your people at Frog and Onion lakes should be prepared for departure at a moment's notice. If they came here now, the fort would be considerably strengthened in the event of trouble."

"I'm confident with Tom's assessment," said Dickens. "He knows these people well."

McLean sensed there was little to be gained by disputing the views of the two men. Dickens understood very little of the native languages but he had been in the northwest for over a decade. Quinn had more experience than McLean, not to mention his family ties with Big Bear's band, but he possessed a bull-headed determination to do things his way no matter what. If the agent and the policeman were content to ignore his advice, then the Hudson's Bay man had business to run and he would concentrate on his work.

McLean raised his concerns again with Quinn later that month.

"Tell me honestly, Tom, how do you feel the inspector will bear up in the event of trouble? The two of us have had many years on the frontier. I know Dickens has been here many years but I feel he still has much to learn. He misses important clues to the mentality of the local Indians, to my mind."

Quinn eyed McLean with suspicion. He interpreted the comment as one intended to undermine the authority of the police, to establish a position that would leave the company in control if trouble broke out.

"Well, granted he has little understanding of the Cree language, but there's more to the man than meets the eye," replied Quinn. "I have no doubts about his courage, nor should you. There was a time he backed down to Crowfoot at Blackfoot Crossing and needed to be rescued, but in truth there are not many among us who would have behaved differently in that situation. My opinion is that he is a little soft on the Indians, but I don't begrudge him that. There are others who are worse."

"I find him indecisive, and that he ignores good advice," said McLean.

"That good advice being yours, of course," interrupted Quinn.

"What I mean is that he does not react well to suggestions from others that might challenge his own ideas. I tell you, Tom, I have lived in this country for many years and have come to believe this and not Scotland is my home. I do not sense that Dickens feels that same kinship to the land. His father was undeniably a man of great power and strength, resilient and efficient. He had to be to produce those fine works, which my family and I read with exquisite pleasure. But I see little indication that those qualities have passed along to the son. I believe at some point the inspector and I will come to a head, and that I might have to take charge. If this happens, I tell you, I'll be damned before I'll willingly place the necks of my family, or myself, in a noose because of Mr. Dickens's failings."

Quinn laughed. "Come now, Willie! Don't be so serious. You and I will be here to advise Frank if trouble breaks out. The three of us will make sure everything holds up."

Quinn regarded McLean closely now and he turned serious:

"I don't need to point out to you that the senior authorities here are the government people, including myself and the police. The company's claim to authority ended when the land was turned over to the Canadian government for cash and land a few years back. Bear that in mind." He brightened: "In any event, I don't anticipate things will get out of hand."

For his part, Dickens felt that McLean resented both the company's loss of control to the government and the police, and the new influx of settlers who were beginning to trickle into the western plains. The government had issued posters in the east in 1883 to attract homesteaders to the plains between Regina and the Manitoba border. It would only be a matter of time before promotion of settlement of the more westerly lands would begin.

"McLean may be an old hand in this north country but he is a company man," he told Quinn. "By all means, the company shall conduct its business dealings as before, but its people must accept the changes that are occurring. Every day more settlers arrive in the West, the railway ensures that. McLean and others of the old school resist that and want to maintain their old control but they must adjust their frame of mind. And they must accept that the police are here to ensure that the change is orderly."

"It's hard for the company to give up the place they had, even after fifteen years, Frank," said Quinn. "They were untouchable for over two centuries. Whatever the people of the country wanted, the company supplied: Good cloth, iron tools and pots, guns and bullets, tea and sugar, liquor…They won the loyalty of the Indians and the half-breeds, and those people are loyal sellers and buyers to them still. The coming of the settlers means death to the old ways, and neither the company traders, nor the natives, nor we, I might add, know what's next. I know what you are saying Frank, and I know that people's expectations will have to change, but it will take time and perhaps a little agony. You must understand that."

# Chapter 23

The winter of 1884-85 along the North Saskatchewan River had not been brutal by the standards of the northern plains. Clear and sunny days had offset the seasonal chill. Now spring was breaking. New shoots were rising from the earth and buds forming on the trees. But underneath the apparent calm in the country there was an undercurrent of tension and human misery. Buffalo were now rarely to be found anywhere in the west and many native bands relied almost entirely on handouts from the government men who had been sent to administer assistance on the Indian reserves.

Much discontent had been expressed by the Metis. Louis Riel, their leader who had fled to the United States after the earlier rebellion in 1870 was said to be at the heart of the malaise. Metis travellers began carrying messages from one camp to another and some made common cause with Indian leaders who saw their people being starved into submission by unsympathetic government agents. Misery had become fertile ground for the seeds of rebellion.

There was talk among Cree militants that their blood relatives, the Metis, would take up arms under Riel and a highly regarded warrior, Gabriel Dumont, to fight the government and the police.

Chiefs and warriors debated whether an uprising could benefit their people, or whether it would lead to worse times, with much blood spilled to no good end. Perhaps, said those who preferred war, the Indians and Metis could sow discord between the red-coated North White Men and the South White Men, or bluecoats, and they would kill one another. But travellers to the east came back with tales of thousands of red-coated soldiers who would surely be sent to punish any rebels. And the towns of the white man in the direction of the rising sun were far larger than any of their modest camps in the west, even Battleford and the Red River country. Anger was palpable in the lodges, but the unanswered question was whether the people were desperate enough to risk war as a solution to their woes.

Some Cree arrived at Fort Pitt over the winter to trade furs. That was normal, although pelts they brought to the fort were ragged and pitiful, ranking low in quality in the experienced and disapproving eyes of McLean. What was new, in Dickens' view, was the conspiratorial nature of some of the travelers, the sideways glances to see who was listening and the whispered conversations. The Cree had always been reserved and stolid, but the usual fun-loving amiability of some of the arriving Metis was missing. Some were hearty enough, to be sure, but he sensed this to be a façade. Dickens strained to hear the content of the conversations, but with difficulty. There was no question now that his hearing was increasingly impaired.

He was definitely suspicious of two Cree who passed through the fort in February on their way to Frog Lake and reserves further upriver. Dickens detained God's Wind and Little White Bear for four days, suspecting them to be runners for the followers of Riel. But after repeated and intensive questioning, he felt there was no good ground to detain them and allowed them to go on their way.

Near the end of March, two horsemen rode along the muddy trail to Fort Pitt on the big river from the tiny settlement of Frog Lake to the northwest. A week of clear spring weather had melted most of the snow along the trail. One man, swarthy and short, wore a large floppy hat that shaded his face against the bright glare of sunlight from lingering patches of snow. He rode a spotted cayuse furnished with a well-used, weather-beaten saddle. A blanket lay behind the saddle and on the right side of his mount was a holstered carbine.

The other, in uniform but with a heavy topcoat, sat with military bearing on a powerful black stallion. He was young and tall, with a ruddy complexion and a reddish handlebar mustache. He seemed in charge of the two riders, occasionally casting side-long glances to make sure his travelling companion did not race off into the surrounding bush. A Colt revolver was strapped to his right hip.

Though the two would engage in brief conversation, they rode mostly in silence. When the shorter man spoke, which was seldom, he talked in French-accented English. The tall man usually began the talking, with a slight trace of a Scottish brogue. The other replied curtly with no life in his voice. His eyes twitched.

"So then, Andre, how long were you at Frog Lake?" This question, probing, had been asked before, as though a different answer might be forthcoming each time.

"Two days. I go with Henri Sayers to bring supplies." He looked sideways at Constable Billy Anderson of the North West Mounted Police, who stared ahead at the road.

"I trust the people there spent a good winter? Did you see Big Bear or his sons?"

"Oui. His son Imasees was there, the one some call Bad Child, and de young one, too. Not de others. Me, I speak to Big Bear only once."

"Any gossip going the rounds, Andre? Did the people complain about food?"

"'Twas a hard winter for food, by God. Never enough food." He considered saying more, but thought better of it and held his tongue.

Andre Nault had travelled the road from Battleford, by Fort Pitt and Frog Lake and on to Fort Edmonton many times. Like many Metis, he engaged in a variety of occupations to make a living, hiring himself out as a freighter carting supplies between posts, trapping and hunting, and on rare occasions working as a scout for the police. His family lived in the Batoche area, south of Battleford, where his wife raised chickens, baked bread and kept a vegetable garden. Much of his time was spent travelling, away from his family, so he was annoyed that Constable Anderson was so curious about his activities this time. Annoyed, but he knew why.

Anderson rode close and reached over to the pouch Nault had slung across the pommel of his saddle. "D'ye have any tobacco in there, Andre? Lord, I'm dying for a smoke."

The Metis slapped the other side of his cayuse so the tough little horse jogged forward a couple of steps and the pouch was now out of Anderson's reach. "Non. I get some at Pitt. Is the company man Simpson there?"

"What do you make of these rumours that some of your friends on the South Saskatchewan are taking up arms against the government?"

Nault thought a few seconds before replying. "Dere's always some who are unhappy, who complain. Damn, you know, each year seem get worse for us. Cree, they even worse off. I feel bad for dem...I don' know anyone who want to fight," he added pointedly.

Fort Pitt was in sight now. The two rode through the gate in the low fence around the post. A few people looked up from their activities, some waved. Travellers along the river had been commonplace this year, and the numbers would increase now that the worst of winter seemed to have broken.

Anderson rode directly to the police buildings, motioning Nault to follow. They dismounted, tied up their horses and Anderson led the Metis into the office.

A shorter policeman dressed casually in a thick wool sweater, heavy leather riding boots and black breeches emerged from a corner room.

Anderson saluted. "Inspector Dickens, I believe you know Andre?"

"Yes, of course," replied Dickens. "Please, sit down, Andre, and warm yourself by the fire. I should like to have a word with you, Anderson."

The two policemen entered Dickens' office, leaving Nault by the open hearth. He reached down and tossed another birch log in the fire, rubbing his gloveless hands.

Billy Anderson followed Dickens into his office.

"I don't trust Nault, sir," the police constable told his commanding officer. "He is known to be sympathetic to Riel and his rebels. You know he is a relative, a nephew, I believe, of Riel?"

"Was he carrying any mail, any messages?" asked Dickens.

"No, but Corporal Sleigh says Nault was always around Big Bear's camp, talking to Imasees, Little Poplar and Wandering Spirit. That's a trio that can't be trusted, for certain. They are very angry with government agent Quinn. And with all these rumours."

"That's exactly what they are, rumours," the inspector said. "I'll talk with Nault. If he has some information to offer, I'll note it, but we have no cause to hold him unless there is some proof. Corporal Sleigh arrived here an hour ago. I'll discuss Nault's goings-on with him."

Anderson saluted and left.

Dickens re-entered his office and motioned to Nault to sit down.. The officer glanced at the calendar. It was Friday, March 27, 1885. Nearly eleven years in this blasted country, he thought.

The Metis doffed his hat. Long black hair tumbled and swept down to his shoulders.

"Andre, you must know why I want to talk to you," Dickens began. "All this talk of a rising. You've been travelling up and down the river. What do you hear?"

Nault pursed his lips and eyed the policeman. He was no admirer of the police, considering them meddlers and agents of a government that had treated his people unfairly. How could he reply without bringing suspicion upon himself?

"I hear de same rumours, capitaine, but don' know de truth. You have more people to listen and watch dan me. I'm just a poor freighter trying to earn my bread."

"That's where you are wrong, Nault. You men who travel up and down the river constantly are our ears and eyes." Dickens casually tapped his pipe against his boot. He reached across the desk and offered Nault some tobacco.

"How well do you know Big Bear?"

"Not well. I told Billy, I speak only one time or two time to him. I see some of his people unhappy wit' him. Many mos' likely to follow other angry men who make dem proud again, and get dem a side of meat, an' best dat it be wild."

"I understand," said Dickens, switching into the French he had learned as a boy while attending school in Boulogne. "You have had some dealings with Wandering Spirit and Imasees. Do they speak of messages sent along the river from Riel?"

Nault chuckled. Dickens' French sounded stiff and pompous to him.

"Ha," he snorted. "Riel has sent messages to the Cree and other tribes for years. His messages flow like the waters bubbling from a spring. Do the people listen? Do you feel that anything has changed? As long as the Cree are fed, they will not rise. They are pre-occupied with food after these many years of hardship."

"My view precisely. But there have been complaints against government agents for being too hard on them, ungenerous with provisions, and much grumbling about how some bad white men have treated their women. We are talking about hungry and desperate people. Men lose their perspective under such conditions. And God knows, the Indians have been patient. And your people, too, Andre. I wonder if my own compatriots, English, Scots and Irish, not to mention your own French forefathers, would have been so accepting. Rebellions have been fought for less."

Dickens looked out the window, stooped to put another log on the fire, then swung back to Nault.

"I think you may be one of Riel's messengers." His remark was half statement, half question, and his eyes narrowed as he watched the Metis' reaction.

Nault sat stiffly silent for a moment, his eyes fixed on the office doorway. "No."

The Metis shifted his gaze to Dickens' face. "How can I be? I have no paper and unlike my uncle, I cannot read. In spite of the priest trying to teach me."

"You do not have to read to be a messenger. Constable Anderson said you had something in your saddle bags. Would you show it to me now?"

"Are you arresting me?" Nault asked with a fleeting smile. He seemed almost relieved as he retrieved his saddle pouch and opened it for inspection. There was a small bag of tobacco, some wrapped pemmican the odour of which penetrated the room, a crucifix, a few coins and a box of lucifers. No paper. Nothing to indicate he was a courier.

Dickens watched him closely. Nault's manner was suspect but there was nothing to implicate him in any conspiracy.

"You may go, Nault," Dickens said in English. "You are heading for Battleford? Eat something first. Constable Anderson will see to your needs. Corporal Sleigh arrived earlier today from Onion Lake. I will have him ride part-way with you to set you on your journey. But here's a word of advice for you: Stick to business, no truck nor trade with any rebels. There'll be no profit in a rebellion that will be crushed. And I promise you, it will be."

Dickens watched as a scowling Nault left the building. He wanted Sleigh to be sure that Nault's destination was Battleford and the freighter would not double back to Frog Lake where he might stir up trouble.

# Chapter 24

Two days after his interview with Andre Nault, urgent messages arrived for Dickens at Fort Pitt. One came from Inspector Morris, the commanding police officer at Battleford, and one from John Rae, the Indian agent for the area.

Both messages referred to a catastrophic defeat that police and a volunteer militia had received at the hands of Metis marksmen and a few Cree allies. Fighting had broken out on March 26 at Duck Lake, southwest of Prince Albert. These were the first shots of an uprising. Dickens now regretted having released Nault so quickly. Perhaps some time in a cell would have loosened the freighter's tongue.

Rae's message implored Dickens to ensure that Big Bear and his band were confined to the Frog Lake area. If the Cree were to join with the Metis rebels, the whole north country would rise in a state of rebellion, Rae feared. More Indian bands and Metis fence-sitters would join the fray. The tone of the letter was desperate. There would be little support forthcoming from Battleford if trouble broke out at Fort Pitt, Dickens thought, and the first course of action should be to consolidate forces. He immediately ordered a doubling of the sentries at the little outpost and sent a messenger to Tom Quinn, the Indian sub-agent at Frog Lake, urging him to come to Fort Pitt. The small white and Metis settlements among the Indians at Frog and Onion lakes should move to the fort, he believed. Dickens also offered to send more police to Frog Lake if Quinn thought that was a better course.

At Batoche, the centre of the Metis settlements along the South Saskatchewan River, Riel's supporters had seized control on March 18. A "provisional government of the Saskatchewan" had been established. Stores were looted for supplies and weapons. Riel had declared the establishment of a new church of North America, drawn up plans for the division of lands in the West, and the Metis council had condemned to death Riel's cousin, Charles Nolin, for refusing to take up arms. Debate raged among Riel's enemies whether the Metis leader, both brilliant and bizarre, was a criminal or a madman. Heedless of this debate, his followers obeyed his commands.

The police commander in nearby Fort Carlton was Leif Crozier. He had foreseen trouble for months, urging the government to send a surveyor to settle Metis land grievances, without success, and failing that, requesting more police to be sent to the area.

No one had ever doubted Crozier's courage. Some questioned whether he was too rash. When disturbances broke out at Duck Lake, Crozier decided the time had come to act. He put together a force of about a hundred police and civilian volunteers and set out on March 26 from Fort Carlton for Duck Lake, twenty miles east, to arrest the troublemakers. The small army rode on horse and on sleigh through slush and sticky snowbanks and encountered a group of Metis and Indian allies who had prepared defences by digging pits and concealing themselves in the surrounding woods. Crozier rode out fearlessly to parley with Gabriel Dumont, the Metis military commander, when a shot was heard. Which side fired first was uncertain, but the police began shooting and the Metis sharpshooters replied.

There was little doubt of the outcome. The strategically placed Metis had honed their marksmanship of necessity, aiming at the hearts of the buffalo and other animals they relied on for life. The exposed police and volunteers struggled to keep their horses from floundering in snowbanks while returning fire. Throughout the battle, Crozier marched up and down his ranks encouraging his men. He would have been an easy mark for the Metis but Dumont, admiring Crozier's gallant display, told his fighters not to fire on the bold policeman.

Dumont himself was wounded in the encounter, and his older brother Isidore killed. Younger brother Edouard Dumont took command and was prepared to annihilate the retreating police when Riel intervened.

"Let them go," he said. "Enough have been killed today."

Duck Lake was a disaster that would haunt the police over the coming months. Crozier abandoned Fort Carlton and consolidated his forces with Irvine's at the town of Prince Albert, about thirty miles northeast. Twelve police and civilian militia had been killed and eleven wounded, a toll that would have been much higher without Riel's intervention. Until that battle, the police had seemed almost invincible. Now, to their enemies, and others who had until then remained aloof, their medicine was shown to be weak. And despite his valour in battle, the fight at Duck Lake would be the beginning of the end of the police career of Superintendent Leif Crozier.

Soon after the battle, Crozier would receive a promotion to assistant commissioner but after that he was continually passed over for higher posts, and he left the police in the following year. His critics attributed the defeat and the loss of life to Crozier's ill-considered decision to ride into a trap. While the official line was that the Metis had executed a well-planned ambush and that Crozier's men had done well to escape, rumour suggested the fighting might have been averted and it was the police and volunteers who fired the first shots.

Dickens, like others, was shocked by the news but in the recesses of his mind there lurked a grim satisfaction. Crozier had acted decisively, perhaps rashly, in his duties before. And Dickens' reputation still suffered from the event at Blackfoot Crossing when Crozier impetuously had risked war with the Blackfoot.

"Perhaps," Dickens mused," it was only a matter of time before Crozier's impetuous nature caught up with him. I'd questioned my own judgment after the Bull Elk incident when I was attacked for being overly cautious. But perhaps I was right."

Dickens grudgingly admired Crozier's bold style, his readiness to risk all in battle and his swift decision-making when he thought he was right. But it had always weighed on his mind that disaster might have been the fruits of Crozier's actions were it not for Crowfoot's wisdom and the esteem the Blackfoot chief had among his people.

A declining relationship between the police and the Blackfoot had been laid by Dickens' superiors and colleagues at his feet, although surely, he thought, the seeds of that change had been planted long before he had been sent to the Crossing. He felt it unfair that the climate of discontent that grew with the epidemics of white man's diseases, the niggardly response of government agents in the face of starvation, and the demands that the police defend those cruel men enforcing the even more cruel orders from the east — that all of these things could be placed at the feet of one scapegoat, middle-rank officer. "After all, I had reached an agreement with Crowfoot that was acceptable to both sides until Crozier took events into his own hands."

But perhaps he was making more of this episode than he should, indulging in an unnecessary bout of introspection and paranoia of the kind that would have given his father sport in his writings.

Surely, Dickens was taking too long to get over his humiliation. Those events at the Crossing had happened over three years before. Yet Crozier's boldness was again foremost in his mind! Until now, Dickens seemed doomed to have Crozier's hitherto unblemished record dangled before him as a comparison with his own shortcomings. But things had changed unexpectedly. Duck Lake had raised the stakes along the whole frontier. Dickens had reserved to himself the notion that his senior officer was in large measure a puffed-up blusterer, who had the good fortune to succeed in past endeavours through a combination of charisma and boldness, not to mention his opponents' willingness and good sense to back away from a fight. At Duck Lake, Crozier had finally been called to account by Gabriel

Dumont, a man who possessed those qualities in equal degree. The superintendent's provocative actions had failed him this time, and in future many others would see it that way, too. Perhaps Dickens would now have an opportunity to rehabilitate his own tarnished reputation and prove his worth as an officer. The thought gave him perverse comfort.

# Chapter 25

There was little question now in Dickens' mind that trouble would spread from the Metis settlements westward along the Saskatchewan. The message from John Rae, the Indian agent at Battleford, was on the edge of panic, urging Quinn and Dickens to do all in their power to stop members of Big Bear's band from joining forces with raiding parties of Crees and Assiniboines that threatened to rise further east. Like many bureaucrats, Rae was confirmed in his mistaken belief that a chief like Big Bear held the power of a despot over the members of his band. The Battleford agent did not countenance the idea that groups of militant warriors might ignore the advice of their elders and join with other rebels.

Dickens sent a message to Quinn.

"Rae expects us to do the near impossible," Dickens wrote. "Come to Fort Pitt. There will be greater safety here if we are all together. If you feel it is impossible to relocate, I will send reinforcements. An increased presence of police might be a deterrent to militants who have a mind of rising."

Quinn remained outwardly confident that the risk of danger was slight and that he could handle any incidents. "I am convinced that by feeding the local Indians and treating them kindly, there will be no trouble," he replied in a return message. He was not comfortable with having more police at Frog Lake. He believed the presence of the redcoats would only be a provocation. So, instead of requesting more help, he urged Corporal Sleigh and his small police contingent to saddle up in all haste and leave for Pitt.

Big Bear's son, Imasees, had taken a sudden interest in the mood of the local white settlers and the government authorities. Messengers had come from the reserves lying to the east along the Saskatchewan with word about the fight at Duck Lake. He was curious to know what the police and government men were saying about the details of the skirmish. He crept into Quinn's office at night and discovered a copy of Quinn's message to Dickens. Imasees then attempted to find a co-operative party who could read it. He approached three Metis whom he believed would help. The trio, not trusting Imasees, chose instead to avoid trouble, telling him they could only read the white man's papers when they were written in French.

When the white men's version of the battle was explained to the Cree, it came from a surprising source. Some Cree leaders had gone to Quinn to ask for food for their famished families. Rations distributed earlier by the agent had run out. As he so often did, Quinn refused their appeal. But to the astonishment of the Cree, Quinn took out the message he had received from Dickens and translated parts of it into Cree, emphasizing the point about the police sending reinforcements. Quinn supposed the suggestion that more police might come would make any potential rebels think twice about rising.

Quinn added that the rebels would be crushed quickly and the transgressors severely punished because thousands of soldiers, all armed with the latest repeating rifles and even greater weapons of destruction, cannons and Gatling guns, were already on their way from the great white camps of the east.

But when Imasees heard the reference to the fight at Duck Lake, he saw it as an embarrassment to the police. And the references to more troops coming simply confirmed his belief that the enemies of the whites must strike hard now before reinforcements could arrive. His eyes gleamed and his mouth curled in a smile.

"It has begun," Imasees whispered to his friend Wandering Spirit. "You see, the white man can be defeated. This is the time to act."

That same night Quinn called a meeting of all the whites and the Metis who worked for the government at Frog Lake. He surveyed the room. John Delaney, the rough-spoken farm instructor, was there with his new wife Teressa. John Pritchard, a Scottish-Cree Metis who was interpreter for the government attended, as did Charles Gouin, a Metis carpenter employed by Quinn. George Dill, who owned a small privately owned store in the settlement, and William Bleasdell Cameron, a Hudson's Bay employee, came to the meeting, as did Tom's nephew, Henry Quinn. Father Fafard, the Roman Catholic priest arrived late, bringing his elderly lay assistant, John Williscraft. The young Gowanlock couple, John and Theresa, who ran the sawmill on the edge of town brought along their foreman, William Gilchrist. Corporal Sleigh represented the police.

Most of the early talk centred on the safest course: that all the whites and Metis should leave and join the others at Fort Pitt. But the brash and outspoken Quinn confidently announced he would stay even though his Cree relatives had warned him to go. Not to be outdone by Quinn's bravado, the tough-minded Delaney said he would remain as well, and his wife said she would not abandon her husband. Then Father Fafard spoke out. "We must show we have confidence in these people, that we trust them." The priest's declaration was the final word. He had influenced the others to remain at Frog Lake.

All agreed, however, that the police should pack up and leave for Fort Pitt. Quinn and others won the day by arguing that it was the police presence that put the civilians in peril more than anything. They believed that the battle at Duck Lake had finally pitted the police against the rebel Metis and Indian allies, and that these groups were seen as the combatants by the local Cree. They rebuffed Corporal Sleigh's suggestion that the women, at least, should go with him. So

Sleigh ordered his men to pack up. Cameron and Constable Loasby loaded nearly all the powder and shot they could find in the police and company stores on two sleds. When all was ready, the police departed at daybreak the next morning, carrying a message to Dickens from Quinn.

Quinn explained that he still felt the Cree were quiet and the whites were certain they were in no danger. "I will send a trusted messenger if anything unusual happens," Quinn wrote. "I suggest however that a police messenger be sent to Cut Arm's band at Onion Lake to ensure that the farm instructor and his wife, Mr. and Mrs. Mann, are safe."

Riding hard, Sleigh and his men arrived at Fort Pitt about midday on March 31st, just before a snowstorm closed in.

On Dickens' orders, the following day Sergeant John Martin rode to Onion Lake through the deep snow left by the previous night's heavy fall and stopped at the home of George Mann, the local farm instructor. Mann was a family man, with a wife and three young children.

Some of the Wood Cree at Onion Lake saw Martin ride in and rushed to Mann's house, yelling in anger and firing guns in the air. Their chief, Cut Arm, soon arrived. He had once been a formidable warrior in forays against the Blackfoot and had received his name for a disabling wound he had suffered in battle. Despite his reputation as a fighter, Cut Arm was not inclined toward rebellion against the whites, several of whom he counted as friends. He resented the treatment of his people by the government but had concluded that war would only bring greater harm.

But today, Cut Arm was angry at disturbing rumours he had heard.

"We hear two thousand soldiers are coming to our country and will kill us all, Martin. Tell us the truth and we will believe you."

Martin mounted the front steps of the house and raised his voice so all could hear.

"What you have heard is a lie spread by evil-minded men. Soldiers may come and punish those who have rashly taken up arms against the Great Mother, but only those who spite her will face her anger.

You should return to your homes and your daily work and continue your lives in peace. Stay quiet and I promise no one will harm you."

Martin's words were relayed to most of the Cree by those few who could understand his language. His message seemed to allay the fears of the Onion Lake people for the time being. They returned to their activities, talking quietly among themselves. Some knew Martin's reputation as an honest man and believed him; others grumbled that he was a liar. He could not help it, they explained. He was a liar, just like all white men.

Martin went inside the house. Mrs. Mann poured him a cup of java and brought fresh baked bread. As he warmed his hands around the mug, Martin told them to quietly prepare.

"Not a word of this to the local people, but you must be ready to fly at a moment's notice. Load your wagon at night and ready your horses, and above all keep your ear to the ground. The Indians are very unsettled and you cannot count on help from the halfbreeds. We are hearing that even Big Bear is losing control of his people, that the old rascal is isolated and nearly friendless in his own band."

"I have heard that Big Bear is out hunting," said George Mann. "He hopes to bring back meat for his band to settle them down. That means important decisions are now being made by Imasees and the war chief in his absence."

"What do you think of Cut Arm?" Martin asked.

"A good man," said Mrs. Mann, while her husband nodded. "We believe he would not see us suffer harm."

"But whether he will go along with others if his leadership is undermined, I do not know," said the farm instructor.

At Frog Lake, the morning of the first day of April had broken fine and clear. The sun shone brilliantly off the snow, which was melting in the warmth of spring. There was no sign of trouble, and everyone seemed in good humour. It was the day for pranks among the whites, and the day the Cree had come to know as Big Lie Day. The young Hudson's Bay clerk, William Cameron, awoke when a messenger rapped on his window and delivered an urgent message from Quinn to attend John Delaney's house. When he got there and opened the door, Cameron was shocked to see Wandering Spirit sitting there in his war regalia with Miserable Man, another of the prominent Cree and a relative of Big Bear.

"Ha," laughed Wandering Spirit. "You have been fooled. This is Big Lie Day." All took the fool's errand lightly and chuckled heartily. The mood in the village seemed light and all concerns appeared to have been banished for the time being.

But underneath the apparent calm, there were disturbing signs of trouble. When Big Bear returned that afternoon from a fruitless hunting expedition of several days, he found that the special lodge of the Warrior Society, the Rattlers, had been raised. That signalled that the Cree camp was now under military rule. Wandering Spirit, the Rattlers' leader, was the ultimate band authority and Big Bear's powers were limited. His reputation as a leader would be taken into account when he spoke, but the final word was no longer his. Already, warrior lodges were being set up on the other side of the lake, and movements of the people were restricted. Curious whites were discouraged by the young men from venturing near the teepees.

Late in the afternoon, a weary Big Bear and other Cree leaders gathered at Quinn's house to make another request for food.

Quinn responded testily. "I have told you what day I will next hand out rations. Listen to me. I will not do it before then. Nothing on earth that you can say or do will change my mind. I am standing by my word. There is nothing for you today. Now you should go and stop wasting my time and yours. Cut some wood, so that you can earn the food that the government will provide you."

The chiefs glared at Quinn in silence, and Quinn returned their stare, not giving one bit into their demands. Finally, Wandering Spirit stepped forward to confront the agent. The two men were about the same age and stature, both tall, muscular and handsome. The war chief was charismatic and eloquent, with a streak of temper that was feared by all members of the band. Wandering Spirit was a man who started his speeches in a low even-tempered tone but as he carried on, his voice rose and became high and shrill, flecks of foam appeared at the corners of his mouth as he raged. The band members knew that this was when he was most dangerous, and might lash out at foe and friend alike. All the Cree were eager to witness this contest between the two strong-willed men. The leader of the Rattlers pointed at Quinn, who half-stood at his desk, unblinking, his jaw set.

"Brother," began the war chief, "I ask you, now. How will things get better between us? The young men are hungry and may do something that we will all regret. You should all go to Fort Pitt like the police have done. The priest, the traders, all of you. You could leave the storehouse for us and one of your people could give out the food, and nothing else will happen. It would please my people to be fed. Then, when the time comes you could come back here to do your work. But go now and let us have the food we need."

Quinn stared at Wandering Spirit with defiance. His wife's uncle, Lone Man and her brother Sitting Horse, had expressed concern for Quinn's safety and let it be known that they thought he should leave. Out of family loyalty, they had until now been very protective of the temperamental agent. But Quinn would not be swayed by others. He had his orders from the government and those commands would be followed to the letter. That meant no food for those who would not work and take up a settlement, and abide peaceably under the rule of the authorities.

"No! I was sent here to do a job and I will stay here. You do not frighten me. Others can go if they wish, but I will remain and do what I am to do."

Wandering Spirit appeared downhearted and his shoulders slumped with exasperation. He felt that he had given Quinn enough warnings to change his course. He warned bitterly that Quinn's decision would mean difficult times.

Imasees now intervened. "My father went out to hunt for food but found nothing. Like a leader of his people, like a man, he has worked for all of us, but there is no game. Why not give him the food for his efforts and we can have a feast to celebrate the self-sacrifice of a chief?"

"Do you think me a fool, Imasees?" shouted Quinn. "I am the only one here who gives out the food. Hear my words: I am not giving you people anything to eat now!"

The Cree listeners were furious. They slammed the walls of the log building and pushed over furniture, shouting and cursing at the Dog Agent. Some took threatening steps toward him, but Quinn did not budge. Imasees held up his hand for quiet and turned to his father.

"In the morning I will go to Fort Pitt and see the policeman Dickens. He knows you well, father, and gives good things to you because you are poor. I will tell him that my father is hungry and that he should give you food."

Quinn turned and walked from the room.

That same night, Cameron stopped by again to see Quinn. He was surprised to see Big Bear and Imasees along with two other Indians he did not know. Big Bear, his eyes glassy, his body slumped with weariness, was relating a vision that he had several years before. He had travelled the prairie in search of buffalo but found none. Then he saw a lake, with the sun glinting off the surface, the light dazzling his eyes. He sat for a while until the sun shifted in the sky and he realized the water was bright red, like fresh blood on the prairie. He shuddered at the image and closed his eyes. The dream was unsettling to everyone and the listeners, especially the Cree, were murmuring gravely to one another. Big Bear had the power to see into the future, his people knew, and they expected his vision to come true. Imasees seemed the most upset. He abruptly rose without a word to the others, and left the building, brooding. When Big Bear departed he rose quietly and stared at Quinn and Cameron with deep concern, as though he might never see them again, but he said nothing.

Not far from the village, warriors were dancing by the lake. As the drums beat and the men danced around a large fire, uttering war cries, they were interrupted by Wandering Spirit.

"Stop," he shouted in his powerful voice. "Tomorrow I will be a warrior again! What do you think of that?"

The assembled men looked at one another but said nothing. After a few minutes they resumed their dancing and drumming.

Wandering Spirit watched the warriors. The drums grew louder and more insistent, reverberating across the ice-covered lake. The war chief scowled and stepped up again, calling for silence. His voice was becoming shrill as his spirit became more excited. The dancing paused again.

"Tomorrow I'm going to eat two-legged meat. Who will join me? The brave and the strong will follow the path I have chosen. Who are those brave and mighty warriors? Those who will not follow can go home and put on their wives' dresses."

This time several of the men loudly shouted their support. Imasees and Miserable Man were among them.

# Chapter 26

Early on the morning of April 2 1885, four men crept through the darkness at Frog Lake toward the log house of Isidore Mondion, a Metis who was also a minor chief of the Wood Cree. Mondion was suspect in the eyes of Wandering Spirit's militants because he was friends with some of the whites. The intruders entered the house through a window and seized Mondion as he slept. While his wife and children were kept under guard by a war-painted warrior, Mondion was tied up with ropes and a gag put around his mouth.

"Make no sound," the guard warned his wife. "Or your husband dies."

Others went stealthily to the compound where the government agent's horses were kept. They stroked the horses gently to keep them calm, then quietly dismantled the fence and led the animals out of the village, and down the trail to the warriors' lodges around the lake.

A third strike was executed at Quinn's home. Imasees and a companion, Chaquapose, stole through a window and crept in silence upstairs to the bedroom of the two-storey house. Quinn's wife was lying awake and in the darkness sensed the presence of intruders. She sprang out of bed between the invaders and her sleeping husband.

Her shouts brought her uncle Lone Man and brother Sitting Horse running up the stairs with guns at the ready. Menacing the two intruders, they yelled that Quinn's wife was their relative and warned they would defend her and the couple's young daughter with their lives. Thwarted in their goal, Imasees and Chaquapose left the house in silence.

Lone Man and Sitting Horse sat with Quinn and his wife, trying to persuade the agent one last time to distribute provisions to the Frog Lake Cree.

"Bad things may happen today," Lone Man said. "You should take this as a warning. We will try to protect you but we can't guard you forever. You should give out food. Maybe then they will go away."

Oddly, Quinn seemed unperturbed by this invasion. The four sat up mulling over the events of recent days as the Quinn's young daughter slept. In the end, Quinn persuaded the two men to take their guns downstairs and place them on gun racks.

That this was a grave error soon became apparent. Just as the sun rose above the horizon, a war-painted Wandering Spirit, equipped for battle and accompanied by a dozen other followers, kicked in the front door and took the guns from the racks before Quinn's sleepy relatives could react.

"Dog Agent, you are my prisoner," the war chief declared. He glared menacingly at Quinn.

Although unarmed, Lone Man and Sitting Horse rushed to Quinn's side and prepared to fight to protect him.

Quinn put up his hand to stop his loyal friends. "No, I will go with them. Now, you must look after your sister and our child."

The two men stepped back and Wandering Spirit, followed by his warriors, led Quinn from the house.

William Cameron had stayed awake late into the night worried about the mood of the Crees, but exhaustion had overtaken him just before dawn and he fell into a deep slumber. Cameron was concerned that trouble might break out while his boss, Jim Simpson, was away on business at Fort Pitt. If the Crees were determined to break into the company store, there would be no way he could stop them, especially with the police gone. Only Simpson's strong persuasive personality could stop a raid on the storehouse. Simpson, the senior Hudson's Bay Company man in the village, was an oldtimer in the West, a blunt-spoken but practical man well respected by all and with strong ties to the native community through his Metis wife and her Cree relatives. Cameron believed that Simpson could have swayed the opinions of the whites had he been at Frog Lake when they met two days earlier, and that he would have urged them to leave for the comparative safety of Fort Pitt. He might also have moderated the views of some of the Cree who were now falling into line behind Wandering Spirit and Imasees, now beyond question the controlling forces in the settlement. Soon after sunrise, Cameron woke with a start, aware of someone in his bedroom. He reached over to a nearby table for his gun, but was relieved when he saw it was Kamistatum, a friendly Cree who, with his wife, had done odd jobs for the company.

"Get up, Cameron," Kamistatum said. "This will be an evil day. Wandering Spirit has taken Tom Quinn. Imasees and others have broken into the company store."

Cameron rose and dressed quickly, then followed Kamistatum to the store. The place, which Cameron had always kept neat and orderly, was a shambles. About twenty Cree warriors were ransacking the shop and tearing cloth from the rolls, then discarding them in a heap on the floor. Some were stacking goods aside for their own use, but the real aim of Imasees was to find the store of ammunition.

"Where are the bullets?" Imasees demanded of the clerk.

Cameron paused. Fearing trouble, Corporal Sleigh and his men had taken all the ammunition they could when they fled to Fort Pitt. There were still some bullets, powder and old musket balls left behind in a concealed cabinet, however. Seeing Cameron glance toward the cabinet, Imasees smiled.

"Open that place up or we will break it open," Imasees said. Cameron took his key and opened the storage place. He was elbowed aside and the warriors rushed at it, grabbing bullets, powder and a stock of large knives. Then they left the building.

Cameron felt ill. He stepped outside, shaking, for some fresh air, trying to grasp the magnitude of the danger that he and all the other whites in the village faced that day. Then he saw a friend, Yellow Bear, who had taught him some of the Cree language. Cameron remembered that there was a stock of Perry Davis Pain Killer, a powerful concoction of alcohol and opium, purportedly medicinal, that had been overlooked in the store. This mixture was often abused as a beverage by some of the whites and Cameron feared it would only inflame matters if the Cree rebels discovered it in their current state of excitement. He asked Yellow Bear to help him carry the case to the Simpson house for safe keeping.

"What's happening?" asked Mrs. Simpson, who opened the door. There was the smell of fresh coffee and oatmeal porridge. Mrs. Simpson, with a red calico apron over her dark blue ankle-length cotton dress, was cutting up scraps of meat to make soup.

"When is Mr. Simpson returning?" Cameron asked anxiously. "We will need his help."

"I think later this afternoon," Mrs. Simpson said. She was a strong, robust woman who was seldom perturbed even when others were dashing madly about her. She played no favourites and was much admired by the whites and natives alike.

"Sit down, Willie, Yellow Bear," she said. "Have some java, boys. What's going on? You can have soup later, too. Big Bear comes later for a feed."

"The truth is, Mrs. Simpson, that we don't know what is happening. The store has been ransacked. Everything of value is being taken. Imasees has been asking for bullets. We thought we should hide this away in case it falls into the wrong hands."

The Metis woman clucked and looked at the case of alcohol. "Here, you can hide it behind the chimney. Put it there for now. When Jimmy returns he will set things right. Willie, you should keep account of things that were taken."

Cameron sipped the hot coffee slowly, gaining some comfort from the warmth of the cup. He had no stomach for food. Mrs. Simpson urged him to take some nourishment, but he shook his head at her persuasions. Yellow Bear drank and ate heartily, asking for more of the oatmeal. After they had finished, Cameron and Yellow Bear returned to the store. There was a message from Wandering Spirit. Cameron was to go over to Quinn's house. Yellow Bear stayed at the store and waited. He was now nervous and torn between loyalties. With the militant warriors in control of the village, he did not want to seem too close to the white people but he feared for his friend.

Quinn, who told Wandering Spirit he had business to attend to, had returned to his house in the company of the war chief and a handful of warriors, as well as Delaney and the Metis interpreter Pritchard. They were sitting there when Cameron arrived, dreading what might happen next. The whites were being harangued by a furious Wandering Spirit, who paced the wood floor.

The frustrated war chief wanted to find out who had the authority to address the problems of his people.

"Who is the government?" Wandering Spirit demanded. "Who do we talk to get help for our people? How could the company have sold our land to government without we who live here seeing any money, or even being asked? Is your chief the Great Mother, or the police, or the company? Tell me these things. We want to speak to them so our people will be treated justly."

Quinn listened to Wandering Spirit with a smirk. His impulse was to respond to the war chief with sarcasm, to make the man look a fool before his followers, but the agent was treading more cautiously now. He forced a laugh.

"These are the same old questions, Wandering Spirit. We have answered them many times before for your chiefs, including Big Bear. The leader of the government is a man called John A. Macdonald. He lives a long way from here, many days travel to the east. Some of the Metis people, including Louis Riel, have been there. They can tell you how far away it is. Macdonald might listen to your grievances and give you help but it will take days or weeks before you get a reply. It would be best for you to return to your lodges in peace until he makes an answer. I can send along your demands, if you wish."

"Pah! We have no time to wait," grunted Wandering Spirit. "My people will starve before an answer comes. What good are your magic wires that send messages? You must get a faster answer!"

"Unfortunately some of your halfbreed friends have cut those magic wires," Quinn replied. "We can get messages through, but it will take time. We will have to ride the whole line from here to Battleford to find where the line is cut, then repair it. That will take days, and then your so-called friends may just ride out and cut it again. They have no interest in us getting messages to the great camps of the white men."

"If government is so far away, as you say, then perhaps we can kill you now and be gone before the many white soldiers come after us," Wandering Spirit said. "Perhaps they will never come. Perhaps the halfbreeds will kill them before they get here. They will not be able to help you anyway, Dog Agent, because you will be dead long before they come."

For the first time, Quinn's face bore a worried expression.

"When they come, you will be pursued to the ends of the earth," he said. "I will promise you that."

"This Macdonald you speak of. Is he the father of the trader at Battleford? I have heard of many Macdonalds."

"No, Wandering Spirit," said Quinn. "He is not a relation of any of the men you know. He lives many miles away, and perhaps if you give us time, we will ask him for more food."

"Our people are hungry now. They need food. Do you have animals that we can kill and eat?"

Quinn looked at Delaney. He and the farm instructor were obviously prisoners. Wandering Spirit's men could take what they wanted. But the Cree leader was engaged in a match of wills with Quinn. He wanted the Dog Agent to cave in, to hand over food voluntarily.

"We do have an old ox that can be slaughtered," Delaney offered nervously. "They can have that now."

Quinn saw Kamistatum's son watching from the side. "You, young Fred. Show the chief's men the old ox, the one with the broken horn. They can take that one to eat. Quick now."

At the Catholic priest's house, Father Fafard prepared for a special mass. It was Holy Thursday and Fafard had invited his colleague, Father Marchand, from Onion Lake to assist. The two were kneeling in prayer when a group of Indians led by Little Bear burst through the door of their house. The priest's handyman, old Williscraft, saw Little Bear coming and attempted to block the door, but the stronger warrior shoved him brusquely aside. A man in his sixties, Williscraft stumbled backward over a chair and fell heavily to the floor. He was slow getting to his feet.

"What is the meaning of this, Little Bear?" an angry Fafard shouted. He was enraged that his prayers had been disturbed in this abrupt intrusion. Fearless, the little priest glared at Little Bear and spoke harshly to him. The two men had had a collision before. Fafard had denied Little Bear's son permission to marry a Catholic Cree girl unless the young man converted to the faith. As Fafard berated the intruders, Little Bear had decided he had enough abuse. He raised his rifle and without warning struck the priest squarely in the face with the butt of his gun. Stunned, Fafard fell back and blood streamed from a deep gash on his nose. He gasped, trying to regain his composure.

Father Marchand stepped forward and took his fellow priest by the shoulders. He reached for a cloth and held it tight to his colleagues face, trying to staunch the flow of blood. He checked Fafard's nose to see if it was broken.

"This is a holy day for us. Will we be able to celebrate the Mass that we have planned for this day?" Marchand asked quietly. His voice trembled as he tried to bring some peace to the ugly scene.

Wandering Spirit had arrived at the priest's house now and Little Bear looked to him.

"Yes," the war chief assented. "Bring all the white people to the church," he instructed his followers. The men left to round up all the white villagers, Catholic and non-Catholic alike. The whites were all led down to the little mission church. Some Metis and Christian Cree were already there, waiting outside.

Marchand took Fafard in hand and washed the streaming blood from the wounded priest's face, putting salve on him to help healing. Then the two priests headed toward to the church.

Fafard, his face now swollen from the ugly welt on the bridge of his nose, began the Mass, but all in the church were uneasy. Twice the priest had to stop the prayers to staunch the flow of blood from his face. Cree warriors with guns lined the aisles of the small church watching uneasily, their fingers on triggers. Many had not seen the white man's rituals before and wondered what magic would be performed, what danger they themselves faced. It was said by some the black robes had power to turn water into blood and a man's blood into water. If this happened to them, would they have the courage to fight? Would the war chief allow this magic to happen?

The Mass had just begun when the doors flew open, slamming back on the hinges, and Wandering Spirit and Imasees strode in. The war chief wore a hood fashioned from the head and shoulders of a wolf. Three eagle plumes were affixed to his hair, and the right side of his face was smeared with black warpaint, with yellow paint on the left. There were white circles around his eyes to make them look larger and fiercer. Carrying his 30-30 rifle, Wandering Spirit walked swiftly toward the altar then, in mock reverence and with an exaggerated movement, knelt on one knee and bowed his head. Fafard, watching uneasily, continued with his prayers. Marchand took a step down toward the war chief, but the older priest waved him away. Then Wandering Spirit spun around, stood and raised his gun above his head, uttering a piercing war cry that shattered the priest's mumbled prayers. Imasees laughed aloud and joined in, encouraging the other warriors. The church was in chaos, the shouts of the intruders drowning the priest's words.

The shocked priests stopped the ceremony.

"How dare you interrupt our holy devotions!" Fafard said to Wandering Spirit, who grinned mockingly. "We cannot continue in these conditions. I want all of you to leave the church until some respect can be shown."

Wandering Spirit signalled to his followers to push all the people, including the priests, out of the church.

Outside, the Cree warriors, the white and Metis villagers and curious Cree women and children mingled together, wondering what would happen next. Big Bear, who had watched events in the church with deepening concern, left the crowd and walked over to the Simpson house where he had been invited for some beef barley soup by Mrs. Simpson. He felt powerless and exhausted, unable to exercise any influence over events as they unfolded.

Henry Quinn, Tom's nephew, feared for his safety and that of the others in the village. He occupied himself setting up his blacksmith shop, arranging his anvil and tools as if he was preparing for a day's work. Then, when others were distracted he took advantage of the milling people by edging into the shadow of the buildings and thence into the nearby woods. He thought he might be able to ride away without being seen and bring back help. Once into the trees, he realized that all the horses had been led away. He looked about hoping to find the nearest mount but there was none to be seen.

Cameron struggled to maintain his composure and headed back toward the store where he wanted to clean up and do an inventory of what goods remained. On the way he was joined by King Bird, one of Big Bear's sons. An amiable, light-hearted young man who had inherited the good humour of his father, King Bird put his arm around Cameron.

"My friend, lend me the company flag for the day. I want to wear it to the dancing that is going to happen later."

In no frame of mind to resist any request, Cameron consented and retrieved the flag, which had a Union Jack in the corner and the company seal on a red background. As Cameron handed the flag to King Bird, the chief's son leaned toward him.

"Brother, be wary," he whispered. "Some here want trouble today and you must go. Stay at the store as long as you are able."

Wandering Spirit was now stalking the village decked out in his war regalia, including a buckskin jacket decorated with Blackfoot scalps. He wanted the white people all in one place and ordered both Cameron and Quinn to go to Delaney's house. As the two walked along, Quinn showed signs that he feared what might be ahead.

"If we come through this alive, we'll have something to talk about for the rest of our lives," he whispered to Cameron.

"Aren't you afraid?" Cameron asked, turning pale. He was astonished by Quinn's newly acquired fatalism.

"They can kill me, but they can't scare me," Quinn growled.

As they walked, Yellow Bear spotted Cameron and Quinn together.

"Cameron," the young Cree said. "You promised to get me a hat. Come with me back to the store."

The young storekeeper looked helplessly at Wandering Spirit. "I want all the whites together in one place," the war chief said.

"But this white man promised he would get me a hat," Yellow Bear protested. "The sun is getting strong and I need a hat to wear. Will we allow the white men to break their promises to us?"

Wandering Spirit grunted and dismissed Yellow Bear and Cameron with an impatient wave. There was only one man the war chief truly wanted. "Go then, but then bring him back here later."

At the store, Cameron rummaged through the piles of clothing that had been dumped on the floor. He took his time, and Yellow Bear seemed in no hurry, turning down several hats the storekeeper offered. When Miserable Man, another Cree arrived at the door, Yellow Bear suddenly grabbed one of the hats he had been presented with earlier and rushed off to rejoin the other warriors.

Miserable Man had a note: "Please give Miserable Man one blanket." It was signed T.T. Quinn.

Cameron gave the Cree warrior the blanket, took out a pencil and some paper, and began listing the items taken from the store.

The war chief had given orders for the Cree camp to be moved about a mile from the village. He told his men to march all the village residents, white and Metis alike, to the new camp. As they started slowly along the path, Wandering Spirit went looking for Quinn. The mood was unexpectedly lighthearted. Even the painted Cree warriors bantered with their prisoners as they all trod along the muddy path beside the lake, still covered with winter ice.

Impatient, Quinn resolved that he would head back to his house to check on his wife and child. He had turned and begun walking back when Wandering Spirit caught up with him and blocked his way.

"I want you to go with the others," the war leader ordered. His steely eyes looked at Quinn with cold hatred.

Quinn, the muscles of his hands and jaw tensing, refused. He challenged Wandering Spirit. "I will not go. I am the agent here; you must listen to me. I have work to do today and, by God, I am going to get it done."

Kamistatum, standing nearby, begged Quinn to obey the chief. Quinn stared directly at Wandering Spirit, not even glancing at Kamistatum.

Wandering Spirit was enraged by this latest show of defiance. He ordered the agent three times to turn around. Each time Quinn said no.

"What am I to do with this bullheaded man who will not listen?" the war chief roared. "I might as well kill you as we did the ox."

Without hesitating, Wandering Spirit raised his gun to his shoulder and in one motion fired a shot. Quinn was only ten feet away and the bullet caught him square in the forehead. The agent, mortally wounded, spun around on the trail, his body falling heavily into a nearby snowbank. His body jerked and blood and brains flowed out into the crusted snow. The roar of Wandering Spirit's gun echoed in waves around the lake and in the low hills. It was as if some evil spirit had ripped down a curtain in the sky, exposing a new world of agony and death. Others in the ragged, doomed parade screamed and turned in shock to look back at the village.

Then, a blurred, fantastic nightmare erupted. The Cree who had been joking minutes earlier with their captives were transformed into an chaotic rabble, their prisoners a terrorized flock of sheep. The first shot set off a bloody purge that last only minutes but seemed to take hours in the minds of those who witnessed it.

After Quinn fell by the trail, Charles Gouin, the government-employed carpenter, panicked and fled back toward the village. One of his guards, Bad Arrow, instinctively raised his gun and fired, as calm as though he was shooting at a deer. The wounded Gouin staggered but kept moving until Miserable Man, still with the gift blanket from Cameron draped over his arm, fired a hipshot at the fleeing man. The second shot struck home and Gouin fell, mortally wounded.

There was no pause to the orgy of violence that now broke out. George Dill, the private storekeeper, and the lumber mill foreman, William Gilchrist, had been last in the procession and were closest to Delaney's house. They turned and sprinted for the shelter of the building but each of them was gunned down by Little Bear and Iron Body.

Big Bear was finishing the last of his meal at the Simpson house. He was warmly thanking Mrs. Simpson, when the first shot rang out. He looked down toward the lake, jumped up and dashed from the house to see what was happening.

"Wait! Wait!" Big Bear shouted. "No more!" But he was unheard over the screams and the continuing roar of gunfire.

The priests' assistant, Williscraft, also scrambled down the trail. "I'm an old man. No trouble. Don't shoot," he yelled frantically. Two shots brought him down at the feet of the horrified young couple, the Gowanlocks.

Theresa Gowanlock screamed and grabbed her husband for comfort but he fell, too, with a bullet in the head. Theresa fell on top of him, and whispered in his ear to stay low. She thought he had only dropped to the ground to duck below the volley of bullets. Then she saw that his mouth gaped open and blood was gushing from a head wound. Her terrified shrieks echoed around the lake.

There was a brief pause in the shooting now, but the killing work was not done. An excited Wandering Spirit, now urging that all the whites be slain, had caught up with the group. He fired pointblank at Father Marchand, killing him instantly. Delaney went down with a bullet in his heart, and Father Fafard was shot while administering last rites to Marchand. Seeing Fafard sprawled on the ground,

Round-the-Sky, the orphaned youth who had lived with the priest, rushed up and finished the job, putting a bullet in the wounded man's brain.

Nine dead men were strewn along the trail. The shooting now stopped but the smell of gunpowder lingered in the air, and blood flowed onto the snow and mingled with the churned up mud of the trail. The only whites who had been in the march to survive were Theresa Gowanlock and Teressa Delaney. In shock, they wailed loudly and clutched the bodies of their dead husbands until they were gently pulled away by some of the Metis women.

"Come," a Metis woman said sympathetically. "It is too late for them. You must come with us to the camp. We will look after you and protect you from this terrible business. It is all we can do now."

Cameron trembled with fright as he heard the outbreak of shooting. He had dropped his pencil and rushed to the Simpson house when Quinn was killed. Cameron saw Big Bear racing down the hill shouting for the warriors to stop shooting. On the way to Simpson's, Cameron encountered Kamistatum rushing up the hill after witnessing Quinn's murder.

"Come into the house, quickly," Kamistatum urged Cameron, pulling the storekeeper by the arm. "It's your only chance."

Cameron, in shock, allowed himself to be led into the bedroom of the house. There Kamistatum's wife and Mrs. Simpson found women's clothes and a large blanket. They dressed him hastily and wrapped the frightened man in the blanket. They exchanged his white man's boots for moccasins and hid him in a company wagon surrounded by trade goods.

"We must go to the new camp," said Mrs. Simpson. "But stay out of sight and say nothing. Keep this blanket around you all the time. We will put you in Kamistatum's lodge. If anyone asks who this stranger is, I will tell them you are my sick sister visiting from Battleford. My husband returns later. He will know what to do."

# Chapter 27

About noon of the day of the murders at Frog Lake, Constable Fred Roby arrived in Onion Lake to pick up a load of stockpiled sawn lumber. The small Cree settlement was about halfway between Fort Pitt and the scene of the shootings. A young Cree rider told him about rumours of a catastrophic event that morning in the next village. The reports were vague. Some who had been out hunting said they had heard volleys of shots in the distance, but no one in Onion Lake would admit to having witnessed the affair, so the extent of the incident was unknown. Roby left Onion Lake quickly, racing back to Fort Pitt to tell Dickens of the reports.

When Jim Simpson, the company trader who had been visiting Pitt, heard Roby's incomplete report he told Dickens he would leave immediately for Frog Lake. He left with a wagon carrying a load of freight. He feared no harm to himself but he was concerned for the safety of his wife. And if respect for him wasn't enough to save their skins, the freight he carried might be useful to bargain for lives.

"If I can do anything to prevent mischief from breaking out, I'll do so," Simpson told Dickens. "Your men should stay put. If I feel help is needed, I'll let you know by messenger."

As Simpson neared Frog Lake, he smelled smoke and heard drums in the distance. Shortly after, he encountered a group of friendly Wood Cree who had ridden out to warn any unsuspecting travellers to turn back.

"The Prairie people have gone mad," they told him. "They are burning the church and all the houses. All the white men have been killed and some of their bodies have been put in the church. Your store and Dill's have been looted, as well as the police buildings. All the animals killed for food. Now they are feasting on their evil work. Go back to Pitt. You will be safe there and we will look after your wife."

"She is unharmed, then?" Simpson asked.

One of the Cree nodded.

"I will be safe, too," the gruff Simpson insisted. "I have some things that can be shared to take the minds of the killers off their bloody-minded pursuits."

He cracked his whip over the horses and plunged on, his Cree friends apprehensive and riding some distance behind.

When Simpson reached the camp, he was joyful to find that his wife was safe but horrified at the extent of the killings. He wanted to leave with his wife and return to Pitt but Wandering Spirit, still in his war bonnet and paint, approached him.

"I want to leave now," Simpson said. Darkness was beginning to fall but he thought he would risk the road back rather than stay at Frog Lake.

"You will come to no harm here," the war chief replied. His voice was hoarse, strangely distant as though he was in a trance. "We do not hurt the company men. You can give us many things."

"Still, I would like to leave."

The fires in Wandering Spirit's eyes seemed to be stoked by Simpson's insistence.

"We would like you to stay here," the war chief said. Simpson recognized this was not an invitation but an order. There was no point in pressing further. He would stay.

Now Simpson feared for the safety of his son Stanley at Fort Pitt. Simpson was uneasy, knowing his movements would be watched closely. But there was no protest when Simpson and his wife set up their own lodge along the lake trail. Simpson was relieved to see that Cameron had survived. The junior clerk had first stayed with Kamistatum despite the threatening behaviour of Cree warriors, and now moved into the Simpsons' tent.

Wandering Spirit wasted no time right after the Frog Lake incident in calling a council of all the nearby Cree chiefs and the Chipewyans from the Cold Lake area to the north. Onapahayo, the leader of the Wood Cree at Frog Lake, and Cut Arm from Onion Lake rode in. The war chief wanted to build a strong alliance of all the local Indians so they would be united as one force. This would not be easy. The Wood Cree were stunned by the ferocity of the attack. They too had their grievances against the government but the bloodshed they witnessed was beyond their imaginings. The killing of so many white men would lead to grave trouble, they grumbled. Wandering Spirit suspected the Wood Cree could not be trusted but was determined to gain their support through intimidation.

The war chief did not have to wait long before his authority was challenged. Soon after the pipe of tobacco was offered to the four corners of the world, and to the sky and the earth, Cut Arm confronted Wandering Spirit.

"We have a white missionary, Charles Quinney, and his wife staying with us," Cut Arm told the assembled chiefs. "I do not want any harm to come to this man of God. He is like most white men, too loud and preachy for my liking, but he has a good heart and has made many kindnesses to our people. Wandering Spirit would have them all killed. It would be no benefit to our people, if he killed them or the captives that you have taken. Hold them as prisoners, if you must, but do not slay them."

This presumption infuriated Wandering Spirit. The war chief's eyes blazed with anger and the pitch of his voice rose. Few men, even his closest friends, dared cross him when his rage took hold.

"Cut Arm is a coward," he accused. "These people do not deserve to live. Did they care for us when we were in need? Prisoners will be a burden to us on the war trail as we drive the whites from our land. I will scatter the brains of any cowards who stand in our way."

Wandering Spirit threatened to shoot Cut Arm with his carbine, the same gun he had used to kill Quinn and Marchand.

A distressed Onapahayo jumped to his feet.

"Our people, both the plains and woods dwellers, had been unjustly treated," he agreed "But there has been too much unnecessary killing for my taste already. The white chiefs in the land where the sun rises are the ones who can give us what we justly deserve. We should appeal to them.

"Wandering Spirit is too quick with his gun," Onapahayo continued. "If it is food you prairie people need, I will give you a cow in exchange for the lives of these white people. Killing such defenceless ones will not feed you. The bloody vision that Big Bear has told us about is too close to the truth for me. Let us banish this bad dream from our lives."

The chief of the Rattlers lowered his gun. He grunted. The promise of meat satisfied him for the moment. But for Cut Arm, Onapahayo's intervention was not enough. He would take the war chief down a notch.

"Cut Arm does not fear the leader of the Rattlers," the Onion Lake chief said, looking about the council and with derision in his voice. "Wandering Spirit calls me a coward. I have fought the Blackfoot many times, without fear gripping my throat. I was in the thick of a real battle, dodging their lances and war clubs. Did I see Wandering Spirit in the forefront? He must have been behind me. His courage is that of the man who carries a gun before unarmed women. I, even with only one good arm, do not tremble before him. Brothers, look at my good hand."

Cut Arm stretched out his strong limb. His jaw was firmly set, his face proud and defiant. He stared directly at Wandering Spirit's dark eyes.

Onapahayo interrupted before Wandering Spirit could reply.

"Enough, brothers. We are here to decide what we will do now. Let us stop these quarrels, they only divide and weaken us. We must stay together."

He turned toward the war chief. "Cut Arm and I will take this road you have chosen but only to see our just claims resolved, not blood lust. It is too late to back down and we must defend ourselves. I am fearful that we will all be punished by the white man for your crimes. But we have no interest in more wanton killing, and now we will watch to see how you treat your captives."

Then an elder, Bald Head, who had been watching the war chief with narrowed eyes, stepped forward and taunted Wandering Spirit.

"I see how powerful your Rattlers are when killing unarmed men and asking questions of your women prisoners. Is that all you will do? Wandering Spirit's name will be remembered with scorn, if his only victory is the slaughter of people with no weapons. There is work to be done at Fort Pitt. The police are well-armed and will fight back. Take the post from the police and that will be a truer test of your power."

The council deliberated but the Rattlers were in control and many moderates were afraid to challenge Wandering Spirit. First, there would be feasting for the hungry and excited people. Then, the old Hudson's Bay post would be taken.

Charles Quinney, the Anglican missionary at Onion Lake, and his wife had been warned by Crees who tapped on their window. When Quinney opened the door, twenty men rushed into their house and began taking food and items of value. Half Blackfoot Chief, one of the men, told Quinney that all the whites at Frog Lake had been killed or made captives. Onion Lake would be next, the Cree said, and then the warriors would move on to Fort Pitt. The Crees took the family to their camp, fed the startled missionaries and then brought them to Cut Arm.

"Don't be afraid," the chief said. He spoke kindly. "No one here will harm you. Some of our people feel unjustly treated by the whites and want to kill them, but your own generosity has saved your lives. I will ride along with you to the trading post to ensure your safety."

Cut Arm and three of his elders accompanied the Quinneys to Fort Pitt in the afternoon. When the small party of riders waving a white flag was spotted by the sentries, Dickens and McLean left the fort to parley with the chiefs.

"We thank you for bringing Mr. and Mrs. Quinney," said Dickens. He asked Cut Arm for further confirmation of the events at Frog Lake. Cut Arm said he had not been there.

"The one man I am sure is dead is Quinn," Cut Arm said. "Wandering Spirit boasted about killing him. I know there are others but I do not know who. The war chief is also holding prisoners."

"There will be a reward for any man who brings any of those prisoners to me alive and well," Dickens promised. Cut Arm nodded, accepted a gift of tobacco, and wheeled his horse in the direction of Onion Lake. Dickens and McLean watched the four Cree ride up and over the high ground to the northwest of the fort.

Dickens and McLean rode back toward the walls of the fort, with the Quinneys trailing behind. Dickens had been shocked by the reported death of his friend Quinn and did not speak until McLean broke the silence.

"Tom Quinn was a courageous man, no doubt, but a foolhardy one, too," said McLean. "For his stubbornness, others have paid with their lives. By failing to come here when there was ample warning, the Frog Lake people have also placed us in greater jeopardy. Quinn should have listened to you and come here, inspector."

"It is not wise to speak ill of the dead," Dickens replied coldly, after some silence. For the first time, McLean felt steel in Dickens's voice. He remained quiet for a few minutes before speaking again..

"So now it is we two who will have to make plans for the defence of the fort and our people." McLean was probing. "It is unfortunate for us that Simpson returned to Frog Lake."

Dickens heard but said nothing. The suggestion that McLean should have equal authority with him stuck in his craw. Dickens sensed that there could be trouble ahead. Most of the civilians in the fort owed their loyalty in one way or another to the company, and McLean was the company boss.

McLean studied Dickens' face carefully for any sign of emotion or reaction. He saw profound sadness but could detect nothing else — fear, determination, anger. The inspector had not reacted to his last statement. Had the policeman suffered another bout of his recurring deafness?

# Chapter 28

*I am compelled to compose the most shocking report of all those I have been required to produce as a policeman. Word has come of a most horrible massacre at Frog Lake. Early rumours had come from people with second-hand knowledge of a catastrophic event at the Cree camp, but now I have the news from an eye-witness who managed to escape the slaughter.*

*At 1 a.m. on April 3, Good Friday, George Mann, the farm instructor at Onion Lake, accompanied by his wife and three children, arrived at Fort Pitt and shouted to the sentries to let them through the gate. Mann explained that the morning previous he had heard shooting from the direction of Frog Lake but dismissed it at first as a hunting party.*

*Not long after, Mann had a visit from some Onion Lake Cree, notably Chief Cut Arm, with whom he was on friendly terms.*

*"You and your woman must flee," said the chief. Cut Arm reported that heavily armed and war-painted warriors had been passing through Onion Lake all day on their way to join Wandering Spirit's Rattlers.*

*"They will kill all the whites in this country," the chief added. "You will be safer in Fort Pitt. Don't take the main road over the hills; you will be watched."*

In the late afternoon, Mann loaded a wagon with a few personal belongings and necessities and hitched a pair of horses. The family drove their team through the less-travelled swampland south of Onion Lake. The ground was soft in spots from melting snow and Mann and his wife often had to jump out, unload the wagon, and, with the elder of their children, push to assist the horses through the boggy terrain and thawing, sticky gumbo. As they moved along, the load on their wagon became increasingly lighter. They left behind a trail of unnecessary goods.

Exhausted, Mann drove the horses into a secluded grove of spruces as darkness came and waited for the moon to rise before continuing the perilous trip to our fort Despite his fatigue, Mann rushed to my quarters to tell me that as far as he knew nearly all the whites at Frog Lake had been murdered.

Later that day, the Quinneys, missionaries from Onion Lake, also arrived, escorted by the Wood Cree chief Cut Arm. They were shaken but unharmed.

After Mann's report I roused all the men at once and by torchlight preparations were made in the event of a sudden attack. My goal was to have the post as secure as possible by daylight. I must confess I used all the techniques I saw employed by Crozier at Blackfoot Crossing. Bags of oats and flour were piled at the doors and windows of the storage rooms. Loopholes were cut in log walls of the buildings to help fight off an anticipated assault. I have been especially concerned by the lack of good sources of water. The river is several hundred feet away and there would be no way to defend that open stretch if the fort was surrounded. Digging a well for drinking or for firefighting is difficult and time-consuming because the ground is still mostly frozen from the winter. A bigger concern is that animals kept inside the fort have likely fouled underground water. Still, water is needed, so every available barrel was used to cart water from the river, while smaller containers were placed outside to collect snow or rainwater. By daylight we were in a position to repulse an open attack, but our danger was always fire.

I then sat to write of our preparations in my journal.

Eyewitness confirmation of the Frog Lake disaster came later that afternoon. Sixteen-year-old Elizabeth, McLean's daughter, was patrolling the post's fences, doing sentry duty. I must say the McLean girls, volunteering for *militia service, have made a great impression on all the police stationed here. They are fully competent and accurate shots as well, but I digress.*

*Young Elizabeth thought she saw someone moving in the winter-dried brown grass part way up the low hill that rises northward from the fort. Looking again, she was absolutely sure. She shouted the alarm and Sergeant Martin rushed to her side.*

*Henry Quinn, a blacksmith and Tom's nephew, had made a long and arduous trip by foot from Frog Lake after slipping into the woods when he saw his uncle gunned down with the first shot. Unarmed,, he decided to flee before he met the same fate. He scrambled away in panic as the shooting continued, heedless of the clutching, tearing brush. He crawled on his hands and knees seven miles through thickly entangled alders and brambles before he felt safe enough to get up and run. Quinn's clothes were shreds and he is suffering from frostbite. His tongue is badly swollen from thirst so that he could not speak for some hours. When he was able, he told me of how from his hiding place he had seen his uncle and others shot down.*

*With the confirmation of events, I prepared the following telegraph for Indian Agent Rae and Inspector W.S. Morris, the senior police officer in Battleford:*

> *"It is with the greatest regret that I have to inform you that the massacre at Frog Lake turns out to be much worse than at first reported. The following have been killed:*
>
> *T.T. Quinn, Indian agent*
>
> *John Delaney, Farming Instructor*
>
> *Pierre Fafard, R.C. priest*
>
> *Mr. and Mrs. Gowanlock*
>
> *Williscraft*
>
> *Dill, Trader*
>
> *Father Lemarchand (sic), R.C. priest*

*Mrs. Delaney is a prisoner.*

*H. Quinn, nephew of T.T. Quinn, escaped by running into the bush; he has arrived here this afternoon. I hear that Mr. Mann only just escaped in time. The Indians are living in the farm houses and mission at Onion Lake. They took all of the horses and Mr. Quinney's money ($250). Mr. and Mrs. Quinney were, I rejoice to say, not killed but were brought in by Chief Cut Arm (and councillors). We expect to be attacked at any minute. Please send reinforcements as soon as possible.*

*"W. McLean's family and Mr. Mann's family, Mrs. Mann, Mrs. Quinney and half-breed women are here. The Chippewyans have joined Big Bear.*

*"I am, sir, your obedient servant,*

*Francis J. Dickens."*

Having finished my message, I read and reread the words, almost unbelieving. I remained sitting and allowed myself a few moments of reflection. What tragic events will now befall us? My message is accurate as far as I know, although Henry thinks Theresa Gowanlock may be alive.

I feel an enormous sense of loss. Tom Quinn was one of my firmest friends on this damned frontier and now he is gone. My feeling now is one of overwhelming isolation and depression at a time when I must think of the defense of the fort. But it is hard for me to contemplate: The untimely deaths of my parents, my brothers, my friends in Bengal. So many losses — when will the toll end?

# Chapter 29

Anxiety rose over an imminent Cree attack on Fort Pitt. Dickens swore in as a special constable every able-bodied man and woman above the age of fifteen to assist in the defence of the settlement. As the defensive preparations began, a showdown was shaping up between Dickens and McLean. The Hudson's Bay man knew the mood of the Indians better, but both had spent years in the west, and both were adamant about their claims to seniority at the post. Fort Pitt had been first and foremost a company trading station, and McLean, although a newcomer, considered the police unreliable interlopers and a danger to the good relations that had existed between the Indians and the company. Under the current hostile conditions, Dickens and the police believed they were in charge. But McLean's forceful personality commanded the respect of most of the fort's civilians, including the local Metis.

Preparations began smoothly. Despite the danger, the post's inhabitants worked steadily and with good cheer. Poplar trees were cut and the poles stripped for a stockade around the fort's buildings. Bastions were erected on the northwest and northeast corners, the directions from which attacks were most likely. At McLean's direction, carpenters plied their trade and with the lumber from Onion Lake constructed a large boat that could be used to carry fugitives and supplies down the ice-clogged North Saskatchewan. Every available container was used to haul water supplies up from the river and these were stored, covered, inside the walls in case of a siege or attempts by enemies to burn out the defenders. Dickens again telegraphed Battleford, the nearest major police post, to request assistance. Soon after the message got through, but before a reply came, that link was cut again.

Day after day passed and no war parties appeared, much to the surprise of the nervous inhabitants. Wandering Spirit's Rattlers were in no hurry to force a battle. Hopeful speculation was that the more moderate Wood Cree would not follow a leader so volatile or mentally unstable. Or that after the looting of Frog Lake and Onion Lake, the need for food and trade goods had been sated, at least temporarily. Whatever caused the delay, generally clear weather, with days lengthening into spring, gave the fort's inhabitants more time to prepare for an attack that most believed was inevitable. Fort Pitt, it was assumed, would be too tempting a target to be ignored. So the people remained apprehensive of the fury that they felt was in store but that was damnably slow in coming. No response to Dickens's urgent appeal to Battleford for reinforcements arrived. Without any foreseeable help, there was an air of impending disaster.

As one quiet daybreak followed another, Dickens and McLean became resigned to the idea that there would be no assistance from any other quarter. Meanwhile, work continued to make Fort Pitt as secure as possible. The company men had now almost completed the large scow. Ammunition and food was stockpiled in storehouses at the centre of the post. Outbuildings and stables that might provide shelter for any attackers were torn down and the wood used to build up the defences. The stockade and bastions would afford the defenders a clear view of enemies. A determined assault with sufficient fighters could still have taken the fort but the effort would have been costly to the attackers. Dickens had estimated that the police had only about forty rounds of ammunition per man, so they would have to conserve their bullets and use them wisely and efficiently. His greatest fear was that an enemy could creep close to the walls in the dark and set fire to the buildings, forcing the defenders into the open where they could be picked off by snipers on the high ground to the north.

Occasionally, some friendly Cree and Stoney stopped by. One reliable friend who had often come to the post to trade and work was Necotan, a Stoney who set up camp just outside the barricades and did some scouting in the vicinity of the fort. He brought no news, however, on the whereabouts of Wandering Spirit's followers.

On the Tuesday following the Frog Lake killings, Corporal Ralph Sleigh was looking toward the river's south shore when he spotted some movement on the bank opposite the fort. He rushed to tell Dickens. Soon nine lodges were erected on the south side and a tall man was waving a white flag and shouting for the police.

The new arrival caused a commotion at the post. The group's leader was Little Poplar, a relation by marriage of Big Bear, and a chief whose behaviour was often erratic. At times he was good-humoured and engaging, but manipulative; other occasions he was surly and hostile. Some people in the fort suspected that Little Poplar's purpose was to report back to Big Bear's Crees and that his followers were only the advance party of the impending attack.

"Sleigh, take some men and go and see what Little Poplar wants," ordered Dickens. "Be cautious and don't get too close in case this is a ruse. I don't want our men caught in a compromising position. Perhaps you can get some intelligence on the whereabouts of Big Bear's men. Lead him to believe that we are expecting reinforcements at any moment."

Sleigh and five men crossed the river in a small boat, dodging ice floes, with weapons at the ready. They anchored in the shelter of a sandbar, out of the main current of the river, which had not yet reached full spring flood. They refused Little Poplar's invitation to land on the south bank. Seeing they would not come closer, Little Poplar bounded down to the shore with a smile.

"We are low on food, corporal," Little Poplar beamed. "Do you have some beef and other provisions you can spare?"

"How many are you?" Sleigh replied. "I will ask what we can spare."

"We are forty," the chief said.

"Where is Big Bear? Are they coming soon?"

"He is in the Big Hills, hunting. They will not be coming soon. The storehouses and other buildings at Onion Lake have been burned by the Rattlers. That is why we are short of food." He watched Sleigh carefully for signs of concern or fear but the policeman was a calm, even-tempered man who did not betray his emotions.

"You should return to your land at Frog Lake and stay there in peace," the corporal said. "There must be food there. What of all the animals the white settlers had there?"

Little Poplar scowled and stared sullenly at Sleigh. The policeman wondered what the enigmatic man would say next. After a long pause, Little Poplar replied.

"The warriors have taken everything. They only share with those who have committed themselves to battle. We want peace."

Sleigh avoided Little Poplar's eyes. He looked beyond the chief at the small group of men and women gathered behind him on the river bank.

"We will come tomorrow with what you need," Sleigh said. "We can bring more later when the big troops of soldiers arrive from the south. They are bringing a lot of provisions along with their weapons."

The policemen rowed back to the fort.

The next day food was taken over to Little Poplar and two days later, the chief moved his camp across the river and just outside the fort. It was apparent the unpredictable chief had no intention of returning to Frog Lake, and so rather than create new enemies the police chose not to press Little Poplar too hard. Then Necotan, at McLean's behest, had persuaded the chief that he would be better off being close to the fort. McLean believed it would better to have the little band outside the post so that Little Poplar's movements could be watched. The company factor felt that Little Poplar, like his namesake, bent too easily in the wind. He also felt sure that the chief had no stomach for war, despite his anger at the government.

A week passed before the massacre at Frog Lake was announced in the East. The Conservative prime minister, Sir John A. Macdonald, rose in the Canadian House of Commons to report the massacre. He read the wire from Dickens, including the names of the presumed dead.

"That is the news which I have received."

"Are there any refugees at Fort Pitt? Did any escape?" asked his opponent, the former Liberal prime minister, Alexander MacKenzie.

"I am not aware," Macdonald replied. "There are very few people at Fort Pitt. It is merely a police station between Battleford and Edmonton. I believe there are very few people there. That is all I know about it. Whether they will hold their own at Fort Pitt, or move eastward towards Battleford, I do not know. I expect to hear every moment, or very shortly what further has happened."

The prime minister then moved a motion that would allow his cabinet the authority to increase the number of police constables to about one thousand, virtually doubling the force. The police would be able to hire up to fifty scouts. Senior police officers in the West had begged for this kind of action for years but it had taken murder and open strife to push the sluggish eastern politicians into action. And there was no chance that these new resources would be ready in time to save the besieged inhabitants of Fort Pitt.

Inspector Morris, the senior North West Mounted Police officer at Battleford while Crozier remained in the field, feared his own post and the nearby town were vulnerable to roaming bands of hostile Stoneys and Cree. Some of the houses on the outskirts of the town had already been looted and burned. Dickens' appeal for assistance was not welcomed by his colleague. Morris's opinion was that the Fort Pitt inhabitants should abandon the small, indefensible fort and move down river to Battleford, which would bolster the town's defensive position. The telegraph wires, repaired once, had been cut again so he sent Johnny Saskatchewan, a veteran scout, to Pitt to deliver that message to Dickens.

Dickens tore open the envelope with a hopeful prayer. Would this be word of a rescuing force? Instead, Dickens was downcast when he read the unwelcome news. Morris believed the Indians were rising all over the northern prairie. Dickens should leave Pitt and take the road along the north shore of the river to Battleford, Morris suggested. Dickens impatiently threw the paper down on his desk. Morris's proposal was fraught with risk and would pose greater danger than if the fort's people stayed put, where at least they had some shelter and would not be exposed to open attack. He shuddered at the thought of a heavily burdened, noisy caravan, struggling through thick prairie gumbo and snowbanks, the danger of a sudden winter blizzard, a slow-moving target completely at the mercy of a superior enemy's surprise attack.

"Dear Morris," Dickens replied. "We at Pitt are unable to move. We have little means of transport as the Hudson's Bay wagons were seized by the rebels at Frog Lake. If we set out on foot, it would be a slow journey and we would easily be overtaken by the Indians. If we are attacked, with a number of women and children, we would be worse off than in the Hudson's Bay Company's post. This is also the opinion of all the civilians. I have heard that you expect reinforcements in a day or two. I beg you, for the sake of our women and children, to send me fifty men. If only our own force of police were to move, we would be sufficiently well-armed to make it through with our own horses and wagons. With the civilians, it will not be possible."

Morris replied quickly to Dickens but his second response was even less encouraging than his first. The Battleford inspector feared a sally by his men along the river would be extremely costly in terms of lost men and equipment. Even when a civilian militia volunteered to go to the relief of their friends in Fort Pitt, Morris refused them permission to leave. He wanted no shrinkage of the defensive forces under his command.

"We are under continuing threat of attack and I have grave doubts about the loyalty of some of the people who have come here, ostensibly for protection," Morris told the organizers of the volunteer force. "Already the Stoneys have raided the outskirts of our town and burned houses. Moreover, any force would have to cross the Saskatchewan's swift-flowing icepacks. I have no desire to lose any valuable men through drowning, exposure or battle."

"Damn it, man," said one of the eager volunteers. "You're condemning those people at Pitt to starvation, torture and death. They're a pitiably small force to defend against hundreds of armed warriors. I got relatives there. Let's go to save them now."

There were cheers and shouts of encouragement from the volunteers.

Morris held up his hand for quiet.

"That's my decision. Furthermore, I am determined to enforce it. Anyone who leaves this place to go there without my permission will be considered by me to be a deserter. Take my word. I mean it. It is more important to defend those hundreds who have rallied here for safety than to take risks to save a handful more."

Morris confirmed his views in a report sent to his superiors. "Even if the river had been measurably passable, I should have deemed it unwise to risk the sending of any considerable part of my available force. The enemy was vigilant and numerous, and I felt that my first duty was to ensure the safety of the fort and the nearly 400 women and children who had sought our protection. When this was seen to, there was not a man to be spared for offensive operations on the enemy."

Commissioner Irvine, the senior commander of the North West Mounted Police, holed up in Prince Albert, east of Battleford, was no more inclined to engage in a rescue mission. He too was more anxious to defend the town, the largest white settlement in the Prairies west of Winnipeg, against a force of Metis and Indians. So the people at Fort Pitt could anticipate no prospect of assistance from that quarter until troops arrived from the east to quash the rebellion.

Police and civilians also considered sending a mixed volunteer force from Fort Macleod northward toward Fort Pitt. This would have been a lengthy and onerous expedition in early April, meaning a crossing of about 320 miles of prairie and hills, likely buffeted by late winter blizzards and icy winds, with crossings required of four major rivers swollen with the first spring meltwater. But the supporters of a potential rescue mission were instructed by Major-General Thomas Strange, the local military authority whose nickname was Gunner Jingo, to forget that notion. Although he would set out later for the Fort Pitt area once given orders from the high command, Strange hated and distrusted the Blackfoot. He felt it would be more compelling for the police and militia to stay where they were to ensure that those Indians, though traditional enemies of the Cree and Stoneys, did not rise and join the rebels.

Morris chose a second experienced guide and scout, Josie Alexander, to deliver the gloomy tidings that there would be no help for Fort Pitt. Alexander was ferried from Battleford to the north side of Saskatchewan, and under cover of darkness set out on horseback to make the 100-mile trip. By travelling on the north bank of the river, he hoped to avoid detection by roving hostile bands of Cree and Stoneys in the Battleford area. The weather was gathering up for a snowstorm, and once across the river, Alexander made progress with difficulty, punished by powerful west winds that blew directly in his face, making the trip almost unbearably cold.

After riding all night, Alexander was only about one-third of the way. He felt safe enough to stop in a small clearing by the Turtle River to make some tea to ward off the chill. His fire had just begun to blaze when he heard something snap behind him. Turning, he saw six Stoneys astride their ponies, wrapped in Hudson's Bay blankets, with eagle plumes in their long hair and brightly painted vermilion faces. They were smiling but their rifles were pointed at his chest. They had followed him along the river, watching until the fire was well started before emerging from their cover.

"Josie, friend," said their leader, Man Without Blood. The Stoney leader was something of a dandy. He wore a white man's vest over a fur-lined pronghorn skin jacket and his feathers were stuck in a woman's blue dress hat. "Do you have some gifts for us?" There was no hostility in his voice.

Alexander threw up his hands. "You have me. I 'spect you'll take what you want." His expression was grim. He did not know what to expect.

"The north wind is bitter, Josie, so first make us some of your tea. Then we will see what you have that is useful to us."

Alexander was well-known to the Stoneys. They knew he worked for the police but his honesty and forthrightness were respected. Man Without Blood sipped tea and bragged about a white farmer he had killed near Battleford a few days before. He watched Alexander's face for signs of fear but seeing none, hastened to add that Josie was in no danger. The two men chatted amiably around the fire, each prodding the other for useful intelligence. The other Stoneys sat impassively, drinking from mugs taken from ransacked houses around Battleford.

Satisfied he had all the information he could gather from the scout, Man Without Blood stood up.

"So, we will take your pouch. Any tobacco? No, just the white man's scribblings. Well, our halfbreed friends may find a use for those. We're hungry now, so we'll relieve you of your food. You wouldn't want to carry all that anyway, because we're taking your horse and saddle, and your rifle. It will be a good walk back to Battleford."

"And what do I git in return?" Josie asked, pressing his luck.

"Our gift to you is your life. Your life, this blanket and these matches. May the Great Spirit walk with you."

The Stoneys mounted their sturdy cayuses and rode off to the east, trailing Alexander's horse behind.

Alexander tossed more wood on the fire and hunkered down a while longer to warm himself, brooding, as more snowflakes drifted down from a steely sky. The rebels would now know that Fort Pitt could expect no help. Rising, he kicked snow over the fire and set off on the long cold trek back to Battleford. Fearing an encounter with warriors he did not know, he kept to the brush as much as possible, walking with a slow and steady pace through falling snow that kept on all day. He fashioned a pair of rough snowshoes from alder branches and bootlaces to help him through the worst places. At night, he burrowed into a snowbank and wrapped himself in the blanket for warmth. He was reluctant to start a fire that could be seen by prowling enemies. His march on foot to Battleford took nearly two full days. By the time he arrived, he was exhausted, frostbitten and famished, without horse, gun or despatches.

Meanwhile, Johnny Saskatchewan, riding in the opposite direction over a circuitous route, had better luck. Travelling mainly at night, he arrived at Battleford at 3 a.m. on April 6 carrying Dickens' urgent call for help. The appeal would go unanswered. Dickens would have no intelligence from the outside world to assist him in making decisions over the next fateful days.

There was a shattering noise beneath Frank's bed and a sound of rushing, clawing feet along the floor. The noise continued loud and deafening in the pitch black of the windowless room, echoing, bouncing off the walls and piercing the inspector's ears. Dickens awoke in a cold sweat and found himself standing by his pine log bed, shaking. This unexpected position made him wonder if he had reverted to the sleepwalking of his youth that so distressed his father.

Slowly it dawned on him that the scraping, and the startling bedlam at his feet was caused by his Irish retriever, who always slept under the bed. He calmed the dog down, urging him into silence and petting its head. The fire had gone out in the hearth and Dickens shuddered, now realizing how bitterly cold his room was. He wondered what had set the dog off. He had a vague notion that the dog might have been roused by the crack of a rifle shot, but as he put on his clothes, he could hear little of the commotion that would erupt if an attack had finally come.

Tension had built day after day as the inmates of Fort Pitt awaited the arrival of the Cree warriors. Everyone who could carry and handle a rifle was taking turns at sentry duty, so that the walls of the post were patrolled day and night. Every shadow in the dark was potentially suspect as the harbinger of attack. The people at the fort felt they were besieged even though no enemy had shown itself at the gates. There were frequent alarms, occasional shots fired into the darkness as the jumpy guards let their imaginations run wild. As days passed, the anticipation became unsettling, even though the peaceful interlude left welcome time for preparation of a defence and, if need be, retreat.

Frank lit an oil lamp and looked at his calendar, then his father's watch. It was now a week since the slayings at Frog Lake, and it was four in the morning. The lamp was just flaring into brightness when he heard the clump of heavy of boots coming down the hallway to his room. Oddly, the steps were accompanied by sounds of giddy laughter among two or three men. There was a forceful rap on the door. Dickens reached across his bedside table and picked up his pistol for assurance, then told the visitor to enter.

There was one man in uniform standing at the door. It was Constable Roby, one of the sentries for the night. The dog eagerly sniffed around the policeman's feet.

"I expect you heard the shot, sir," Roby spoke first.

"I was sleeping, Constable, but I believe I was awakened by it."

"Just an accident, sir. 'Grizzly' Leduc was patrolling the east side of the stockade and thought he saw some crouching figures crossing the open ground near the fence. They were moving slowly and stopped occasionally. He fired to sound the alarm."

"Did they run, Roby?" the senior officer inquired.

"Pigs, sir," said Roby. In the flickering light, Dickens could see the constable was grinning broadly. "They were three pigs that had escaped from the pen."

Dickens, relieved, forced a smile. "Thank you, Roby. It's not the first false alarm and I reckon it will not be the last. Carry on."

Roby saluted and turned to go back to his duties.

"One more thing, constable. Will we be having roast pork for dinner tonight?"

Roby chuckled. "No sir, Leduc missed. If we could spare the bullets, I'd suggest the men be called out for some target practice."

"Damn, a wasted bullet," Dickens said. The two men laughed.

As the door closed, Dickens recalled the moonlit phantom expedition that happened with his father many years before in Kent.

"If only this would turn out the same way as that little adventure," he mumbled, shivering and returning to his bed.

# Chapter 30

A string of fine spring days in the second week of April gave tempo-
rary relief to the gloomy atmosphere at Fort Pitt. But contact with
other settlements was now completely cut off. Charles Quinney, the
Anglican missionary who had been in the country for many years,
persuaded Dickens and McLean that he should ride out to his mission
house at Onion Lake to reconnoiter. He found that the Cree had
completely abandoned the village after burning the buildings, and had
taken all the useful provisions they could carry.

The morning of April 13 was sunny and warm. Sheltered snowbanks in the coulees, hidden from the sun's rays, were noticeably
shrinking and fresh shoots were now appearing in the brown, winter-
dried prairie grasses. Spring crocuses provided splashes of colour. The
honks of the first of the returning geese and the babble of the cranes
were heard in the distance. Most of the ice in the Saskatchewan River
had broken now, and the stream's flow was nearing a peak.

Dickens had kept busy overseeing the construction of defences.
When he was not, he closed himself in his office and worked on his
daily routine reports, hoping to keep his mind off the constant threat
of attack. Details of organizing sentry duty he had left to Sergeant

Martin and Corporal Sleigh. Dickens realized that the fort's inhabitants could not withstand a long siege. Food would soon run short and ammunition supplies were already low and dwindling. Some people now inside the barricades, he feared, could not be trusted. In the event of a determined and lengthy attack, some of the Metis and hitherto friendly Indians might lack the will to confront their kinsmen and disappear, or worse, switch sides and become a hostile element inside the hastily erected walls. The defenders would be trapped inside the fort and doomed. He felt that he was lacking key pieces of information. He desperately wanted to know the whereabouts of the rebellious Cree. If they were west of Frog Lake, he thought, it might be a good time to pack and make a dash for the greater safety of Battleford before the enemy realized what was happening. He wondered about the presence of Little Poplar near the fort. Was he a spy, sending intelligence back to Big Bear's band? Even if he were not a spy, he had a loose tongue and would readily give up crucial information to the hostiles.

After weighing the options in his mind, the inspector sought out McLean and expressed his thoughts.

"Are you asking my advice, or looking for confirmation of your own decisions, inspector?" McLean asked. Dickens was put off by the tone.

"You have been in the west many years. I want to know your thinking about our situation."

"Well, then, I believe we are better to stay put," the Hudson's Bay man said. "We have women and children to move, too. If we're discovered making a run down the river, we would be extremely vulnerable to attack by a force of hundreds of warriors. I just do not believe we can move quickly enough and I too fear there are some here, a few only, but we need only one, who would betray our movements in exchange for safe passage. No, Captain, I think we are best to stand firm here."

"My difficulty, McLean, is that we are like sitting ducks. We have no hope of outside help, we have no idea where Big Bear's band is, and we remain here, paralyzed and outnumbered, like dumb animals waiting for the axe to fall. I fear we cannot survive a long siege. We'd run short of food, water and fuel. I would like to send out a party of two or three scouts to determine the whereabouts of the hostiles, and once we know that we can make our next move."

"My opinion is that sending scouts would be rash and I would advise against it," said McLean. "One of the sentries reported seeing signal fires last night. The guard dogs seemed edgy, too. Perhaps we are being more closely watched than we know. To send out two or three men now could mean the loss of their guns, ammunition and horses — losses we cannot afford."

Quinney happened along as Dickens and McLean strolled the post's grounds, deep in conversation. They pulled the missionary aside.

"Mr. Quinney," said McLean, "The captain would like to send out a scouting party to find out the whereabouts of the Cree. What is your opinion?"

"I've been out scouting myself," the missionary replied. "There's a risk but I have known the Cree here for a long time and I truly believe they would not hurt me. Sending out police, however, would be a terrible blunder, inspector. All we have heard suggests that the police are the special target of the rebels. What if the men are lost? I believe Wandering Spirit's men are spying on us constantly, and agree with you that Little Poplar is likely a spy. They are hoping that we will act precipitously so that an attack would be more likely to succeed. In short, I'm with McLean on this."

Dickens listened to the views of the two with some dismay. Others in the fort had appealed for the police to act in the face of a threatened attack. Granted, McLean and Quinney were both well-experienced on the frontier but he believed that something had to be done. Rather than passively wait for the inevitable, he would have the police under his command make the first move. It would be his decision to make.

By the time he returned to his office, he had made up his mind. Dickens summoned Sergeant Martin to his office and told him to enlist three men for a scouting party.

Martin had misgivings. But he did not wish to challenge his superior officer, so suggested two men. Corporal David Cowan and Constable Clarence Loasby had both been spoiling for some action to break the monotony of being cooped up in the fort. The sergeant also proposed that they be accompanied by Henry Quinn as a special constable. Tom Quinn's strong and perceptive nephew knew the Frog Lake area intimately and was also acquainted with some of the rebels, which could be the salvation of any scouting party. Dickens confirmed Martin's suggestions, and the three men prepared to saddle up later that same morning.

McLean was enraged when he saw the preparations. He dashed over to the stable to confront Dickens, who was standing with Martin.

"This is foolishness, captain," he protested. "You are sending out three men to their doom. Two of them are raw recruits and have little experience in Indian ways. The only thing you will succeed in doing is to weaken our defences. I fear the worst — that your men will be killed and their weapons and horses turned against us."

Dickens clamped his teeth hard on his pipe. He resented the intrusion from this meddler and reminded McLean that he was not the senior civil authority at Fort Pitt.

"I have an obligation to the people here, McLean. They are fearful and anxious and we have no idea of the intentions of Big Bear's followers. We must make an effort to find out where the enemy is and then to prepare ourselves for any eventuality. I do not have the patience any longer to wait here until they come to us."

"May I remind you, captain, that this is a Hudson's Bay Company post and has been since its construction, and that I am the senior company man here." McLean retorted.

Dickens held up his hand.

"Enough, McLean. I might remind you, sir, that we are living in a state of insurrection, and I repeat, I am the senior civil authority here. As such, I am responsible for the well-being of the people. Do not question my authority, or it may fall back on you in future."

McLean grimaced, and replied sharply. "Well, Dickens, perhaps you are the senior government man. We've seen what befalls government representatives in this country when they fail to heed warnings. I have my family here. I know where my responsibility lies. I have watched over them for years out here and their safety is my obligation. And I'll be damned before I'll put the safety and welfare of my own family in your hands."

McLean spun around and left Dickens. The inspector nodded toward Martin, who had been standing by watching the bitter exchange.

"Are the men set, Sergeant? Then send them on their way."

The three scouts hugged the north bank of the Saskatchewan, riding northwest toward Frog Lake. The bush there was heavier going, but they had no wish to take the main wagon road that was two miles north, only to risk a meeting with a rebel war party. Smoke still billowed from the direction of Onion Lake where the remaining buildings were smouldering. They ignored the fires at Onion Lake and made good time, riding westward toward Frog Lake. When they arrived at the low hills surrounding the settlement, they dismounted. Cowan and Quinn quietly crept to the top, looking down at about thirty teepees, fewer than expected, while Loasby stood watch. Quinn looked for the Soldier's Lodge but it was not to be seen. He wondered what that meant — had the band members decided not to fight, or had the warriors moved on? The Frog Lake buildings were all burned, too, but the camp was very quiet. Only a few women and children were visible.

"They've gone," whispered Quinn. "Only a few old men guarding the camp. The warriors must be off somewhere. But where?"

He pointed Cowan to the place where the shootings had occurred. "Over there's where I slipped into the woods. Crawled and ran on foot all the way to Pitt. Jesus, I was a-scared. I sure hope they buried my poor uncle."

"I wonder if there are any prisoners here," Cowan whispered. "Should we try to rescue them?"

Quinn looked wide-eyed at Cowan, as if he were a lunatic. The young corporal had a reputation for being hot-headed. He seemed determined to live up to it.

"Don't be mad, man. There's only three of us. You don't know what's inside those teepees. They could have left some warriors behind. And just because those fellows are old doesn't mean they've forgotten how to handle a gun."

Loasby was signalling them. Some Cree guards were coming up the hill. The scouts had seen enough. Most of the warriors were not here, but the question was, had they headed toward Fort Pitt, ridden southeast along the river to link up with fellow rebels at Battleford, or gone upriver to threaten Fort Edmonton?

The trio decided to head back to Pitt and report what they knew. Perhaps they would find some sign of the Cree movements on the way back. First they rode to the other side of Frog Lake, looking for tracks. But now it was late in the day and darkness was encroaching so they looked for a place to camp.

About 2 o'clock on Monday afternoon, a sentry at Fort Pitt spotted movement on the low hill about a half-mile north of the post. Soon after, about two hundred and fifty Cree warriors, all astride horses, showed themselves on the hill and, with some women who had come with them, began setting up camp. There was no indication that an imminent attack was threatened. The Cree rounded up a group of the company's cattle that had been foraging in the dry grass near the fort, shot them and began cooking a feast of fresh beef. The warriors would eat before making war.

Once bellies were full, a party of men started toward the fort under a white flag. Among the group was Francois Dufresne, a Metis who had worked as a cook for Tom Quinn. He carried a letter written for Big Bear by Henry Halpin, the manager of the Hudson's Bay company post at Cold Lake. In the days between the Frog Lake killings and the arrival at Fort Pitt, the rebel Cree had gone north to Cold Lake to badger the local Chipewyans there to join them. Halpin would be a useful prisoner who could send written messages to the other whites. Big Bear had given him the role of his secretary. Big Bear had also told Dufresne he was free to stay with others in the fort. The crafty old chief thought it would be useful to have someone who could speak fluent Cree to stay at the post.

The chief had now regained some of the power he had lost to Wandering Spirit. Many of the Cree had been shocked by the ferocity of the Frog Lake killings and were now urging moderation, giving Big Bear their support.

Big Bear's message called upon the people in the fort to surrender to his band, and for the police to turn over their guns and ammunition and leave. The chief also asked for tea, kettles, tobacco and a blanket.

McLean was the first to receive the note. Although he was still seething over their earlier confrontation, he took it to Dickens.

"Mr. McLean, I recognize that this fort is indefensible against any sustained attack from a war party of that size. My concern is that the Cree are divided. Big Bear might promise safe conduct to us, but does he truly control the men? If we hand over our weapons we would be utterly defenceless against slaughter by Wandering Spirit's militants, who may owe no allegiance to Big Bear."

Henry Quinn's account of the massacre at Frog Lake did nothing to ease his mind. Dickens refused Big Bear's demand for surrender.

"I will hold the fort as long as there is a man able to point a gun," Dickens said.

"I agree this is not the time to surrender," McLean said. "The Cree will not risk a headlong assault at this point. They would likely overrun us, but it would be foolish and too costly. That means we have time. But let's provide Big Bear with the other things he wants. It will create a climate of amiability."

"Agreed," said Dickens.

Later that night a second message arrived, addressed to McLean alone. Big Bear wanted to meet with the company man by himself. McLean discussed the note with Dickens.

"I think I should go. I would be able to get a sense of the attitudes among the Cree, how prepared they are to fight. I'm not afraid. I have dealt with them long enough to have the advantage of their friendship."

"I'm agreeable to that," said Dickens. "But be careful in case it is a trap."

McLean left the stockade with Dufresne and walked halfway toward the camp. He was met by several smiling men, who told him that Big Bear wanted to meet with him at ten o'clock the next day. There would be no attack that night.

"Take your rest tonight. You will not be disturbed. But in case of trouble, keep your family close to you."

They shook hands with McLean and he returned to the barricades unmolested. He did not tell Dickens of the arrangement for the next day.

# Chapter 31

The Crees kept their promise not to attack the night they arrived at Fort Pitt. The sentries at the walls remained vigilant, watching the shadows closely and listening to the noises of celebration from the great campfires on the higher ground, but the warriors made no approaches toward the besieged post. The chill northern night was broken by rhythmic beating of drums and hypnotic singing of scores of warriors, their songs alternating between fierce, high-pitched shrill chanting and a low ominous rumble.

As dawn broke, a weary Sergeant Martin received another message from Big Bear. The old chief knew and respected Martin from previous encounters. Big Bear again demanded surrender by the police but the message, written by Halpin, told Dickens that the chief regarded him favourably.

"Tell your captain I remember him well, for since the Canadian government has had me to starve in this country he sometimes gave me food. I do not forget, the last time I visited here he gave me a good blanket. That is the reason I want you all out without any bloodshed. We had a talk, I and my men, before we left camp at Frog Lake and thought to let you off if you will go. Try and get away before the afternoon as the young men are all wild and hard to keep in hand."

Dickens studied the note and thought about it carefully. Was this just a ruse? Could he trust Big Bear to keep the young warriors under control? He looked at the messenger. He would offer an alternative.

"Tell your chief we will stay for now," Dickens said. "But also tell him that if your people return to Frog Lake and promise to stay quiet, then all of us — the police and the others — will leave Fort Pitt."

Dickens then ordered all hands to prepare to repel any attack.

Dickens called McLean to his office and explained what he had told the messenger from Big Bear.

"I believe our best course is to try to persuade them to return to the reserves. If there is a large group favouring peace, perhaps they will accept that option."

"You and I agree on that, captain. I too feel that's the best resolution. But I fear that the peace faction may still not hold the upper hand. You must remember the ways of the Cree: the camp is now under military rule. Many of the warriors are under thrall to Wandering Spirit and are not disposed to listen to Big Bear."

Despite their meeting, McLean thought best not to inform Dickens of his agreement to meet with Big Bear later in the morning. He could barely conceal his fury over their confrontation of the previous day and lacked confidence that Dickens would be able to bring his family and the rest of the civilians to safety from their perilous situation. Now, McLean was prepared to take matters into his own hands and go out alone to meet the chief. He would not tell the police inspector of his movements. He believed that Dickens would refuse to allow him to parley with the Cree leaders, and that the inspector might even place him under arrest if his secret meeting was disclosed.

After talking with Dickens, McLean returned to his family quarters. He dressed warmly, not knowing how long he would be away, and put his black stetson on his head. He first strapped a gunbelt and revolver around his waist but then removed it. He would carry no weapons, to prove to the Cree that he had no hostile intent.

On his way to the outer barricades, he told the company's interpreter, Francois Dufresne, of his plans. He wanted Dufresne to go with him.

"Oh, no, monsieur, it is too much risk," Dufresne protested. "They will not let you back. For sure, they will keep you prisoner."

"Francois, we must do something. I am of the opinion that there is a large faction of Cree who are friendly toward us and will lay down their arms. But I need you to pick up the nuances as we speak. That's why I want you along. If there is some way out of this without bloodshed, I want to find it. It is a risk I will take."

McLean kissed his wife and each of his children, and then he and Dufresne stopped to talk to the sentries before they struck out across the open ground.

"I am going out to parley," McLean said. "If you see me taken forcibly behind the hill, do not hesitate to fire. Don't concern yourself about hitting me, just shoot. I will wave my handkerchief as a sign if everything is all right."

"Does the inspector know you are going?" asked Corporal Sleigh, the senior police sentry. "You should speak to him, don't you think?"

"I do this of my own free will," said McLean. "You can say, if you wish, that the inspector does not bear any responsibility for my decision. But I must do this."

The McLean family and the guards watched, worried, as he and Dufresne marched away from the walls of the post. Sleigh sent a messenger to Dickens but it was too late. McLean did not hesitate as he strode along. Dufresne's eyes darted about nervously as the two men neared the camp. A group of Cree leaders had started down from the brow of the hill to meet the two men. They shook McLean's hand.

"We want you to come to our camp," said Big Bear, who was wrapped in the blanket sent by Dickens. "We will have more time to talk then, in the warmth of our lodge and where you can have some hot tea."

McLean was visibly upset. "I thought we would talk here," he said irritably. "My people in the fort are not expecting me to go into your camp. I do not know how they will take this."

"Still, we want you to come. No harm will come to you, I promise. We have many things to discuss."

McLean felt he had no option. Standing well clear of the chiefs, so none of the sentries would mistakenly think he was compelled to go, McLean took out his white handkerchief and waved it toward the fort, signalling that all was well.

"They are taking Papa," said Amelia McLean. She was alarmed, fearing that some of the warhawks in the camp might do harm to her father. "He said nothing about going to the camp."

Mrs. McLean put her hand to her mouth. She felt ill. She gathered all the children to her and hugged them as she kept watching the hill for signs of her husband.

Dickens had been patrolling the open area behind the fort nearest to the river with a pair of constables. He glanced at the sun, noticing that it was surrounded by a sundog, the double halo that folklore said signalled snow was on the way. A heavy snowfall might give the people in the fort more time, he hoped, thinking that Cree might not attack during a blizzard. He noticed that Necotan had gone and that Little Poplar's small band had vanished. As he headed back to the other side of the post, he was astonished to see two men walking toward the Cree camp.

"Who the devil is that?" he demanded of the closest sentry. "What do they think they are doing?"

The messenger sent by Sleigh rushed up and told Dickens that McLean had arranged a second meeting with the chiefs.

"The fool! That arrogant, pusillanimous, mean-spirited fool! He will be a prisoner. They will not let him come back. They will use him as a pawn to weaken us."

In the Cree camp, the chiefs gathered for their meeting with McLean. A calumet was produced, and after the sacred tobacco was lit, the pipe was offered to the four corners of the earth. Each of the chiefs drew on the pipe but when it came to McLean, it was seized by one of the hostile leaders and was about to be passed by him. McLean took this as an ominous sign. But Cut Arm protested.

"Let this man take of the pipe. He has come in peace. What has he done to you that he be treated so shabbily?"

Cut Arm turned to McLean: "Brother, we know you come in peace and we want to hear your wisdom. Here, take the pipe so that your words may be found in harmony with ours and that peace for all will come to this land."

Cut Arm glared at Wandering Spirit and handed McLean the pipe.

McLean looked around the teepee at the chiefs. He was surprised to see Little Poplar there. The enigmatic chief flashed him a quick grin. Some of the leaders appeared hostile and suspicious; others seemed more welcoming.

Now McLean became the sounding board for all the grievances and slights felt by the Cree over the last thirty years. The slaughter of the bison, the diseases that drove entire villages to extinction, the restrictions on movement of the once independent prairie people, the sale of the country without the knowledge or any benefit to the people who lived there, and the personal affronts and maltreatments suffered by individuals — all became fodder for their complaints. Big Bear himself spoke of rumours that ten thousand American soldiers were coming to their aid and would drive the Canadians from the land. The Metis were powerful and organized and were making overtures to the Stoneys, the Sioux and the Blackfoot, who would likely rise in their turn. There would be many great fighters who would take back the land from the whites, who were less numerous and had grown soft from their easy lives. What did McLean have to say?

"Do not believe the false tales that Americans will come to help you," McLean argued. "The white men have treaties among themselves that would prevent this. And even if they did, are your memories so short? Do you recall the fate of the Sioux and Sitting Bull, and Joseph and the Nez Perces? Do you truly believe that you will be better treated by the Americans? No, my brothers, if the long knives come, they will stay forever and even more whites will come to this country."

The chiefs murmured, some nodding agreement, others gesturing in anger.

"I would rather die in battle as a warrior, as did the Sioux and Nez Perce, than live as a slave on a small scrap of land given to me by this government, unable to live freely, digging the earth like a woman instead of living as a man should live," Wandering Spirit said.

Big Bear spoke up. "None of our anger is toward you and the company, brother. We do not know you well, as you are new here, but we have heard from our relatives to the north and east that you are a just and fair man. Nor do we hate the company. For many years the company men have brought good and useful things to us. We know they do not covet the best hunting land but only want to make trade. That is why we want you to come under our protection, to get away from the men we may have to fight."

McLean raised his hand to speak.

"I would not be a friend to you if I did not warn you that any war on the government will bring greater evil upon you than you can ever imagine. These police you have trapped in the fort are nothing compared with the many thousands who will come against you to fight. Your people will be scattered like dust before the wind. They will be driven from one river to another, and from the dry coulees in the south to the swamps of the north and back again. They will have no rest and no food, until they and their children perish in despair. I say this, not in a threatening way, but as a friend, fearing the consequences for you whom I have come to admire and respect. I have seen the power of the white man in the villages of the east and even across the great waters, and I know well what he can do."

"Your words are wise," said Cut Arm. "But it is too late for us. We have made promises to Louis Riel and we have already begun to fight. Can we go back on our word now and stop and remain unpunished, too? The police and the soldiers will come and they will kill us, anyway. The government men will refuse us food. They will not make distinctions between those who have fought and those who bury their weapons. No, friend, we are like the buffalo herd set to running. There is no stopping along the path we have taken."

Wandering Spirit came forward and stood face to face with McLean. He cradled his rifle on his arm. McLean's face froze with concern. He had heard much of the volatile nature of the war chief, whose moods were feared even by his closest friends.

"We have heard too much from you. We know you are right when you talk about the company. But we do not believe your words about government. Why do you keep so close to the police? Do not speak on behalf of our enemies. That fort was built for trading with us, but your company has allowed it to become a camp for white soldiers who oppress us and deny us food and freedom. That is the only thing we have against you. We will not harm your family. But when you and your family come out of the fort, we will kill all the police like young ducks. They will be ghosts before the sun goes down."

McLean protested. "But the police have done you no harm…"

He was stopped by Wandering Spirit, who put his hand on McLean's shoulder, gripping it tightly.

"Do not speak too much," the war chief warned, a dark fury shining in his eyes. "The Dog Agent could not stop his talking. That is why I killed him."

# Chapter 32

Cowan, Loasby and Henry Quinn stuck close to the river, away from the main trail, as they rode southeast toward Fort Pitt with their scouting mission coming to an end. They had to cross the main road between Frog Lake and Fort Pitt at one point and what Quinn saw made him tremble.

The mud revealed the tracks of many passing animals, heading southeast, and one of them had left a clear imprint. As a blacksmith, Quinn recognized the print as that of a horse he had shod himself.

"That belongs to a horse Wandering Spirit took from my uncle on the morning of the massacre," he told the others.

Cowan was unconvinced and dismissed Quinn's remark. He was a brave and audacious man who craved adventure but had little patience for reasoned argument.

"Those could be tracks of men from Pitt rounding up cattle, Henry," the corporal said. "The tracks of those horses show they are all shod. Big Bear hasn't moved. We saw all those teepees standin' at the lake. The men were probably off huntin'."

"I put those shoes on myself. I know them," Quinn countered. "The Cree are riding horses they stole from Frog Lake."

"Losin' your nerve, Henry?" Cowan sneered. The two policemen moved on, ignoring Quinn's warning.

They soon learned that Quinn was right. The camp that they had been seeking for the last day lay before them, overlooking the fort.

The three men reined up together in a grove of poplars, considering what to do.

Quinn suggested waiting until nightfall. Then, he said, they could attempt to slip by the Cree camp in the dark, or double back and then come in on the river side of the fort. Another possibility, he suggested, was to ride for Battleford and try to bring back reinforcements.

"If we try to sneak back to the fort at night, we could be shot by our own people," Loasby said. "They're pretty damn jumpy."

"And if we go to Battleford, it's risky and it could be days before we get back with help," said Cowan. "We should just ride like hell through the camp and take our chances. That's what I want. Surprise 'em."

"Shit," said Quinn. "That's a half-mile of open ground. We'd never make it."

The impatient Cowan had enough of talk. "Henry, I'm senior man here, and I say we make a run for it."

Without further talk, Cowan spurred his horse forward at a gallop. "C'mon, Loasby," he shouted. The constable, despite misgivings, followed.

Quinn chose to play it safe. One narrow shave with the Cree at Frog Lake was enough. At the first shot, he decided he would veer off to the right and try his luck through the poplar thickets to the west of the Cree camp. If need be, he would hide out in the thick brush until nightfall.

The mad dash by Cowan and Loasby might have succeeded except for the unpredictable. The pair began their run on the northwest side of the hill. A wind had come up and the horses had to gallop across a log bridge that traversed a small creek. The beating of the hooves on the squared timbers was amplified and the sound carried toward the camp by the wind, alerting the Crees to the presence of charging horsemen.

A handful of women and youths stood near the lodge where McLean and the chiefs had been talking when the two policemen emerged from the bushes.

They raced to the teepee. "Redcoats! Redcoats! They are coming to kill us!"

The sounds of panic had come just as Wandering Spirit had ominously warned McLean to stop speaking further about the government. The war chief, sensing betrayal on McLean's part, glowered at the white man and ducked out of the lodge to take charge of his warriors. Most of the other chiefs followed, dashing from the teepee for their weapons. McLean was left alone with Big Bear, a shaken Dufresne and a couple of the older men.

"Damned fool," cursed McLean, guessing that the commotion involved the returning scouts that had been sent out by Dickens. He went to the teepee entrance but Big Bear stopped him from going out, scrutinizing the trader's face for some sign that he might have been aware of this unexpected foray.

"Have you betrayed us?" Big Bear asked, staring up into McLean's face and searching for an answer.

McLean shook his head. "I knew nothing of this. I would not have ordered it."

Outside, the warriors now realized this was not an attack but an attempt by the police scouts to gain the security of the fort's make-shift barricades. They mounted their own horses and raced after the two fugitives, whooping and firing as they gave chase.

Hearing shots from the direction of the Cree encampment, the anxious guards at the fort shouted the alarm. Defenders rushed to their designated posts and looked toward the hill. It was soon apparent this was not the long-awaited attack by the Cree but the return of the scouts.

"There are only two," said Sergeant Martin, fearing the worst for Henry Quinn.

"Provide covering fire," Dickens shouted as the riders neared.

"By golly, I think they are going to make it," yelled one of the constables, as others excitedly cheered on the fugitives.

Then, disaster struck. Cowan was within firing range of the fort's walls when his panicked horse abruptly stopped running and refused to budge even when the corporal jabbed his spurs hard into the animal's side. Loasby, racing close behind, almost collided with Cowan's mount. Cowan dismounted and began to tug the reins, hoping to get his horse moving again but, spooked by the shooting from behind, it reared up with flailing front hooves. Cowan mounted again, shouting the horse's name in its ear and again jammed his spurs hard into the animal's flanks, all without success.

Cowan gave up and began running for the fort, about five hundred yards away, but one of the pursuing Cree warriors on horseback caught up with the breathless man.

"Don't shoot, brother," Cowan begged. The rider, satisfied with the honour of coming so close to an enemy, leaned over and counted coup by tapping Cowan in his chest with the barrel of his rifle, and then peeled off, whooping in triumph. But then a bullet from another warrior pierced the policeman in his upper right chest.

Loasby, seeing his comrade in trouble, had turned his horse around, hoping to ride back to rescue his beleaguered friend. But now the constable was hit in the left leg by a bullet fired by Lone Man, Tom Quinn's in-law, who had sought to show his loyalty by joining the rebels after Frog Lake. Riding a striking white horse he had stolen from Montana in a raid the year before, Lone Man fired again and his second shot struck Loasby's horse in the neck. The animal crumbled beneath the constable and rolled over, fatally wounded. Lone Man was so close now that his own mount tumbled over the policeman's horse, so that both men were on the ground. Loasby had lost his pistol but struggled to his feet and began limping toward the post. As the constable gimped along, Lone Man recovered his rifle, sank to one knee and with careful aim fired. Loasby was hit square in the small of his back.

Cowan was writhing in pain on the ground when he was approached by Louison Mongrain, a Wood Cree chief, and Dressy

Man, one of Big Bear's followers. They looked to see if he was still breathing. Fearing he was dying, Cowan appealed for mercy from his assailants. But there would be none. Dressy Man bent to feel Cowan's chest to see if he was still breathing. A barrage of shots was now coming from the fort and the Cree feared they would be hit. "Don't, brother, don't," Cowan pleaded as Mongrain raised his repeating rifle and fired two bullets into the prone policeman's head. For good measure, Dressy Man took his war club and smacked the corpse in what remained of his skull.

Loasby lay in the grass, face down. He was aware that Lone Man was close behind him and felt his best chance was to play 'possum. He was also counting on the intensifying fire from the fort to keep the Cree at bay. Lone Man crawled along the ground up to Loasby, turned the wounded man over, and cut off his revolver belt before scurrying to cover. Loasby closed his eyes and held his breath while Lone Man was near him, praying desperately that his adversary would not stab him with the knife for good measure.

The shooting from the horrified defenders in the fort was having its effect. Several of the attackers abruptly fell to the ground, although the police could not be sure if they had been hit or were simply diving for cover. But now the warriors were retreating in triumph, supposing both policemen to have been killed.

Sensing Lone Man was gone, Loasby staggered to his feet and began limping as quickly as he could for the safety of the fort.

"Loasby's up," shouted Sergeant Martin, and he and Stanley Simpson, leaped over the barricades and dashed out to help the wounded man to the walls of the fort.

"Cowan's gone," gasped Loasby, as he leaned with relief on the shoulders of his rescuers.

Concern mounted now for the missing Henry Quinn. The defenders scanned the open ground and the nearby woods for any trace of the disappeared scout but there was none. Loasby told Martin that Quinn had decided on his own to try another route to the fort. "We should have listened," Loasby moaned.

Quinn had again been spared. The gunfire from the Cree camp had persuaded the shaken man to stay put until nightfall. He dismounted and led his horse into a dense alder thicket near the river bank. He would bide there until dark and then make his move to safety.

McLean, isolated in the Cree camp, now feared the worst. He had good cause. At the first shouts of alarm, Wandering Spirit had again directed his penetrating stare at McLean, as though he was trying to read the white man's thoughts. Now the war chief returned to the lodge, confirmed in his belief that McLean was just another of the hated white skins and could not be trusted. He lowered his rifle at McLean's temple. Perhaps this man would represent the third of his eagle plumes in this new war.

Little Poplar had rejoined the other Crees once the band appeared on the hill overlooking Fort Pitt. Seeing the anger in the war chief's eyes, he stepped forward and embraced McLean.

"Don't shoot, Wandering Spirit. This man is a friend to the Cree." Grumbling loudly, the war chief turned sharply and left the lodge with his other supporters.

McLean believed the return of the scouts might have sealed his doom. Big Bear seemed to read his mind.

"Do not worry, my friend. We will not kill you. This is the promise of Big Bear. We know this is not your doing."

The chief's words served to confirm McLean's feeling that many of the Cree, perhaps most, wanted no more killing. Still, he feared for the lives of the police, especially after Wandering Spirit's threats. When the war chief and his followers returned, McLean acted on his intuition and said the police should be allowed to leave without being attacked. He was comforted to see that Big Bear was nodding in agreement.

"These men that you feared were attackers were not charging your camp," McLean said. "They had been sent out as scouts yesterday and were only returning to the fort. This was a tragic blunder. They did not expect to encounter your lodges. See, they did not fire any shots at you or try to kill anyone. They were only riding for their own safety, to rejoin their people. Don't use this mistake as an excuse to kill the redcoats in the fort."

Wandering Spirit shot McLean a menacing look. McLean wished he could see inside the mind of this man who held his life, and that of all the others, in his hand.

"Hold up your arms, McLean."

The captive, for that was what he now knew himself to be, shuddered. Was this to be his last moment? He began to pray.

"I want you to swear an oath to your God and to the spirits of the earth, in the heavens, under the ground, and in the air around us. You must swear that you will not desert us or fight us, and we will spare your life and take care of you and your family."

McLean sighed with relief. He was reluctant to promise anything but knew he had no choice. He agreed not to leave the Cree without their knowledge.

"Write a letter to your wife and children," the war chief said. "Tell them to join us in this camp. Their presence in the fort is stopping my warriors from making war on the police. When your family is here my men can attack and then be happy in their great victory. We will set fire to the fort. Then when the police come out, we will pick them off as we pick off lone buffalo on the outside of the herd."

McLean felt brave enough to speak out now. "If you attack the fort, many people will die needlessly. The dead will not just be the police but many of your own followers, Wandering Spirit. The police will be fighting for their lives from behind the barricades, and although they are not many, they will fight to the death. They will make their bullets count and they will take a toll. You should not doubt their bravery. Are you willing to risk the lives of your brothers and sons in this foolish attack that would weaken your band forever?"

McLean paused to let his words sink in.

"In truth, it is possible Captain Dickens will not allow my family to leave. I am sure he regrets my decision to come to speak to you. He feels responsible for the safety of all the people in the fort."

"The policeman should worry about himself," said Cut Arm.

"We will soon bring McLean's wife and family to him, whether the police like it or not," a young warrior vowed.

"I beg you, let the police go. I will write a letter to my family asking them and all the other civilians, I believe there are forty in all, to come to your camp."

Big Bear stepped forward. "Yes, give them a choice. Those who are not soldiers can come to us or stay with the redcoats as they wish. They should know they will take their chances if they stay with the police. But also write a letter to Captain Dickens. Tell him we will give the police until two hours before the sun sets to pack up and leave the fort. They must leave behind their horses, saddles, harnesses and wagons. We will need those to carry our guests and supplies. Tell him that we do this as a favour and they must move quickly because I fear we cannot control some of the young men."

Wandering Spirit scowled at Big Bear, but Cut Arm and Onapahayo, the two most influential Wood Cree chiefs, agreed. "Well, they may die as they retreat," the war chief grunted.

McLean wrote a letter to his wife. He expressed regret at coming to the Cree camp and said he was at a loss to know what was best now that he was a prisoner. For now, he thought, the family and all others but the police would be safest with the Indians.

"I candidly believe it best that you should come, as the Indians are determined to burn the fort if the police do not leave. They have brought coal oil with them for the purpose and I fear they will succeed in setting fire to the place. The Indians promise that beyond doubt after you all come out they will retire and give the police time to get off before making any move...May God bless you and guide you all for the best."

Then he wrote a second letter to Dickens:

"I am now a prisoner. I fear I have no choice but to protect the safety of my family and the company people...Take the flat-bottomed scow and make your way down the river to Battleford. I suggest that you carry with you the bales of furs. Those can be piled along the sides of the boat to protect you against shooting from the river banks. God speed to you and your command."

Outside, there were sounds of another commotion, and Cree voices rising in astonishment. Amelia and Eliza, McLean's two oldest daughters, had left the fort and were coming to the camp looking for their father.

# Chapter 33

The police and civilians cheered as Martin and Simpson half-carried, half-dragged the wounded Loasby back to the safety of the fort. Several officers rushed to help, clapping the two bold rescuers on their backs.

Mrs. McLean ordered her daughters to bring clean sheets to bandage the wounded man. Staff-Sergeant John Rolph, the police doctor, raced over to inspect and dress Loasby's injuries. A wagon was brought over and the box taken off. The wounded man, shaking with cold and pain, was placed on a feather bed and blankets put over him. Loasby bore his agony stoically, grimacing and grinding his teeth to keep from crying out.

Dickens had gone with Rolph to see to Loasby's needs and then patrolled the makeshift barricades of the fort, urging the men to stay alert at their posts. He told them to keep the loopholes clear, use bags of flour and oats as protection against bullets and to shout alarm if they noticed any further incursions by the Cree warriors.

"Remember that we are low on ammunition," Dickens said. "I want no needless shooting. Every bullet must count."

Mrs. McLean and her daughters were now distraught over the fate of their husband and father.

"I will go to the camp to find out what they have done with father," Amelia declared.

"You can't go alone, Amelia," said Eliza. "I'm going, too."

Mrs. McLean said nothing, but stared at her daughters with a look of apprehension.

Corporal Sleigh, who had been standing nearby, protested.

"You are brave girls, but you can't go. They will take you prisoner, too, and God forbid what might happen."

"We've made up our minds," Amelia interrupted. "They know us as friends. They will not hurt us."

"Then I will go with you," Sleigh said with determination.

Amelia pulled Sleigh aside.

"Ralph, you must understand. The Cree know we are no danger to them. But you yourself are in danger, simply because of your uniform, so you cannot go. You need to stay and defend the fort. It is our father who is a captive now. I am more afraid for him than for myself. We have learned their language during our time in the west and we will do what we can to persuade the Cree to release him. Let us do this."

She placed her right hand on his shoulder, giving Sleigh a look of admiration.

"You are right brave girls, Amelia. Few would be as bold as you," the corporal said. "But if you don't return within the hour I will speak to the inspector about sending a party."

"You don't know we McLeans very well, Sassenach." She smiled and patted his cheek with her right hand.

Minutes later, Amelia and Eliza started toward the Cree camp, waving a white handkerchief tied to a stick. The besieged and the besiegers both looked at the two young women with amazement as they crossed the open ground and marched up the brow of the hill toward the Cree lodges. The young women were easy targets and could have been picked off by any willing sniper. But no one even raised a weapon. Soon, from the camp a small but growing group of warriors, daubed with war paint and decked out for battle, came out to meet them.

Dickens stared in astonishment and concern, fearing for the safety of the young women. The disastrous return of the scouts was bad enough. Now he felt that because of McLean's ill-considered action he had lost control of events at the fort. He raged inside at the conduct of McLean, which he regarded as a betrayal of himself and all those under his protection. Now McLean's behaviour had even put his own daughters at risk.

The McLean girls were within a few steps of the closest warriors.

"Aren't you afraid of us?" Lone Man asked. His left cheek and hands were still smeared with Loasby's blood.

"No," said Amelia in Cree. "Why should we be? Our father has taught us never to be afraid of Indians."

The warriors exchanged surprised looks, impressed with the young women's boldness.

Inside the lodge, McLean was finishing his letters to his wife and to Dickens. An anxious Dufresne stood next to him. When his daughters came into the teepee he looked up in surprise.

"Good heavens, girls. This is not a safe place for you. Why did you come? They will not allow me to return."

He stepped forward and embraced each of them in turn. There were tears in Amelia's eyes.

"We feared so much for you, Papa. Why won't they let you go?"

"They want all of us to join the camp here. That is, excepting the police. It is a guarantee of safety, most of the chiefs say. There are some here I do not trust, but if we put ourselves in the hands of Big Bear and Cut Arm, I believe our chances are better than if we stay in the fort. I have written your mother to have all our family, the company people and the other civilians to come here. Big Bear says he will allow the police two hours to prepare to abandon the fort and take the boat on the Saskatchewan. Whether he can hold back the warhawks I do not know, but I think it is our best chance."

"Father, Amelia and I want to travel with the police," said Eliza. "I can understand that you want mother and the younger children to surrender and not be involved in any fighting, but we are capable of fighting and have proven we are good shots. We took our place on the walls…"

"No, lass," McLean said, surprised at Eliza's suggestion. "I forbid it. You'll come with us. Don't you see that this is the best chance for the civilians? If you two are thought to be with the police, that will make it harder for the rest of us in the Cree camp. You must come with us."

"But father," protested Amelia. "We can take the place of the two hands the police have lost. They need as many people who are capable with guns as they can get."

"I'll hear no more, Amelia. You'll come with us. Damn Dickens. I warned him not to send out the scouts, and what I foresaw has come to pass. Now he tries to turn my own daughters against me."

"He said nothing to us, father," said Eliza. McLean held up his hand for silence.

He angrily scribbled his signature at the bottom of the papers and folded the letters, then turned to Big Bear.

"Will you allow my daughters to return to the fort to take back these letters? I have proposed to Captain Dickens what you asked — that the civilians come out and join your camp, and that the police leave the fort and go downriver."

A look of relief passed over Big Bear's face, as if the weight of scores of bloody spirits was now removed from his soul.

"Yes, they can go, your girls. The civilians can come with us or stay with the police, as they choose. There will be no attack while your family is in the fort. But your daughters must tell the police to hurry, because I cannot be sure how long the young warriors can be held back."

The Cree chief turned to Amelia and Eliza. "Tell the police they must leave quickly. I do not want their deaths on my conscience. I know I will be blamed for any ill-fortune that befalls them, because the white man does not know our ways."

"I understand," said Eliza, and the two young women were gone, heading back down the hill to the camp.

"Two people coming," shouted Sergeant Martin. He looked through his field glass. "It's the McLean girls. William is not with them, nor is Dufresne."

Frank Dickens was perplexed. What message would they bring? What had happened to their father. He presumed from their lively step and the way they carried themselves through the brown, trampled grass that McLean had not been harmed.

"This is for you, mother," said Amelia, handing one letter over as she reached the walls of the fort. "And father has written one for you, captain."

Dickens's hand shook as he unfolded the letter from McLean. He stepped into the entrance to the police headquarters so he could read privately, then cursed as he scanned the contents. He motioned Martin to come over.

"Confound it, Sergeant, McLean proposes to split us up from the civilians, whom I am bound by duty to protect. He has played directly into the hands of the chiefs. We will be divided and weaker. Now we will be forced into a dangerous retreat, or will have to make a stand here."

Dickens called together his officers, Stanley Simpson, Mann, the government farm instructor, and Quinney to explain the situation. They assembled at his quarters.

The inspector appeared pale and shaken as he read aloud the contents of McLean's letter.

"My duty is to protect all the civilians," he said. "My preference would be to make a stand rather than to run the river with such a large group and in that small boat. I fear the pusillanimity of Mr. McLean has placed us all in greater danger than before. I do not put much faith in the word of Big Bear that he can guarantee your safety, if the reports that he has lost control of his band are true. But Mr. McLean has made a bargain with the chiefs and you will have to make that decision for yourselves. I will say that if you decide to stay with us, we will do all in our power to defend you."

Dickens paused. There was silence, then a few men spoke among themselves.

"I'll take my chances with Big Bear," said the missionary Quinney at last. "I know him, and I have my wife to look after. If McLean says it is safe to stay with them, I take his word for it. I see no other alternative, inspector. In a fight with Wandering Spirit's warriors, we could all perish. Surrender is a risk, but it is all we have."

Mann, the government farming instructor, said he would do the same.

Simpson had not ventured an opinion yet.

"What of you, Stanley?" Dickens said.

Simpson paused before replying. "Well, Mr. McLean is my boss. And my father and mother are already in Big Bear's camp, taken from Frog Lake. I will go with them."

"We must see if there are contrary views. Everyone should make their own decision," said Dickens. "Sergeant, call all the people in the fort together. We'll meet near the barracks."

All the police, company people and their families, and other civilians, with the exception of a few sentries, assembled at the open space in front of the police barracks. On his way to the assembly, Dickens noticed the McLean children were already making preparations to leave.

"Quiet, please," Dickens said, as the fort's inhabitants chattered excitedly. "I have a letter here from Mr. McLean. The Cree have made a proposal, and you must decide very quickly. I must warn you that there is a risk whichever decision you may make. If you remain under the protection of the police, we will be responsible for your safety. If you choose the other course, which I will describe shortly, your fate will be in your hands alone."

Some of the crowd stood in stunned silence while others gasped or spoke quietly to their neighbours. Dickens noticed Dufresne's wife was weeping. He took her arm.

"Tell us," someone shouted.

"Big Bear has offered to take all the civilians into his camp, where you will be looked after by Cree families. You will be, in reality, prisoners and subjected to the whims of the chiefs. But Big Bear, if he retains command of his tribe, says you will be safe. I am obliged to warn you that I cannot vouch for that, but Mr. McLean puts some stock in that promise. I understand there are some survivors of the killings at Frog Lake who are in Cree hands now.

"My men have been given some time to leave the fort. We are told we must leave behind our horses, wagons, weapons and most of our supplies. Our other choice is to stay and defend the fort. If we decide to leave, we will be taking the scow down the river to Battleford. That, too, is a risk with the ice floes and high flood in the river."

A babble of voices arose as the listeners shouted out questions, or talked about the stark choice with their neighbours.

"What will you do, Mrs. McLean?" someone asked.

"My husband is a prisoner in the Cree camp," she said calmly. "To me, there is no choice. I will join him with my children. We have been told the fort will not be attacked while my family is here, so we will take our own good time in preparing to leave so the police will have a chance, but I will go to Big Bear's camp with all of my family."

Dickens shook his head, muttering to himself. He knew that Mrs. McLean had no alternative. Still, he knew that her decision would influence all the others.

"What about you, Mann?" Dickens inquired. "You are a government man. Are you certain you will be safe with the Cree?"

Mann seemed to waiver. He thought carefully about his answer.

"I am concerned that you will be attacked at the first opportunity, Inspector. Both alternatives offer evil prospects, and I fear putting myself in the hands of the war chief."

"I know my husband will speak for you and your wife, Mr. Mann," said Mrs. McLean.

"Then I will join the others," said Mann.

The other civilians who had been wavering now made up their minds. All forty-four would take their chances with the Cree.

Dickens was exasperated. McLean had turned all the civilians against the police, he felt. He paced up and down.

"Very well," the inspector said, his face flushed. "You have made your choice. I wish you good fortune. I fear you will need it. Now prepare yourselves for your surrender."

"Perhaps you could come with us?" Mrs. McLean suggested.

"No," Dickens said sharply. "We are the targets the hostiles want. We cannot put ourselves into the hands of the enemy. We will not allow ourselves to become sport for the rebels, nor hostages either."

He marched off, without a glance in the direction of the others.

Dickens now met with Martin, Rolph and Sleigh to discuss the options for the police. They all agreed that they would be vulnerable, isolated, cut off from water supplies and overpowered by a Cree force ten times larger than their own. Any sustained attack would undoubtedly carry the fort, and there was the chance of a massacre like that at Frog Lake as the aftermath. There was no prospect of relief from Battleford or other locations and Dickens had absolutely no news of what was happening in the world outside of Fort Pitt. Even the slim chance that the police could fight off their numerous opponents might put the lives of the civilian prisoners in peril from Cree seeking revenge for their losses in battle.

"The civilians have decided to go, so they are no longer our responsibility," said Dickens. "We can do nothing to protect them. Our obligation now is to the safety of our own men, and I believe our best choice is to abandon the fort and make our way down river. We must make haste to prepare. We have only a short time."

# Chapter 34

Dickens ordered the men to take enough staple provisions to last a week. No extras. All the men would be issued a supply of ammunition and weapons, but any superfluous bullets, powder and guns were to be destroyed or dumped in the river, so as not fall into the hands of the enemy. Warm, weatherproof clothing would be necessary, as well as medical supplies. The men carried the baled furs, as suggested by McLean, down to the scow.

The inspector scanned his office. A few maps would be needed, and any sensitive documents must be destroyed. He tossed extra reports into the smouldering hearth in his office, and the singed paper burst into flame, small flakes of burning paper drifting up the chimney. He would carry his logbook and final reports of the events at Fort Pitt and Frog Lake.

Dickens went to his room to look over his possessions. He selected his warmest and most waterproof clothing, but he knew he would have to travel light. That would mean leaving behind his store of books, including several precious volumes given him by his father. They would stay in a trunk and Dickens hoped that they might be left undisturbed so that he could return at some future time to recover them. His dog, sensing something out of the ordinary, came over and pawed at his leg. He petted the animal absent-mindedly. The dog would come. Not only because he loved the loyal animal, but it would also be useful sentry for the retreating men. Dickens took out his father's watch. "I must not forget this," he mumbled, and put it into the pocket of his warmest topcoat.

The other men had been instructed to take the barest of personal possessions. Some of the junior constables were responsible for collecting the necessary food, under Sleigh's direction. A few heavy bags of cereal and flour would be all they could carry. Most of the supplies would be left behind. The horses, too, would be left for the Cree. Martin recruited a group of the men who were finished their own preparations and they now half-slid, half-lifted the heavy scow down toward the river, concealing it on the bank behind a grove of poplars. The baled furs were placed carefully along the sides. Bundled in blankets, Loasby was carried down to the riverbank in a buckboard wagon, each turn of the wheels a painful jolt to his tormented body.

Snow appeared imminent. The storm would provide some cover for the escape, Dickens thought, but it would mean a miserable time for the men exposed on the river. The temperature was dropping sharply now, with the wind rising and the first sleet beginning to fall.

Mrs. McLean checked with each of the families to find out if they were ready now to join the Cree. The civilians preparing to turn themselves over to Big Bear's band dressed warmly and scanned their possessions to see what they might carry and what they would be forced to leave behind. They knew that everything they left, and for that matter, anything they took with them, would be fair game to be exploited by their captors. Those goods deemed necessary were loaded on the wagons that would be driven up the hill toward the Cree camp. Everything else was abandoned.

"I will miss the organ," Eliza told her mother. "I was learning so much on it, too. Do you suppose we will ever have one like it again?"

"There are other organs, child," said Mrs. McLean. "Certainly, if the Lord is willing, we will make music again."

She was reluctant to say more. Who knew what fate would befall them in Big Bear's camp? They would be in constant danger from the more militant of Wandering Spirit's followers. If they moved about the country with soldiers in pursuit, they might be regarded as extra baggage, unwanted mouths to feed, and abandoned to fend for themselves in unfamiliar country, or worse. And there was always the chance they could be slain in crossfire between the hostile Indians and Metis and the government troops they expected would ultimately come to their rescue.

Dickens had gone down to the river with John Martin to survey the possibilities of piloting the boat downstream to Battleford. The water was steel gray, hostile and cold, with great chunks of ice rushing along in the stream. If the boat foundered, he thought, there would be little hope of survival for most of the men. No one could survive for long in that swift, cold river. But, to be sure, the fort was indefensible, especially now with the reduced forces at his command.

"We won't get very far tonight, Sergeant," Dickens said. "We'll cross the river at the first opportunity and camp on the south side, set up defenses for the night. I don't think the Cree will attempt a river crossing after nightfall, so we should be safe unless there are war parties on that side from the Battleford area."

He was musing about the choices that had to be made and the dilemma the police were in when Elizabeth McLean and her children appeared at his side.

"We are ready now, captain. If you wish, I will delay our departure for the Indian camp for as long as you need."

"Thank you, madam," said Dickens. "I think we are as ready now as we can be. When you leave the fort, we will use your departure as cover. I expect that the Cree will be preoccupied with your arrival and it may give us more time to get off."

"Very well, then. God speed to you and all your men. I wish we could do more."

"We can, mother," said Amelia. "We will stand here, between the officers and the rebels to give them more time to escape."

"We'll also release all the horses," said Dickens. "They'll likely mill about close to the fort, and that will make it more difficult for the Cree to see what we're about."

Glancing sideways, Mrs. McLean saw her older daughters bidding farewell to Sergeant Martin and Corporal Sleigh. Amelia stepped forward and embraced the corporal and he kissed her tenderly on the cheek.

"You're the bravest of girls," said Sleigh. "None of us will forget your courage."

Amelia buried her face in the shoulder of Sleigh's tunic and hugged him, then turned away to join the rest of her family.

"Such goings-on," Mrs. McLean mumbled and smiled at Dickens. She knew how attached her girls had become to the two officers. Dickens had a wistful look in his eyes, as though his thoughts were far away.

"Your young ladies are a credit to you, Mrs. McLean. I only wish we would not have to part from you in these circumstances." Dickens stopped dead, there was no point in continuing. Then he cleared his throat. "All right, Sergeant. We must go."

Martin saluted and headed smartly toward the boat to give the men their orders.

As soon as he saw the civilians leave the fort and head toward the hill and the camp, Dickens went to the river to join his detachment at the boat. He whistled, and his Irish retriever came running and trotted along by his side. Constable Richard Rutledge, an Ontario man who had piloted boats on the logging rivers of eastern Canada, had volunteered to steer the scow.

Wet snow was now falling, sticking to the men's coats and covering the ground. Chill winds from the northwest had picked up as well, penetrating the men's winter clothing. It was now approaching twilight, as well, a mixed blessing. While the encroaching darkness would make their departure harder to see, it would also mean they would not be able to go far and would make hazards on the river less visible.

The men heaved mightily to push the loaded scow into the river. Rutledge hopped in but was startled by what he saw. Water was pouring rapidly through the seams. The boat had been improperly caulked.

He called over the inspector.

Dickens felt his stomach churn when he saw the leaks.

"Is this useable at all, Rutledge?"

"By hard bailing, we can make it across the river, I think, sir. But it'll take all hands to keep 'er afloat, and that's as far as it'll be safe to travel tonight."

"Well, we've no choice, Rutledge. If you are of the conviction that we can get across this stream, then we'll take that chance and leave now."

Dickens shouted to Sleigh. "Corporal, take a couple of men and go back to the fort to collect more caulking and anything we can use for buckets. Be quick, sir, time is short. The Indians may soon be upon us."

Standing by the boat, Dickens could hear the booming voice of Charles Quinney leading the hymn A Mighty Fortress is Our God as the straggling train of civilians made their way up the hill to the camp. The voices joined in the hymn were soon drowned out by the warriors beating drums and chanting victory songs. Some of the Cree women went forward and met the families, leading the prisoners to the lodges where they would stay. William McLean, watched closely by a pair of armed men, was joyfully reunited with his wife and children. They were directed to the lodge of Little Poplar, who despite his quirky behaviour had retained some degree of influence in the band. Big Bear also urged his kinsman to take the family of Mann because he felt that there would be many who would not think twice to take the life of any representative of the Canadian government. Because of Little Poplar's family ties, no one would violate the sanctity of his lodge.

The new arrivals now met up with the survivors from Frog Lake, Mrs. Gowanlock and Mrs. Delaney, Bill Cameron, and some other prisoners taken at Cold Lake to the north. The captive women greeted the new arrivals, their companions in misery, with tears and relief. Cameron was exultant that McLean and Jim Simpson, in particular, were fellow prisoners. He had feared for his life, and now the larger numbers of captive white men made that terrifying prospect more remote.

With the excitement around the surrender, few in the camp noticed that the police were now close to finishing the preparations for their own escape. Iron Body, one of the warriors from Frog Lake, however, saw the thin line of police down by the river, and rushed to Wandering Spirit.

"The red coats are getting away," he shouted. "Let's kill them now."

He leaped on his horse, gone before Big Bear could tell him to stop, and he was followed by a dozen of the young men. The pursuers rode with all speed toward the fort. The ground was slippery now from the sleet and wet snow and when the horse of one warrior slipped and fell, throwing its rider heavily, the attacking Cree slowed their pace.

Sleigh and his two companions were heading back to the boat with a load of caulking and some buckets. Sleigh saw riders racing down the hillside toward them.

"Here's trouble, lively now," he shouted to the others. The men raced for the boat and clambered aboard. Dickens was the last man aboard, lifting and shoving the scow to free it from the wet mud on the bank as the others strained on their oars. As he pushed, the watch tumbled from his coat pocket onto the muck. With the Cree coming into rifle range, there was no time to go back, and the inspector watched forlornly as the boat drifted out into the river, leaving behind that prized gift from his father.

The men leaned to their oars as Rutledge struggled to direct the boat out into the fast current.

"Bail hard, lads, and row as hard as you can," Rutledge shouted over the roar of the rushing water and the thumping of ice against the hull of the boat. The men with oars pulled with all their strength and the others bailed the water pouring into the boat with all available buckets. The scow rocked back and forth in the raging stream and some blankets piled near the gunwales slid over the side, lost to the current.

If there was need of further encouragement of their endeavours, it now came from the bank they had left. Iron Body had arrived at the place of departure and dismounted, levelling his rifle and firing on the boat. Others followed, including Wandering Spirit. Mostly the shots went astray; a few hit the side of the scow but buried themselves into the fur bales that padded the sides. Rutledge had now manoeuvred the boat into mid-river and the fast-flowing water carried the leaky vessel about a mile downstream, soon out of range of the Cree guns. As Dickens anticipated, the hostile warriors would not try to cross the icy river now.

"Pull in over there," the inspector instructed Rutledge, looking toward a clearing on the far shore. "We'll set up for the night now and get an early start tomorrow. First order of business will be to build some good fires and keep them going all night. A good rest and some hot food and tea to warm our bellies will prepare us for a long day. We must stay warm or perish from exposure."

The police were soaked through from the sleet and splashing water. Despite the wintry chill, their exertions had made them hot and sweaty and now that they were ashore the bitterly cold night froze their sodden clothes, which stuck to their skin. But Dickens was proud and thankful that the men under his command had made their escape without further casualties. They all knew there would be a dangerous journey ahead, but at least they were alive.

Wandering Spirit, Iron Body and the others who had pursued the police down at the river bank turned back to investigate what was left behind in the abandoned fort.

# Chapter 35

With the disappearance of the light, Henry Quinn crept from his hiding place by the bank of the river and made for the fort, moving quietly through the woods. Fear that he might be discovered had kept him frozen to his place of concealment the whole day. The blacksmith was weaponless; in his frantic rush into the bush, he had lost his pistol and was afraid to ride back to find it. He had released his horse and driven it off with a hard slap to the rump. Quinn had heard a volley of shots fired from the direction of the fort after he split up from his companions and assumed they had come from the defenders. But after that barrage had died down, he heard only an occasional shot, so he believed the police still held the post. From his refuge he had been unable to witness the day's events and so was ignorant of all that had transpired.

Shaking with cold and desperately hungry, Quinn relished the idea of a hot meal and warm, dry blankets, even if the future of the fort remained in the balance. He was relieved to have escaped the presumed fate of Cowan and Loasby.

Through new-fallen snow, Quinn scrambled silently up to the walls of the fort. He heard voices but could not make out who was speaking or what was being said. There were lamps, too, and sounds of wood being chopped to build a fire. He slipped in through the gate on all fours, surprised that it was partway open and there were no sentries to challenge him. Then he realized he had made a terrible mistake.

He hid behind some water barrels on the inside of the fort walls. There were no police, no company people, only a pair of Cree warriors in buckskins and blankets coming his way. Others stood by a newly lit fire, adding wood that had been ripped from some of the walls. Now he heard the crashing sounds of buildings being ransacked, furniture broken and glass jars hurled to the muddy ground.

What surprised him most was there was no sign of any fighting. No bodies heaped on the ground, or dragged toward the fire where they could be stripped of clothing or valuables. What had happened to the police and the civilians who two days earlier had seemed so determined to defend the fort against attackers? Afraid of being captured or killed, he thought to slip back out through the gate and return to his hiding place. Better to endure another cold night than to be tortured and murdered. But it was too late now, more warriors were arriving. There was no way he could avoid being seen. He slipped back behind the barrels wondering how he could save himself.

The Cree militants were in a mood of celebration with the taking of the fort. They had captives to bargain with if any army of soldiers arrived from the east. The police, enforcers of the hated government's rules, were in full retreat. They had left behind piles of booty, horses, cattle and chickens, clothing, blankets, perhaps guns, and luxuries that would make the Cree rich.

Without waiting for commands from Wandering Spirit, his jubilant, laughing followers tore into the stores, ripped apart furniture and trunks in search of precious items. The war chief went with some followers directly to Dickens' office and pulled out a heavy trunk. They were disappointed to find it contained only books, papers, a collection of letters and clothing. The books were torn apart and dumped on the fires but the box was quickly abandoned when the men noticed that others were finding much more interesting leavings. Supplies of food and alcohol or opiate-laced medicines proved to be the most popular, although the Cree found that some items left behind, like the pickled walnuts enjoyed by the police officers, were foul to their taste. Provisions like canned sardines and sweet, sticky honey and syrups, however, were objects of desire. Some unwary celebrants swallowed down alcohol-based medicines and later felt uncomfortable side effects, paying dearly the next morning for gluttonous ingestion of medicines that were intended to be taken by the spoonful.

Quinn watched in amazement as the warriors tore apart the buildings, destroying what they could not take, then danced and sang as they set fire to all. As the flames roared higher, and the light illuminated his place of hiding, Quinn decided he had no choice but to join in celebration. He smeared mud on his face to darken it, crept carefully to a pile of blankets and wrapped one around him, found a hat with a feather, which he placed on his head, and joined in the dancing, cautiously sticking to shadows so that he could not be seen too clearly by the others.

He was startled to see Little Poplar arrive, pulling a reluctant Amelia McLean by her arm. The looters had not known what to make of the organ, which had been carried outside near the fire. Little Poplar told the young woman to play a tune on it, but when she obliged with a mournful hymn, several of the Cree who had never before heard the wailing instrument, ran off screaming that it was the moaning of evil spirits and ghosts.

"Stop," they cried. And when Amelia ended her tune, they rushed at it with axes and smashed the organ, then torched it with a brand from the big fire.

Others broke out the abandoned clothing. The most stylish clothes, usually the least effective against the cold of winter, had all been left behind and were donned indiscriminately. As the alcoholic medicines took their effect, the attire worn by the looters grew increasingly bizarre. Women's feathered hats were complemented by men's breeches, with corsets worn over outer clothing. The men laughed as they dressed in the most outlandish fashion they could find. Perfumes, ointments and powders became part of the adornments of war-painted warriors. With the men clad in dresses and the clothing left behind by the police, the revelry resembled a grotesque Halloween party.

One of the warriors went down to the river bank to see if there were signs of the police. Across the river, about a mile away, he could see the faint glow of their fires. He turned to walk back, then spotted something in the mud that reflected in the glow of the burning buildings. He picked it up. It was a watch. This would fetch a fine price from the halfbreeds, he thought, and stuffed it in the policeman's Norfolk jacket he had taken from the barracks.

When the food was eaten, spread on the ground or carried off to the camp, and the flames from the burning buildings reached a climax, Wandering Spirit stepped to the centre of the fortress grounds and shouted in his booming, menacing voice.

"You see that we have another victory. The cowardly police have fled, and we have many white prisoners. There will be more triumphs, and they will continue until there are no more white men anywhere in our land. For many years to come, our people will rejoice in the victories of Wandering Spirit and his brave warriors. We will be giants to our children and grandchildren. Follow me, my friends, and glory will be yours."

As the other buildings were burned or dismantled, and the destruction continued, the war chief, waving his Winchester above his head, led a victory dance to the drumming and chanting of his followers.

Henry Quinn stuck to the shadows, dancing when someone looked in his direction. He had hoped not to be discovered until he could find a way out of his dilemma. He noticed one of the warriors was watching him suspiciously and he tried to edge away, but the man kept following him wherever he went. He knew that to make a sudden break would spell his doom.

After a time, the man spoke to him in Cree. Quinn knew some Cree but enough to know that his speech would betray him, so he kept dancing and didn't answer, hoping the man would give up and leave. But Quinn's lack of response only made the warrior more curious. The man called over a friend and the two stared at Quinn, watching his every movement. Soon, one of them went to find Wandering Spirit.

Quinn decided now that he had no choice but to make a run for the woods on the western side of the fort. He broke from the gate and raced back toward his riverbank hideout as fast as his short legs and stocky torso would allow. A bullet skimmed his boots, as he disappeared into a thicket of alders and ducked behind the stump of a fallen cottonwood. Panting, he prayed for God's deliverance. Wandering Spirit and ten other pursuers were close behind.

The war chief and his men passed Quinn's refuge and kept going down river. The darkness away from the fires of the fort provided the fugitive cover as he waited breathlessly. He feared the loud and rapid beating of his heart would betray him to his pursuers.

Then, as Quinn adjusted himself to sink deeper into his hiding place, his boot slipped on the rotting bark of the cottonwood. The last warrior in the group, Isidore Mondion, heard the sound and investigated. Sharp eyes scanned the black mass of the stump and spotted a shape that looked like a white man's boot. The Wood Cree stepped back and cocked his rifle in Quinn's direction.

"Come out," he said in a loud whisper. "I see you now. Don't fear. I'm gonna protect you. Come fast before Wandering Spirit returns. You must come now. It is your only hope."

There was nothing to do. Quinn rose and stepped out, his hands up.

Mondion checked Quinn for weapons and then called the war chief. "I have the white man here."

Wandering Spirit came running back along the riverbank, his rifle lowered at the prisoner's chest.

"No, Wandering Spirit," Mondion said, stepping between the war chief and Quinn. "This man is my captive. I caught him. His life is mine and I give it to him. That is our law. From today, we are brothers, Henry and I."

Angry, the frustrated Wandering Spirit kicked at the stump.

"Very well," said the war chief. "He is your prisoner. But he dies if he causes any trouble."

Quinn's heart jumped. It must be Irish luck to be spared again, he thought. Though he was the war leader, Wandering Spirit still had to respect the Cree code that gave a captor authority over his prisoner. With Mondion's arm around his shoulder, Quinn was marched back to the Cree camp where he joined the other civilians, content for now just to be alive. Mondion's Metis wife brought a bowl of broth filled with chunks of scrap meat and some bannock. It was not much, but to Quinn the greasy mess would remain in his memory as the best meal he had ever tasted.

Across the river, Dickens surveyed the camp that the police had established. He had ordered some of the men, under Rutledge's supervision, to re-caulk the boat overnight. The superficial job done earlier had almost cost the men their lives. Nearly all, he calculated, would have been lost if the boat had capsized, throwing them into the raging cold water, with its thick floes of ice. Those who might have survived could have been picked off by Cree snipers, weaponless as they emerged from the stream, wet and freezing in the icy wind. He shuddered as he imagined the dreadful scene. For a successful escape, the boat would have to be absolutely waterproof. He admired the skill of Rutledge, whose performance in steering the unwieldy vessel seemed to be superhuman. They all owed their lives to him.

The men had turned over the scow about one hundred feet in from the riverbank, forming a defensive wall in case of attack. McLean's fur bales were stacked on the ground, in front of bow and stern, to serve as a further barricade. The men had sought out wood to build large fires to warm themselves. Dickens had sentries changed every half-hour, so that none of the men would grow excessively cold in the miserable, snowy night. The tents were erected between the boat and the shore. He was confident that if an attack came, the police could make a good account of themselves.

Dickens went to see Loasby and Staff-Sergeant Rolph, the doctor. They were bedded down in a tent that was close to the main fire. Loasby was shivering under a pile of blankets.

"How are you, Constable?" he asked.

"I never thought a pleasant afternoon ride would be so painful," Loasby joked through his agony.

"I've removed the bullet in his leg, Inspector," Rolph said. "I fear there is not much I can do about the one lodged in his back under these circumstances. I'm changing his dressings frequently. We'll have to wait until Battleford. The constable is a brave man."

"Courage, my friend," Dickens said to Loasby.

He drew Rolph aside. "Will he make it?"

"Yes, sir," said Rolph. "It is not a fatal wound. The only fear I have is that of infection if we are delayed in our voyage."

Dickens left and went to the bonfire to make notes in his personal log:

"The men are suffering greatly tonight. The snow has stopped but the cold is becoming more intense. Uniforms are wet and now the cold freezes the cloth to our skins. I fear many men will have severe frostbite. The men are brave and in good spirit, considering their pain. Their only complaint to me has been their frustration that they cannot exact a measure of revenge for the death of their comrade Cowan and the wounding of Loasby. To my own despair I have lost father's watch, but perhaps it will be a worthy exchange for our escape."

He stood up. "Get a good rest tonight," he told the men still around the fire. "We will leave for Battleford at sunrise tomorrow."

Dickens headed for canvas shelter, to be greeted by his happy but wet dog.

He had just settled down when outside there were sounds of drumming and shots fired. The wild celebration seemed close by, with the noise carrying on the wind blowing fiercely across the river.

Corporal Sleigh entered the tent.

"Inspector, they've set the fort alight."

Dickens went outside to look. He trained his glass on the orange glow of the flames in the distance. He could hear the drums and whooping, now softly muffled, now shrill and loud. The Cree would revel in the fort's capture, and the possession of the goods inside, he knew. That was good. Their preoccupation would give his men more time to get away.

But before he slept, Dickens wondered how his abandonment of the fort would be regarded by his superiors and his companions in arms. Would their judgment be that it was a cowardly abdication of duty, an abject defeat, especially allowing all the civilians to leave his protection and be taken prisoner? Or would they see his retreat as a judicious move, allowing the men, who would have been overwhelmed in the end, to fight another day? He could not be sure. As his eyes closed, a familiar image came before him. He again saw the tiger of Bengal, ripping the little antelope to pieces on the margins of that faraway forest glade.

# Chapter 36

Dickens awoke when it was still dark. His sleep had been restless and he could hear the wind howling outside the shelter he had shared with Sergeant Martin. Snow had fallen heavily during the night and it weighed down the canvas. He punched the roof of his tent and the snow rolled off. He was still not quite sure of his whereabouts, then the terrible anxiety of the day before came back to him. His men were camped on the south side of the river, vulnerable to any raiding enemies. The strong northwest wind was blowing the smell of burning wood in the direction of the camp.

Dickens rose quickly and dressed in his warmest clothes to ward off the bitter chill. He looked out. The snowfall was lighter now than it had been when the men turned in, but powerful gusts of wind would stir up the new powder and swirl it about, so that it was difficult to see any more than a few feet.

"Sergeant," he said to Martin. "Rouse the men. It is still early but we must get started down the river as soon as there is light, to put distance between us and the Cree."

At least the wind would be behind them, he thought. He could hear the grumbling of weary men as Martin made his rounds, waking the constables from their slumber. Corporal Sleigh emerged from his tent.

"What a wretched night!" Sleigh said to no one in particular before turning to Dickens. "We've got several men with frostbite. Some shelters collapsed from the weight of snow during the night and the men were so exhausted they continued sleeping. Now they are suffering from exposure."

"Fetch Sergeant Rolph," Dickens said. "He will do what he can. But we must be on the move."

By the campfire, Rolph examined about a dozen men for frostbite. The skin of the ears, cheeks or hands of several men had a dull waxy appearance and the flesh was hard and numb, but there was no sign yet of the ugly blistering or swellings that marked severe frostbite. He dipped cloths in lukewarm water from the fires and wrapped the affected parts, urging the men to keep covered as much as possible.

"There's little more I can do now," he told Dickens. "Particularly without shelter and with our need to get on down the river. But I'd rather treat them for frostbite than for bullet wounds."

Dickens looked back at Fort Pitt across the river. When the wind abated and the snow settled, he could see buildings were still burning and the smoke blowing from that direction mingled with that of the police campfires. There were no signs of life at the fort, and he could not see the Cree camp. He was still angry at McLean and wanted to see him punished but thought it best to put that behind him for now. There was a bigger task ahead.

Constable Rutledge was already checking out the caulking job that had been completed by the others the night before.

"Is she seaworthy, Rutledge?" inquired Dickens.

"I believe so, Inspector. Only way to be sure is to try 'er out."

"We all are very grateful, Constable. You saved many lives yesterday with your skillful handling of the craft. I shan't forget that when I report to our superior officers."

"Thank you, sir." Rutledge, his shoulders and legs stiff from yesterday's exertions, stood and called for assistance from his comrades to prepare the scow for the morning trip.

The men ate a hastily prepared breakfast of oatmeal porridge and tea and then made ready to leave. First, blocks of ice that had scudded into the river bank during the night had to be cleared before the boat could be launched. The sun had crested the horizon by the time all supplies were loaded and the men were aboard. Rutledge took the tiller and, taking advantage of the current, steered the unwieldy craft to mid-river, while the other men poled or rowed.

Dickens looked back to the place they had left. He felt grateful that they were now on the move and that fate had spared them an attack during the night. The weather, he reckoned, would be a shield for them, as great a deterrent to would-be attackers as it was a punishment to his own small but stalwart party.

At first the travelling was uneventful and the pace was quick, but the refugees were only a mile down river when they encountered a number of thick and broad ice pans that blocked passage of the boat. The men rowed up to the edge of the floes and vaulted over the gunwales onto the stable ice, slipping in the slush as they pulled the scow up onto the pan. With all except Loasby hauling on the boat, the men waded through boot-high punk ice as they struggled to drag the scow across the pan, where they jumped back into the boat for the next stretch of water. They grunted and cursed as the officers urged them on and water ran into their boots. They were loathe to rest, fearing that if they lost the momentum of the heavy, sliding boat, the scow would stick and freeze to the floe. Despite the cold wind and blowing snow, the men were sweating and when they stopped to rest, their damp clothing clung to their bodies, adding to their misery.

By the third of the large pans, the muscles of the struggling men cried out for relief and even the fittest were panting with exertion. Dickens could see their strength was ebbing but there seemed little else to do but to continue across each of the floes. They had some brief moments of rest as they drifted between floes but it was not enough for complete recovery of their strength. By the middle of the pan, with gloves soaked and boots filled with ice water, their power had been spent and the scow came to a halt. Martin and the other officers urged them on but it was no use — the boat could not be moved.

They all knew that it would be difficult to start the heavy vessel again but rest was imperative. After ten minutes of drifting downriver on the pan, Martin and Sleigh tried to test the men's resolve again. This time, Leduc, O'Keefe and Anderson got up first and grabbed on to the gunwales.

"Come on, lads, lend a hand here," shouted Rutledge, and the rest of the troop rose to work at the boat, some chipping or shovelling away ice and slush from under the bow, and others pushing with all their strength. Dickens, too, pitched in and the men gratefully made room for him. The boat began to move, slowly at first, but with gathering momentum until finally it was sliding toward the open water on the other side of the pan. To a man, the police cheered as the bow of the scow hit the water. Even Loasby, lying in the boat bottom, shrouded in ice covered blankets, looked up and smiled.

The edges of the last pan, however, were soft and hiving off. Two men plunged off the crumbling pan into the frigid water and only Sleigh's quick thinking in tossing them ropes stopped the two from being swept down the river by the current. Once they were in the open water, the shivering men huddled in blankets in a fruitless effort to ward off the cold.

The third ice pan was the last of the big ones to be traversed, and there were now larger expanses of open water. But the river was high, and Rutledge had to ensure that he stayed clear of the ice chunks that were floating down river at the same velocity and in the vicinity of the boat. The winds continued to be a problem. An occasional gust would pick up the snow and push it far over the river, making the visibility almost negligible. Rutledge steered blindly when those whiteouts occurred, hoping that he was not piloting them into greater dangers. The men suffered from the discomfort of frozen hands and faces, and their clothes were soaked when the warmth of their bodies penetrated through their garments. They shook with the cold.

Under the river's surface there were other hazards. Large sandbars that in summer were islands had been submerged by the spring freshet. With the flood, these sandbars were constantly shifting in the river bed, disappearing in one place and recreated in another, so that maps of the channel were useless. Even the most experienced of river-runners had to take care from one year to the next. Some of these hazards had been anchored by vegetation, small bushes and trees that given time would have resulted in the creation of new permanent islands in the river.

Dickens had a man stationed in the bow of the boat to watch for log jams and shallow areas. But the river current was so rapid, the water so murky with silt and the whiteouts so numerous, that it was difficult to see dangerous spots and cry alarm before the scow was upon them.

At one of these sandbars, there were bushes under the flood water, and a large cottonwood stump had caught on them. Too late, the watchman in the bow noticed the ripple in the water.

"Snag! Look out!" he shouted.

Rutledge tried steering around the obstacle but as he swung the bow out with the tiller the force of the water pushed the scow sideways and he momentarily lost control. The scow swung across the flow of the river, caught on the stump, and was now at the mercy of the raging stream. The water pummelled the upstream flanks of the boat, tipping it so that the gunwales on the other side were level with the water. Large chunks of ice were hammering the sides and Dickens feared that the unseasoned wood used to build the boat could not withstand the constant pressure. They were very near to being swamped.

"Look alive, men," he shouted, and two officers jumped up with long oars, trying to push the boat off the snag. They were off balance and one man's oar snapped as he struggled. Then the boat suddenly broke free of the snag but the scow was drifting backward down river, Rutledge strained with all his strength to turn the boat around, and a couple of others rushed to his aid but to no avail.

"Just let 'er drift for a bit. I'll try turning 'er in calmer water."

They were off the bar now but had no control over the direction the boat was taking. Then another oar was lost, stuck in the river bottom as the men struggled to keep the boat clear of more snags.

They were drifting backward toward shore and now a new danger appeared. Ages ago, the river had breached an esker, a long sinuous deposit of rocks and sand left behind by the glaciers. Rutledge recognized that there would likely be rocks close to shore that could puncture or break the spine of the boat. Once again, now perspiring and near exhaustion, he struggled to steer away from the riverbank.

Dickens saw Rutledge's strength was sapping.

"Come, lads, lend a hand here," he yelled over the sound of rushing water. "Push us out into the main stream."

Their efforts made no difference. The boat drifted backwards and jammed into a pile of rocks, and though the rocks were rounded by ancient glacial streams, the force of the collision was enough to crack some boards in the bottom of the boat. The boards groaned, creaked and snapped under the tension. Water began pouring in and Loasby, lying on the bottom planks felt the icy water through his clothes. The rudder had been rendered useless, broken in two when it slammed against submerged boulders. Several men rose and with oars or paddles leaned with all their ebbing strength into the river bottom on the downstream side to steady the boat so that it would not be caught up in the powerful current and swept downriver. They were grounded now on the rocks. Dickens was discouraged by the lack of progress but saw no choice but to take a respite from the journey.

"We'll stop here for today," Dickens said. "We'll have some hot tea and then we'll need repairs. Corporal Sleigh, build a fire so the men can dry themselves. Then take out a party and see what suitable wood you can find for repairs."

The men began unloading the boat. Rutledge was slumped over in frustration and pain, every muscle of his body shrieking in agony. He reached out for a bucket, dipped it in the icy, brown water and drank deeply.

"Here, Constable," said Dickens. "Don't drink that. We can find you better water."

He reached over and helped Rutledge to his feet, supporting the larger but exhausted man to a clearing where some of the men were already setting up camp. He took some blankets from the boat and wrapped them around the steersman.

"You've done your duty for today, man. Rest is what you need. We will be counting on you tomorrow."

Rutledge nodded. He was too overwhelmed to speak. He lay down to rest and pulled some blankets over himself. Dickens looked on with concern. Rutledge was a man the group could not afford to lose.

Later in the day, Rolph inspected the men who had suffered from frostbite. Their recovery would be painful but nearly all the men in this country had experienced it in the past and knew what to expect. Dickens broke out a little brandy that had been packed with the medical supplies and passed it around to the men warming themselves by the fires.

About mid-afternoon, the winds had died down and the sun broke through the clouds bringing some blessed relief. Dickens was grateful that the temperature was on the rise and the day had been transformed into a pleasant spring interlude. The snow from the previous night was melting rapidly, turning the clearing into muck under the men's boots. Dickens looked at his charts with Martin. They had just reached Frenchman's Butte, travelling only eight miles this day. They would have to do better than that in future. Could the boat be adequately repaired, he pondered? Or would they have to start out on foot the rest of the way? Without horses and wagons, and a wounded man to carry, it would be a difficult journey. He scanned the bluffs lining the river. In the event of an attack, they would be extremely exposed to enemy sharpshooters concealed in the wooded bluffs above the camp. He ordered the sentries to patrol the slopes.

Sleigh had returned with some wood that Rutledge, now recovered from his ordeal, thought could be sawn and used to repair the rudder and replace the damaged boards in the boat.

At dawn the next morning yellow fingers of light stretched from the rising sun to the east, breaking up a mass of cloud that had passed over them during the night. It could be a good day for travel. The wind was at their backs and the air was becoming warmer. By seven o'clock, the men — now in better spirits — were on their way. The second full day of the voyage stayed fine, with bright sunshine and only occasional cloudy periods. The river however was packed with ice and several times the scow was caught between floes, hampering progress down the river. Sleigh feared the boat would be crushed but Rutledge stayed calm and methodical in his work, ordering the men to push aside the floes and circumventing dangerous passages where ice jams clogged the river. The replacement boards allowed some leakage of water into the boat, so after two hours on the water, Dickens ordered the men to stop for a warm meal. The bottom of the scow was repacked with caulking at each stop and the voyage resumed. There was little point, Dickens thought, in pressing the journey too hard and risking the possibility of a calamitous mishap that would destroy the little vessel that they all counted on to carry them to safety.

The third day of the voyage was cloudy and cold, and the men had to leap out from the scow on several occasions to drag the scow over sand bars and rocky shoals. The ice was heavy again in the river and Dickens, after consulting with Martin, Rolph and Sleigh, decided to stop for the night on an island in the middle of the river. The travellers would be safe from attack there and there was shelter in the trees. The men could dry their sodden, uncomfortable clothing and enjoy a rest for the next part of the gruelling journey.

# Chapter 37

The police had now completed three full days on the river. Repairs made to the boat after the damage inflicted by the sandbar on the first day had held up and Rutledge had done well to keep the scow out in the rapidly running stream. Few of his comrades in arms had experience in piloting boats under these conditions. When the police were trained, their officers anticipated they needed horsemanship and marching drills, but their instruction did not include how to handle river craft in spring flood on the prairies. No one had remotely suspected it would be necessary. Rutledge had taken time when the men stopped each night to instruct others in the art of steering of the boat under adverse circumstances, how to read the swirling waters and what dangers to avoid. The policemen felt very alone in their world on the icy river. There had been no sightings of other people, not friendly, not hostile.

On the morning of the fourth day, April 19th, the river seemed unusually quiet. Dickens and his junior officers had decided the best course would be to camp on islands for the rest of the journey, and they had stayed overnight on Slapjack Island, one of the larger ones in that stretch of the North Saskatchewan. The water was down markedly, Dickens noted, as he strolled the riverbank while the men under his command were loading up.

"What do you make of this, Rutledge?" he asked the steersman. He, like the others, had come to rely heavily on the constable's calm and canny judgment and heroic efforts on this retreat from Fort Pitt.

"I can't say, sir. There's less ice in the river today. Peculiar, but I don't know the cause. Perhaps the worst is passed and it'll be smooth sailing from here on. How far is it to Battleford?"

"I'd estimate that we are a little more than halfway now," Dickens said. "We made good time yesterday, caught up some of the time we lost the first two days. I think we can anticipate more water than what we see today over the next weeks. The snow would just be starting to melt in the mountains, but I expect we'll reach Battleford before that peaks."

The gear was packed and Loasby was placed on board carefully. The wounded man seemed cheerful. He had made great strides. The other men seemed more optimistic too. The voyage had gone well the day before and all believed that soon they would join forces with their colleagues. In their isolation, they hoped for the best although no one knew the fate of their counterparts at Battleford or whether new battalions of troops were on their way from the east.

The weather was clear and fine when they departed shortly after seven, a welcome spring sun reaching over the prairie. Purple crocuses were in bloom on the sunnier slopes of the river valley. The repeated cursing and grumbling that many of the men had voiced during the adverse conditions of the first days of the journey had largely gone. Some of the men broke into song, and even Loasby joined in.

Behind them, up river on the previous afternoon, a large pan of ice had drifted onto a sand bar and held fast. A second floe came to rest against it, cracking and shoving the first block and anchoring it firmly on the river bottom. A sunny break in the clouds allowed some melting of the edges of the ice and the two blocks welded together. Smaller pieces collected on the upriver side, some caught in riverbank trees, and others drifted and jammed together with the larger chunks.

As the pileup continued, a bridge of ice gradually formed across the stream. The force of the oncoming water tilted some of the larger pieces downward, diverting the river's flow into older, less active channels, where it ponded. As nightfall came and the temperature dropped sharply, all the ice, and some of the water flowing over it, cooled and froze, transforming the blockage into a long ice dam that stretched across the river. The stream continuing flowing but much of the water and ice had been held back.

By early afternoon of the day the police departed Slapjack, the warmth of the sun had weakened the icy grip that had held the dam in place. Under the swift flow of the river and the continual pounding of more blocks coming downstream, the ice dam strained, cracked, screeched and roared as water sought weaknesses to penetrate the barrier. Finally, the whole blockage could no longer hold back the force of the river behind it. The ice dam gave way and a huge wave swept down the river, flooding the treed islands, lifting stumps and logs, which now became speeding battering rams racing along downstream and tearing away at rocks and sand. The water that had backed up into side channels now sought a lower level and gushed back into the main riverbed, rushing in a huge torrent of water, ice, trees, sand and small boulders.

Early in the day the men in the scow had found the travelling easy. There was still no sign of enemies and the police were making good headway to their goal. After a run of five hours, they had stopped for food on an island in mid-stream and took some time to rest from their labours. Dickens estimated that if all went well, they could be within forty miles of Battleford by nightfall.

They were well started in their afternoon run, when the current seemed to pick up, and the water was choppier than before. There was little need to use the oars because the stream was carrying the boat at a rapid pace. Rutledge was puzzled how the flow of the river had changed over the course of the day.

Loasby was sitting up in the bottom of the scow looking at the shoreline they had passed when he saw something odd in the distance.

The river was suddenly wider than it had seemed when they passed a curve about a mile back, lapping up against banks that had been previously exposed. He pointed and shouted the change in the river flow to Dickens, who picked up his spyglass.

Behind the boat the river was indeed wider and higher too, halfway up the trunks of some of the trees they had passed minutes before. There was a faint roaring sound of rushing water, growing louder by the instant.

"Pull for shore," Dickens shouted. "A wave is coming."

Rutledge turned sideways and saw to his horror that a wave, half the height of a man, was sweeping toward them at a terrible speed. He knew that the boat could be overwhelmed and sunk if the wave caught them in mid-stream. What concerned him even more were the deadheads, the trees he could see caught up in the furious torrent that now surged toward the vulnerable boat. At this velocity, those logs could ram and splinter the boat beyond repair. Lives would be lost for certain in the icy, roiling water; perhaps all would perish.

Rutledge urged all the men to pick up their oars and row for the nearest shore, where they would still be buffeted, but at least would stand a chance of reaching shallower water if the boat was overcome.

The men struggled to put their oars in the locks but the scow was rocking so much that this was difficult and each valuable moment lost put them in greater peril.

"Head for that island over there, we need shelter," yelled Dickens.

They were two-thirds of the way to the banks of the island, at an angle to the river flow, when the wave caught them. Water poured in over the stern of the scow, and at times Rutledge almost disappeared from sight. Still the boat kept afloat and those not rowing or poling the boat were bailing furiously, a struggle that seemed doomed to failure. They had escaped the worst brunt of the wave in the middle of the river, but the sides of the scow were now being hammered by the pounding of floating logs and ice. One large tree smashed against the upstream side of the boat and rocked the boat so violently that water flowed in over the downstream gunwales. In the collision, one of the constables suffered a broken arm. Connemara, who was lying on the top of the fur bales, pitched forward into the water. The dog was carried off downstream. Some sideboards on the scow were bent, then crushed. Water poured in through the splintered sides. Still, those men able to row pulled with all their strength.

The boat was sinking. Now it was half full of muddy, icy water. Supplies, food, blankets and clothing, were afloat in the bottom. A few men jumped over the side into the river to lighten the load, while hanging desperately on the gunwales to avoid being swept away. To their dismay, they found they were touching bottom, a sandbar that had formed about thirty feet from the island shoreline. The boat now settled on the bar, mercifully grounded for the time being. Now others jumped out, backs against the current, feet planted in the shifting river bottom, hoping to hold the scow back on the sand. The boat was now two-thirds filled with water and vital supplies were being swept out, bags and bales of fur that had been a protective lining were racing down river. Much of the food was gone and the soaked bags of flour weighed the boat down on the sandbar.

"Salvage what you can and head for shore," Dickens shouted over the roar of the stream. "God knows how long this will hold."

Ralph Sleigh, holding a rope attached to the bow of the boat, took two steps toward shore and completely disappeared under water. The sandbar that had saved them was high enough to ground the battered vessel but there was a good thirty feet of deeper water between the boat and the shore.

The men frantically dragged Sleigh, somehow still clinging to the rope, back toward the sandbar. He was almost there when a chunk of ice slammed his forehead, gashing him badly. By instinct, he still held onto the rope and was helped back to his feet by the others.

Rutledge groped in the bottom of the flooded scow until he found a claw anchor with a long length of sturdy rope tied to it. He spun the anchor above his head and hurled it with all his remaining strength toward the island. At the first throw it caught on something but Rutledge felt the bottom giving way in the cascading waters. Spent, he passed the anchor to Grizzly Leduc who threw it well onto the island banks. This time it caught on the stump of a dead cottonwood.

Leduc tested the strength of the anchor and found it would support his weight, then plunged into the water, hand over hand toward the shore. He tied the rope more securely around a sturdy cottonwood. Others followed, one at a time. Rolph and two comrades had lifted Loasby above the water onto the sides of the scow and now they made a makeshift sling, pulling the wounded man across to safety. Soon, all were ashore. Dickens shook with relief that all the men were saved, but he grieved for the loss of his faithful dog.

The worst of the river surge was over, and now some of the men went down stream to salvage what they could of their missing supplies. Others built a warming fire, and looked to the few weapons they had saved. A fire was necessary to dry out the shivering, exhausted men, but it could also attract unwanted attention. A sustained attack by a determined enemy force would have been the end. Most of the ammunition was soaked and many of the guns were lost in the river.

Rolph changed Loasby's dressings. The wounded man seemed to the doctor to be very low, in sharp contrast to his state earlier in the day. He shook with fever and his eyes were glazed. Rolph swathed Loasby in what dry blankets were available and built him a fire. Then Rolph looked to Sleigh and bound the corporal's injured head.

Sergeant Martin, Sleigh, Rutledge and Dickens stood by the water looking with anxiety at the damaged scow, sitting on the sandbar.

"Where are we?" asked Martin.

"Pine Island, I believe," said Sleigh, holding his hands to his aching head.

"The boat must be repaired," said Dickens. "We cannot travel the rest of the way by foot. We've lost a considerable amount of weapons and food, and still have a good distance to go. We'd be an easy mark for any hostiles."

He stared downriver, as if he hoped for sight of a friendly settlement, or rescuers. There was nothing to give him any optimism.

"We'll stop here for a day. Give the men time to recover. Repair the boat. I want a parade tomorrow to restore morale and discipline. Check out what weapons we have and repair any that are damaged.

Sergeant, would you take charge of getting the boat to this side? We'll use the hull as part of our defences."

The men set to work. They cut two large poplars, peeled and trimmed them, and bridged them across to the sandbar on the upstream side of the boat. These were lashed together three feet apart. Some of the abler men then swung across to the boat and bailed out as much water as they could before hefting it up onto the log bridge. Then the others on the island pulled the bow of the disabled boat across the slippery poplar logs to the shore. Martin led a party to search for suitable timber that could be used to repair the crushed walls of the battered scow so that it could be used again. The wood would not be seasoned, but there was little choice. The police would stay close to shore, and travel more slowly rather than seek out the rapid flow of the deeper main channel.

Dickens worried about the loss of weapons and supplies. There was no promise that he and his men would reach safety. The police were on the south side of the island, midway between the reserve lands of Poundmaker and Thunderchild.

"From here on, we'll have to be very wary of enemies," he told Martin.

The next day, after the men had eaten, Dickens called upon his detachment to line up for parade. They were a ragtag group now, with parts of uniforms lost to the river, and the men wearing whatever they could find to keep themselves warm in the mid-April morning chill. Even those parts of uniform that had been saved were worn and dirty. The constables had tried to clean themselves but most of the necessities had been lost — towels and soap swept away — or had been left behind at Pitt. Dickens contented himself with the idea that they were doing their best and no one seemed to be "bucking" orders. That was a mercy, because even in the best of times there were some men who were rebellious and would challenge their officers. He credited the lack of protest to the fact that they were all together in dire straits and no one would benefit if some of the men did not pull their weight.

Martin did weapons inspection. Less than half the men had guns of any description now. Boxes of ammunition had been dumped in the river and the forty good rounds each man had when they left Fort Pitt was now reduced to about ten.

After the parade and inspection, some of the men sawed boards or patched and recaulked the forlorn looking boat. Once the labour was complete and sentries posted, Dickens told the off-duty men to rest for the remainder of the day.

Dickens went to see Rolph in the early afternoon. The inspector was feeling some pain in his chest and he had been unable to sleep. His ears were aching. He was delighted to see, however, that Loasby appeared to have passed the crisis of the day before and was in good humour.

Rolph examined Dickens.

"You have been under considerable strain, inspector," Rolph said. "As senior officer, more so than the rest of us, with the exception of Loasby. This has not been an easy journey for anyone. Some physical effects of the strain are bound to reveal themselves in you. I hope that soon we will reach our destination."

Rolph did not add the thought that was haunting all of them — that Battleford might have been taken and they would be in greater peril than ever.

# Chapter 38

*Something warm and wet was on my hand. Startled, I sat up sharply from my blanket, fearing that it might be blood — that I might have been attacked and wounded. But there was no pain, other than the anticipated aches that would be expected on a trek such as ours.*

*I opened my eyes, at first bewildered, barely cognizant of where I was. Imagine my joy when I saw it was faithful friend Con lapping at my hand. My retriever had been feared lost to the river but now had returned, wet and filthy, having survived the dunking.*

*I raised the flap of my makeshift shelter — the tents were lost in the events of recent days — and there stood several of the men, who gave out a cheer, believing it to be a good omen that the animal has reappeared and they would all now survive, no matter what obstacles remain.*

*The men were packing up now to prepare for our sixth day on the river. It's something of a miracle that we have survived this perilous journey without further attack. Much of the previous day was spent finding adequate timber to repair the scow, and then cutting the green wood, making it fit with what primitive tools had not been lost to the river, and patching the leaks. I have not regretted resting on Pine Island for a day, although we all will be gratified to reach Battleford, if the place still exists. But we all needed a rest* from the ordeal we have gone through. I sense now that all the men are in better humour after stopping for a day, more fit for travel and eager to complete the journey.

Martin and Rolph appeared and saluted. The men were ready now. Their clothes were still damp, or stiffened from being left too close to the hot fires, but that couldn't be helped. We all have to move on. A safe haven was more important than comfort now.

"How is Loasby today?" I inquired.

"Much better," said Rolph. "The day's rest has done wonders for him. He is a man of strong physique and stronger will."

I only wish I felt better myself. My body is in agony, my muscles screaming with exhaustion and tension, and though the men had set to work longer before Connemara awakened me, I had not heard a sound. My hearing must be getting worse. It had already begun deteriorating long before Fort Pitt.

Although I was glad of a day's stoppage, I fret about the days lost as we seek the safety of Battleford. It would have been a two-day trip by horseback but now we have little food to sustain us, are short of ammunition and weapons. Further delays could be catastrophic. What is happening outside the little world of our river? Are troops on their way from the east to put down the rebellion? Are the prisoners of Wandering Spirit's Cree still alive? Was it the best decision to abandon the fort and to allow the civilians to follow McLean? Will I be reprimanded once we reach our destination? Does Battleford still exist? Or has it, too, been overwhelmed by a widening uprising by the rebels and their Indian allies? We have no idea how many Indians or halfbreeds have risen.

What day is it? I think it might be April 21 but cannot be certain. Each day on the river melds into the next. I reach for my log. Yes, I'm right about the date. A good guess. How many more days will it be before this perilous expedition is over?

My thoughts recently have become obsessed with the notion of Time. I can't help but feel guilty over the loss of my father's watch, his legacy to me. I both idolized and feared my father. What would he say now if he knew of the predicament I am in? Would I again be scornfully dismissed as a failure? Or would father have understood the decision I have made.

*I am sure that accounts for the unsettling dreams I've had of late. I envisioned the glare of my father's piercing eyes, his beard waggling as he speaks and a scolding finger poised in front of my face. All of this weighs on my mind, yet it also makes me more determined. I must rise to the challenge and prove to my father's spirit and other doubting relatives, and my superior officers, that I can finish the task of bringing this ragged but still good-spirited company to safety.*

*My recurring dream has me pleading before Father, the way a grievous sinner might prostrate himself before a vengeful god. "Please Papa, I am simply an ordinary soul," I hear myself say. "Exceptional bravery is not the lot of everyone. If it was so, heroism would be routine, meaningless." What I look for is redemption only. There are recognizable heroes. I know some myself. The rest of us merely play our role in history without ever knowing whether we will be celebrated or scorned by our descendants.*

*Enough of this. There is another day to live and carry on.*

*I continue to admire the way the men are reacting to days of persistent adversity. They are certainly more than the "armed mob" that one cynical officer once described.*

# Chapter 39

Inspector Morris, preoccupied about his own situation in the besieged town of Battleford, was nonetheless being pressed by some of the townsfolk to do something about the people at Fort Pitt. No word had been received from that beleaguered settlement in days. Some believed a brigade should be sent to relieve their friends and relatives and bring them to safety. Others demanded punitive action be taken against the rebelling Cree. Morris feared weakening his own defences.

"Inspector Dickens is an experienced officer, and he has good advisors in McLean and Jim Simpson," Morris protested. "I believe they are capable of looking after themselves."

The fort at Battleford had been established on high ground between the convergence of the waters of the Saskatchewan and Battle rivers. The town was nearly a half-mile distant, but fear of attack had driven all the townspeople from their homes and into the enclosure, which was about 200 yards square. In the mind-set of the besieged, their fear was warranted. Several houses had been looted and burned. But the few buildings inside the fort were inadequate to house the numbers that had flocked to the post for protection. The police barracks, the commanding officer's quarters and storehouses, were all built from logs and the fort's location had not been well chosen for defensive purposes. Not only was food in short supply for the 530 people enclosed within its walls, but the police had to drive a cart to the river, five hundred yards away, to load up on water.

People were crammed into whatever space was available. More than seventy refugees alone occupied the commandant's house, and dozens more dwelt in tents that had been set up in the yard, churned into a sea of muck with the spring thaw. If this rebellion was not ended soon, the fort's inhabitants faced another risk — that of rampant disease worsened by malnutrition and starvation. It was this prospect that Morris feared most.

Constant pressure from the civilians persisted and eventually overcame his preference, which was to do nothing but await the arrival of troops from the east. After daily protests, Morris agreed to send a pair of scouts to investigate the fate of the people at Fort Pitt.

James Bird and Pierre Pambrun, freighters and couriers who had worked for the police out of Battleford, were eager for some diversion from the boredom of being cooped up in the post. They volunteered to ride to Fort Pitt to see if they could establish the fate of the police and civilians. On the evening of April 18, under cover of darkness, they left Battleford and were rowed across the ice-choked Saskatchewan on a scow. In the twilight, they watched the river as closely as they could and inspected trails for any sign of a large party of fugitives, or of a hostile war party. They did not get far before they ran into a rain storm and made camp for the night.

By hard riding, the next afternoon they reached the brow of the sloping ground commanding a view of the abandoned fort. There were signs of a recent Cree camp but at first no one was to be seen. Spread among the ashes and debris left behind were some women's dresses, empty tin cans, broken open with the contents consumed or spilled, as well as discarded white men's items that were of little use to a travelling band of warriors.

Bird and Pambrun looked toward the fort and saw that the buildings and defences had been scorched and pulled down. Some were still smouldering. Riding closer to get a better look, Bird spotted the body of a man against a tree. He had been stripped of clothing and there was a deep, gaping wound in his chest. His heart had been cut out and jammed onto a stake planted in the ground. The body had been scavenged by wild creatures.

"A white man. Probably police. Recognize him?" Bird asked his comrade.

"Seen him. Don' know his name," Pambrun said. "Sure, a police."

The two men dismounted and walked over to the body.

"No one livin' here," Pambrun said. "What d'you make of this stuff scattered about?"

"Looks like they were attacked, overwhelmed. God knows what happened to 'em. Prisoners at best, I reckon. May be all dead. Like that poor devil."

"But not here," said Pambrun. "Nothing more we can do here. Just bury this poor soul so he get some rest."

The scouts lacked an implement to dig a hole in the muddy ground and so carried Cowan's remains in an old blanket to a pit that had been dug for the defences. They covered the pit over with lumber and placed heavy rocks on top to prevent further depredations by animals and birds. The work was nearly complete, when they sensed they were being watched.

An Indian stood by a grove of trees northwest of the fort. He was clad in a buckskin jacket and trousers, wrapped in a Hudson's Bay blanket and wearing a black top hat with a feather. He carried no weapons. Pambrun nudged Bird, who quietly drew his Adams revolver.

"Little Poplar, I think," said Pambrun.

"Any others?" Bird had his gun aimed at the Indian. He scanned the grove, looking for any hidden enemies.

"Peace, brothers," said Little Poplar in Cree. "I come in peace."

"Are you Little Poplar?" Pambrun asked in the Indian tongue. "What has happened here? Do you know where the police have gone?"

"They left after a big fight," Little Poplar said. "Two police killed. Four of Big Bear's men. The redcoats took a boat down the river."

Pambrun translated for Bird.

"We saw no signs on the river," said Bird. "Do you think they may have capsized? Drowned?"

"I saw no more," said Little Poplar.

"Were you in the fight?" asked Pambrun.

"No. I would not fight the white police. They gave me food for my family. I was the man who helped them. Remember that. I told Big Bear to let them go. It was me who saved them."

Pambrun had a doubtful look. He whispered to Bird in English.

"This man is known as a liar. He'll say anything to get good treatment. I don' think he can be trusted. He's as likely to boast in the lodges of how many white police he has killed."

Little Poplar sensed Pambrun's skepticism. "You see there are no other dead police. Here is the mark in the ground where the white men dragged the heavy boat to the river. When they had gone, Big Bear's people came in and took everything. Then they burned what they could not carry."

"You said there were two dead white men. Where is the other?"

"They took him in the boat. He is sure to have died now. He was badly wounded in the back and leg."

"Why did you not bury this poor dead man?" Bird asked through Pambrun. He was angry at Little Poplar. "He needed to be treated with respect."

"I was afraid," said Little Poplar. "I thought the war chief might kill me."

Bird looked around again, poking through the ashes and peering into the thickets surrounding the burned buildings. Pambrun continued talking to the Cree chief, keeping a watchful eye for trouble.

Bird came back. It was true, he told Pambrun, that there were no other signs of dead. They gave Little Poplar some tobacco and tea and started back to Battleford. This time they watched the river intently but saw nothing more to indicate the police had escaped.

Once they reached Battleford, the scouts went immediately to report to Morris.

"Fort Pitt is destroyed," said Bird. "We saw no one, except one dead policeman and that maverick Little Poplar. Everything was taken or ruined and left behind. Little Poplar said they had escaped by boat but we saw no sign on the river. We suspect they are all dead or prisoners."

"Hell," said Morris. "Maybe some escaped."

Privately, Morris was worried sick. The bloody fate of Fort Pitt might be visited on those in Battleford next. Marauders were making closer and closer incursions on the settlement near the fort, and he was responsible for the hundreds, including three hundred women and children, who had crammed into the small police post. An attack by a determined, outnumbering force would be disaster. If they were not all killed by well-armed rebels, they could be starved or burned out. He was nervous about the judgments that superiors might make of him for failing to attempt a rescue of the people of Fort Pitt.

Word soon got around of the scouts' return and the besieged citizens of Battleford assumed the worst. The police had been massacred, most believed, or had drowned in the flooding river. No telling what happened to the civilians. The town's inmates felt more isolated than ever.

At about nine o'clock in the morning on April 21, Billy Anderson was scanning the river bank to the south when he spotted riders, about five or six. There was no sign from them that they had seen the boat, which was now moving through a shallow and braided river channel. The water had dropped somewhat and there was now less ice, thanks to better weather. The travellers still had to be vigilant for unexpected sandbars and half-submerged logs that could damage or upset the boat.

"Indians, I think," said Anderson.

Martin was looking through a glass.

"Stoneys," the sergeant said. "We should stick close to the north side. No telling what their frame of mind is."

"Some may have joined the rebels," said Dickens. "For that reason, we'll stay away. Have they seen us?"

"They have now," said Martin.

The small party of warriors were hellbent for the river bank now, whooping and urging their ponies on. Three of them had rifles, and one was taking aim.

"Are we out of range?" asked Anderson.

A shot, and a bullet skimmed the water about fifty feet short of the boat.

"Rutledge, as far as you can to the north bank," Dickens commanded.

A dozen of the police had their rifles trained on the south bank. Others watched the north shore closely for any sign of attackers.

Anderson fired back at the Stoneys and could see the bullet hit the water close to shore.

"We're out of range," said Martin.

"Yes, save your ammunition. We may need it later," said Dickens.

The inspector looked back to the south side of the river. The Stoneys were still there, following along the bank, but the fast current was taking the police further away from them. Still, they might catch up by nightfall. That small group would not take on his men in battle, but there was no telling how far away a larger war party might be. With so much of the ammunition water-soaked and many of the guns lost or useless, Dickens was concerned the police could not hold off a sustained attack.

They had travelled a few miles more down river when Martin spotted a man, alone, standing on the southern shore. It now was early afternoon. The stranger wore a floppy leather hat above his weather-beaten face, and a fringed buckskin jacket, gabardine pants and high moccasins. His rifled was cradled across his chest, his horse tied to a nearby tree. The man looked intently across the river at something — a boat? — floating along. He took out a glass for a better view.

Now he could see it was a boat, and some of the men aboard were wearing red jackets.

The lone rider mounted his horse and went along the bank for a better vantage point. Martin had seen a glint of sun off the stranger's glass and was peering back at him, too.

"Inspector," the sergeant called to Dickens. "There's someone over there."

Dickens took the glass and squinted for a better view.

"By God, I believe it's Josie Alexander."

The others in the boat felt relief but were still cautious. How did they know for certain? The man could be one of Riel's Metis, too. Could the inspector be mistaken?

"Halloo," Dickens yelled.

The man made no response at first, making the travellers nervous. But he did not appear to be threatening or hostile in any way.

"Halloo," Dickens hailed again.

This time the man waved and shouted something that could not be heard over the sound of the rushing water.

"Steer closer to shore. But keep on your guard," Dickens said.

The men on the right side of the boat prepared their guns for action.

As they neared the shore, Dickens could see for certain it was Josie Alexander.

"God 'a mercy," the scout shouted. "We thought you was lost."

"One man killed, one wounded," Dickens replied. "How far to Battleford?"

"Half a day on the river," said the scout. "You won't make it before dark. You'd be faster by boat than walkin'. Safer, too, I'd reckon. Do you want to continue?"

"We'll travel by boat," said Dickens. "The men are too exhausted to march."

The scout nodded.

"Any hostiles about?" Dickens asked. "We saw a small party of Stoneys west of here. They fired on us."

"They's mostly on the other side of Battleford. There's a small island about three mile down. Camp there for tonight. Constables Hynes and Allen are along the bank. We'll ride and alert Inspector Morris."

"What news?" asked Martin.

"Troops are on the way from the east. Soon'll have them durned rascals on the run."

"Damn me, it's good to see a friendly face," Dickens said.

The men in the boat, unshaven, dirty and faces etched with exhaustion, cheered.

The scout waved farewell, and rode along the bank to rejoin Hynes and Allen. The three left at a gallop for Battleford.

The island Alexander had mentioned was little more than a thinly treed sandbar in the middle of the river. The water was lower now, and as the scow approached the island it scraped bottom and grounded heavily into rocks and sand. The men tried pushing it off with the oars but they were stuck solidly.

Rutledge and Sleigh jumped from the boat and waded through boot-deep water to the island. The two men scouted for a suitable place to camp. The sand of the island was wet and gave way under foot. Most of the driftwood on the island was damp as well. They found a place to make a fire and then returned to Dickens.

"The ground's very wet, sir," said Sleigh. "Most of the wood on the island's too wet to burn but there's enough to make a fire for tea or soup. I think the men would be better off sleeping in the scow tonight. If the river rises in the dark, we could find ourselves flooded out."

"Unless we get the boat off and go to the north bank," said Rutledge.

"I think Alexander was right," said Dickens. "If there are wandering war parties about, the island, despite its discomforts, will be the best place tonight. If all goes well, we'll make Battleford tomorrow, by mid-morning, I'd judge."

Josie Alexander, followed closely by the two constables, galloped up to the barricades at Battleford and raced through the muddy yard toward Morris' office. He jumped from his horse, and let it wander, leaving the two policemen to tie it up. The open ground where most of the besieged Battleford people were confined, was crowded as fort's residents enjoyed the last of what had been an unusually warm spring day. Bystanders, unaccustomed to seeing the normally level-headed scout so excited, speculated about what his news could be.

"Inspector!" Alexander shouted. Morris was going over some maps spread over his desk with a couple of junior officers. "Captain Dickens and his men. They's upriver in a boat. They's stoppin' for the night but will be here by mid-mornin'."

"Thank the Lord," murmured Morris. "Have they suffered losses? Any wounded?"

"Just the one man dead that Bird and Pambrun saw at Fort Pitt. Corporal Cowan, I believe. They fought off a Cree attack, some of the men say. One other man is wounded. The rest are weary as hell, frostbite, blisters, some small wounds, a broken arm, but they're safe. They's short of food. Had trouble on the river."

"Then we'll make them a feast they won't forget to celebrate their escape," said Morris. "We can afford it now. Relief is coming. Lieutenant-Colonel Otter with his men are but two days away. With Dickens' men and the arriving soldiers, we'll be safer than ever before. Good work, Josie."

Morris turned to his senior NCO. "Sergeant Bagley, we'll give them a hero's welcome. Lord knows, there hasn't been much to celebrate lately. It'll be good for the morale of the civilians, too. Get the band ready in the morning. And prepare a bed for the wounded man. He'll need serious attention after this hard journey."

For the first time in almost a month, Morris felt secure and relieved to hear of the imminent arrival of both Dickens' men and Otter's soldiers. The rebellion was at a turning point, he thought.

The fine spring weather continued the following morning. Excitement grew as crowds of the refugees, accompanied by armed police, streamed from the fort down to the south bank of the Saskatchewan. For many, it was the first time that they dared leave the protection of its walls. A half-mile wide at the landing where the spectators waited, the river flowed swiftly along, the water muddy and ice-cold. Fred Bagley, who had been the force behind the creation of the police band, had the men polish their instruments that morning. An honour guard in full-dress uniform, led by Morris, stood where the arriving boat would come in.

It was nearing ten o'clock, when an alert young boy, peering out into the river, shouted: "There they come! I see them now."

All eyes strained, peering toward the river. There was indeed something flashing upriver, reflecting the late morning sun. It soon became apparent that it was water glistening from the oars as the men in the boat pulled with all their strength toward the cheering crown gathered on the riverside. Bagley started the band playing, God Save the Queen and Rule Britannia soared over the waters, then a selection of hymns and as the boat neared, some marches. The excited crowd was now wild with joy, shouting and screaming as though their deliverance was at hand. The men in the boat were now waving happily toward the assembled people.

The scow, battered, leaky and patched in many places, hit the landing dock with a thump and screeched along the side of the posts. First off the boat was Dickens' retriever, bounding up and down with excitement. The cheering ceased for a moment as the police carefully lifted Loasby onto a stretcher and he was carried up toward the fort. The wounded man was evidently in pain but smiled and waved as he went by, and the happy applause was renewed.

Most of the arriving police wore what was left of their uniforms, which Dickens had requested of them that morning. A few had lost their red coats in the swamping of the scow but that could not be helped. As each man climbed from the boat, the cheering soared. Dickens himself was the next to last man off, and Morris put his left hand on his fellow officer's shoulder and shook his hand vigorously. Morris could see the trip had taken a toll. Despite the wide smile on Dickens face, he appeared haggard and weary, and close to collapse, exhaustion showing plainly in his eyes. The last man out was Rutledge, and Dickens turned and raised the constable's arm in victory. The crowd roared.

Dickens had his men form into line and, with their remaining energy, they shuffled slowly and painfully in formation up to the walls of the fort, for the moment forgetting their joints that were stiff from days in the boat and the constant dampness they had endured. The band led the way, playing marches, and the rejoicing throng of men, women and children followed behind. At the fort, Morris had ordered a feast prepared for all, so sure he was that more food would be on the way with Otter's column. Medicinal brandy was broken out, in a sly breach of regulations, to toast the new arrivals, because it was evident to Morris and the medical staff that a small dose would go along a long way to restore the health of the exhausted men.

Young, strikingly handsome Ralph Sleigh was particularly popular with all. "You ladies have prepared us a grand dinner," he said to the delight of the women. He related incessantly to all who would listen the adventures of the police at Pitt and after, and spoke with heartfelt admiration of the three older McLean girls toting their rifles and taking their turn as sentries on the barricades of the abandoned fort. "They must be rescued from their cruel imprisonment," he said, as the crowd of men and women about him nodded their heads.

After all had eaten, Dickens addressed his men. "Enjoy the remainder of the day and make certain you are rested, because we are not yet out of danger, and we still have duties to perform."

Morris approached Dickens later in the afternoon, when the celebrations had subsided.

"Frank, you are now senior officer here. I will hand over command to you as soon as you have your rest."

"Oh, man. My health has been severely damaged by this adventure and my body's worn out. I will need time. Please, continue in charge. I will take on some administrative duties."

If the people imprisoned in the fort had believed the arrival of Dickens would be their salvation, they were soon reminded that they were still in danger. On the same night that the prairie mariners from Fort Pitt reached their safe harbour, Frank Smart, a volunteer freighter on picket duty, was slain by a defiant sniper. Stores belonging to the Hudson's Bay Company were destroyed. And even the arrival of Otter's troops the following day was no guarantee of security. More houses in the town were burned, including the home of the local magistrate, Charles Rouleau.

# Chapter 40

With Lieutenant-Colonel William Otter's column came a journalist from the east, Charles Pelham Mulvaney. He was a writer and clergyman, a younger son of an aristocratic Anglo-Irish family. Mulvaney soon searched out Dickens and demanded that the inspector tell him the story of Fort Pitt. The creative account that Mulvaney produced for his book on the rebellion and in reports that he sent east bore only a slight resemblance to the truth of the affair. Mulvaney in fact saw himself as a propagandist for the Canadian government, which desperately needed some good news for its eastern voters. A successful retreat in the face of overpowering odds was an accomplishment in itself, the first remotely positive event of the campaign. But Mulvaney transformed the half-hearted defence of the abandoned fort into a great victory, much to Dickens's unease.

"It was a glorious defence and a masterful, dignified withdrawal, inspector," said Mulvaney. "A grand example of British pluck. Do not deny it. Others will try to disparage your actions, but you must take the credit that is due."

"It was a retreat from an untenable position, and if we had stayed, it would have cost many lives," Dickens replied. "That much I will accept. It was against my opinion that the civilians surrendered to Big Bear's band. Mr. McLean should not be held blameless. Why, my men say that even his daughters wanted to stay with us. I'm sure you have heard from my men — their greatest admirers, surely — that those young women performed wonderfully, handling the same turn of duty as the men. And you should ask Sam Steele what he knows of Pitt. Inquire of him whether he thought the fort could have been adequately defended with the resources we had."

Steele had formed his own band of scouts to fight against the uprising. At that moment, Steele was preparing to join the pursuit of Big Bear's band in the country north of Fort Pitt.

"You had two casualties, inspector. Cowan and Loasby. You killed many more of the attacking enemy, I gather?"

"What I reported was that when the two scouts returned to the fort, there was a volley from our side and four Indians dropped 'as if' killed. Two others had evidently been hit. Given the circumstances, I was not able to confirm the casualties. Sadly, we had not enough time to even give poor Cowan a proper burial."

Under Mulvaney's hand, the brief skirmish at Fort Pitt became a pitched battle, with Dickens depicted as "one of the coolest and most intrepid soldiers in the West" calmly puffing on his pipe as he sniped at fierce attackers. "No more heroic fight or successful defence in the face of overwhelming odds illumines the pages of modern history," Mulvaney wrote.

Even Frank had to smile at that one.


As weeks passed, more troops arrived from the east and went into combat. Only a few of the police joined the military actions against the rebels. A notable exception was a contingent that went with the troops pursuing Big Bear's band. They caught up with the Cree at Frenchman's Butte, east of Fort Pitt, above the place where Dickens and his retreating men had stopped after their first full day on the river.

Cut Arm was killed in that fight. The reluctant warrior, who had intervened on at least two occasions to save the lives of white people, was hit by cannon fire as he emerged from his lodge when the battle began.

Dickens was bitter about another needless encounter that cost the life of one of his most prized junior officers. Otter was champing at the bit to get the troops under his command into action. Against orders from the campaign chief, Major-General Frederick Middleton, Otter led 325 men out from Battleford on May 1 to attack Poundmaker's band at Cut Knife Hill. A group of the police had volunteered to join with Otter. Ralph Sleigh, the cool and courageous corporal who had served Dickens so well, was the first casualty in a battle where the Canadian troops were outmatched. A bullet caught him in the mouth during the first rush on the Cree positions and Sleigh died instantly at age twenty-seven. Dickens grieved at the death. "No finer man has ever worn the Queen's uniform," a colleague said, and Dickens could only heartily agree as he sat down to write a private letter of condolences to Sleigh's father in Kent. Dickens thought of the McLean girls then, how close they seemed to the young corporal and the inevitable sadness they would feel at the news of his death — if, in fact, they themselves would survive.

The whites had not chosen the battleground well. Cut Knife was the site of a legendary Cree victory over the Blackfoot earlier in the century. That day would be no different. Fine Day, Poundmaker's war chief, in a superb demonstration of frontier generalship, pinned down the raw Canadian recruits through the superior marksmanship of the Cree warriors. Otter was forced to retreat with the loss of twenty-six killed and wounded.

Dickens himself sold the possessions Sleigh left behind; a painful duty. As if he had a premonition of death, Sleigh had given his watch to a friend before setting out on his final march. The corporal had kept his gold watch chain and pipes, as well as a few other items. The $31.25 the kit brought in was sent by Dickens to the corporal's father, along with his sympathetic letter. He received a grateful response from the father, who told Dickens in a heart-breaking reply that he was proud of his son's service, and that Ralph was the second son he had lost in military actions.

With his health permanently impaired, Dickens wanted no more part of active duty. He implored his superiors for leave, pointing out that he had none in the eleven years he had served with the police. Dr. Rolph was ready to attest to his increasing infirmity. But Commissioner Irvine refused or ignored Dickens's continuing requests. When Superintendent William Herchmer, a friend of the prime minister who had been newly appointed over Crozier, arrived with Otter's column, he had been appalled at Dickens's reluctance to take command at Battleford. He ordered Dickens to take full charge of the detachment from Morris. Depressed, Dickens became increasingly morose and his health grew worse.

There was a curious mix of attitudes among the townsfolk, ranging from nonchalance to fear. On May 9, the police held a cricket match on level ground in the town, with Dickens making the first pitch. The next night sentries were fired on again. On May 14, Constable Elliott was killed while on patrol.

Still, the rebellion was soon crushed. Poundmaker sued for peace. Riel was captured, then Big Bear, after a merry chase that one officer characterized as "systematic aimlessness." The McLeans and all the other prisoners were freed without any permanent harm. All had survived the harrowing experience, although some, including McLean himself, had been threatened with death by the militants and a few Indian women who had lost their husbands in battle. By mid-summer, nearly all the key rebels, except a handful of Cree who had fled south with Big Bear's son Imasees to Montana, were in custody.

As a Justice of the Peace, Dickens was required to take statements from many of the prisoners, including Poundmaker. One of the proudest and most respected of Cree chiefs, Poundmaker had come in later May to make peace at the camp of Middleton, the British officer sent to command the Canadian troops. Now the chief was charged with treason-felony, a crime that could bring a death sentence with a guilty conviction..

Poundmaker, whose reserve was one of the closest to Battleford, was in his forties, not much older than Dickens. He had generally been regarded as a friend to the whites and had not himself taken up arms until his camp was rashly attacked at Cut Knife by the adventuristic Otter, spoiling to prove himself in battle.

More than any other chief, Poundmaker had tried to adjust to the changing times on the plains. It had been Poundmaker who was the first to take up farming as an example to his people that the old hunting days were at an end. Poundmaker guided the party of the Canadian Governor General, Marquis of Lorne, into Blackfoot country barely four years earlier. And it was Poundmaker, adopted son of the Grand Chief of the Blackfoot Confederacy, Crowfoot, who sought to bring peace between the warring tribes on the plains of the West.

He believed it was suicide to fight the white men and their big guns. "Those guns are something terrible, like the Devil," he told Dickens in his testimony.

Poundmaker, like Big Bear, had seen his authority in his own camp undermined by Metis rebels and militant Stoneys from the Eagle Hills. "They frightened us, and told us that if we did not join Louis Riel, he would treat us as he was treating the white people. We were afraid." At one point, it seemed that fighting might break out among the Crees and the Sioux-speaking Stoneys over a group of teamsters who had been captured while freighting supplies to Battleford.

The taking of the teamsters, most of whom were Metis uninvolved in the warfare, was more blunder than premeditation. A party of Cree and Stoney warriors had inadvertently crossed paths with the muleskinners. Both sides were startled by the chance encounter but the warriors acted swiftly and decisively. They seized the wagons and supplies, with the exception of a handful of teamsters who slipped their horses and rode off helter-skelter toward Battleford. The Stoneys wanted to kill the prisoners, but Poundmaker stood firm. Only their continuing threats and warnings had prevented the chief from riding to Battleford himself to discuss peace.

Even then, Poundmaker had not fought. At personal risk, he had protected the prisoners until Otter arrived with his big guns.

It was clear to Poundmaker that the weight of numbers would mean the end of rebellion. There was no use of further resistance or loss of life, so he chose to make peace. He arrived at the military head-quarters in Battleford on horseback with fifteen lesser chiefs and band councillors. A tall, graceful and handsome man with a long, hawk-like nose, he wore a cap made from a grizzly bear head with a tuft of eagle feathers. One long lock of hair at each temple was twisted with brass wire. His leather jacket was studded with brass nails and beads, and he wore brightly-colored beaded leggings and moccasins. He strode with confidence to where Middleton sat, imperious, pompous and obese. If Middleton thought Poundmaker would grovel, he did not know the man.

Dickens witnessed the surrender, standing amid a crowd of police and soldiers.

"What a contrast!" Dickens thought. "It's fitting that Poundmaker should represent the Cree. No finer leader of his people can be had. But how arrogant and self-indulgent Middleton appears."

"Why did you fight against the Queen, after all the government of the white people has done for you?" Middleton demanded.

His question had to be translated into Cree as Poundmaker spoke neither English nor French. With the translation, some of the men smirked and made noises of derision.

"I did not fight until the white soldiers came to our own reserve lands — given to us for eternity by treaty — and fired on my people," Poundmaker replied. His voice was calm but forceful and contrasted with the shaking bluster and anger of Middleton's.

"Who raided Battleford at night and murdered the white men Payne and Tremont?" the general asked.

"I cannot name them," replied Poundmaker. "They are not of my people, they are not Cree. My band has not attacked anyone but only fought to defend themselves. Nor did warriors under my control raid any white men." Honour prevented Poundmaker from naming the Stoneys.

At that moment, an Indian woman with a blue kerchief called out. "I want to say something."

Furious, Middleton ordered her to be quiet.

"We do not listen to women!" he barked.

"Then what's the reason the Queen sends her word here?" the woman retorted. "Isn't the Queen a woman?"

"She has councillors who are men," replied the red-faced Middleton, startled by the impertinence of this vanquished enemy.

Regaining his composure, Middleton again demanded to know who killed Tremont and Payne.

"I did."

Man Without Blood, a young Stoney warrior, stepped from the surrounding crowd. He wore buckskins decorated with brightly coloured beads, and a black wide-brimmed woman's straw hat with a brilliant green plume.

"I said I would give myself up to save my people. We came upon Tremont greasing his wagon and we argued whether to kill him or not. I had a bow and arrows and some said 'Shoot him with an arrow' but another said 'You cannot kill a man for nothing. Let him be.' Anyway, a spirit told me to kill him, so I took a rifle from another man and shot him. It was me."

"Who is this impudent man?" raged Middleton. "Arrest him! Take him away!"

The police closed in around Man Without Blood, who made no effort to escape. Instead, he continued to speak loudly and defiantly.

"Remember, my people," he shouted, as the police grabbed his arms. "In the winter, the grass on the prairie dies. But the earth remains the same forever. In the spring, the grass will grow again and life returns…"

"Enough!" roared the general. "Take him away."

"…to the prairie, and so will our people…"

"Shut him up," Middleton ordered. A soldier placed a gag around the young man's mouth.

August had just begun when Dickens heard the clinking of chains outside his office. He looked up in surprise as a tall, subdued Cree came through the door in the custody of two constables. The man looked vaguely familiar but he could not place the dejected soul who stood before him now. The Indian hung his head as if ashamed. There was a large bandage around his waist, and blood had seeped through.

"Wandering Spirit, sir," said Constable O'Keefe, one of the guards escorting the humiliated war chief. "He was caught August 1st. Tried suicide by stabbing himself in the guts. I suspect he's sorry he failed at that, too."

Dickens was stunned and felt emotions well up. This was not the haughty and swaggering Wandering Spirit that he remembered. But he knew this devil had killed Tom Quinn in cold blood, likely a priest besides, and had instigated the murders at Frog Lake. The policeman raged inside, but knew that rationally he had to do his duty as an officer of the law. He took a few minutes to compose himself and then signalled for the prisoner to sit. Dickens paced about, then stood behind his desk He turned to the interpreter.

"Tell him I want to take a statement from him."

Wandering Spirit said nothing. He stood head bowed, his eyes fixed on a far corner of the room as if they were staring at an unseen spirit. Dickens eyed him closely. In an odd way, he almost felt sympathy for this man despite his crimes. This assassin of Dickens's closest friend at Fort Pitt did not seemed like the feared menace that he had been weeks before. The once-proud warrior appeared so vacant and defeated that Frank could empathize. He felt much the same way himself. He stared at Wandering Spirit but the man would not return his gaze. Where was the flash of anger, the intensity and charisma that once made this man a deadly force to be reckoned with?

"Told me before he wants to be a Christian," the interpreter said.

Hearing the word, Wandering Spirit looked up. Dickens peered at him intently, searching for some evidence in the war chief's eyes that this was a fraud, a lie to escape the punishment he was due. There was nothing on the prisoner's face that suggested a subterfuge.

Dickens asked some questions which were dutifully translated but the prisoner said nothing.

"Take him back to his cell," Dickens said, after a few minutes. "He's not ready to speak."

"Do we need extra guards for this man?" O'Keefe asked.

Dickens again looked the Cree in the eye. Wandering Spirit avoided the inspector's stare and looked toward the floor.

"I think not," said Dickens. "He is not credible among his own people. His endeavour has failed. His friends are in prison or have fled. No one will rescue him and I am confident he will not try to escape. Only make sure he has nothing to do himself further harm. I have seldom seen a man more defeated, crushed." Perhaps myself, he thought despondently.

One of the constables lifted Wandering Spirit's left arm and he arose. The guards opened the door to return to the jailhouse. The humiliated war chief looked back over his shoulder.

"I sorry," he said. The words were plainly English.

Dickens, startled, answered: "Sorry? What are you sorry for?"

The interpreter asked, but there was no response from Wandering Spirit.

Dickens was left wondering. What was he sorry for? That he had killed Quinn and others? That his rebellion had failed? That he had botched his own suicide?

Dickens opened his desk. He reached in and pulled out a plug of tobacco, offering it to the defeated enemy. Wandering Spirit cupped his chained hands to take it. The links clanked together. Those once-fierce, blazing eyes were clouded, but in them was a spark of gratitude. He spoke no words, but turned away to be led back to his confinement, and ultimately, death. The moccasins of the most feared Cree would dangle in the wind in a place he had seldom seen, the Place of Bones, known to the whites as Regina.

The inspector returned to his paperwork. He was glad that Wandering Spirit had shown no defiance. He had wondered if he could have contained his own rage if the war chief had shown any combative spirit.

A few days later, Dickens encountered William Bleasdell Cameron on the streets of Battleford. The Hudson's Bay clerk had spotted Dickens and hailed him.

"I have something for you, captain," Cameron grinned. He reached in his pocket and pulled out something on a gold chain. It was his father's missing watch.

Dickens eyes widened in astonishment.

"How did you come by this?" he inquired.

"One of the Cree sold it to Alfred Schmidt, a halfbreed of my acquaintance. He came to me and asked if I wanted it. Paid him $15. It's stolen property, rightfully yours. Of course, I wouldn't mind being compensated."

"Why, certainly, Mr. Cameron. I thank you so much for returning it. Never for a moment did I think to see it again."

The recovery of the watch was one of the few bright moments for Dickens after the rebellion. He was frustrated at his encounters with the eastern bureaucracy, the denials of his request for leave. He wrote letters pointing out that the police under his command had not been paid since March. When the government sent funds for the April pay, he discovered that two different employees in the ministry had sent money for the same month and the second amount would therefore be deducted from the men's pay, instead of leaving it for the May salaries. He had to argue for everything. Some food was over-supplied and going bad. Other necessities were not being sent.

He now recognized that his problems in dealing with the bureaucrats for leave were not necessarily personal. He produced a chain of letters making requests for supplies for both the men and their horses, asked for new sashes and windows to keep the Battleford police quarters winter-proof, made demands for books, chess sets, boxing gloves and fencing foils to keep the men amused during the long boring winters.

He wrote a letter on behalf of Mrs. Burke, whose police officer husband had been killed in action, and who wanted to move from Battleford to settle with her children in Winnipeg. "As she is destitute, I wire you to ask authority to pay her passage. Please wire reply." Chafing at the slowness of a response, he paid her way anyway in the expectation that the government would eventually make good.

# Chapter 41

Frank Dickens rose from his bed and parted the curtains in his small room, the sun in the east shining brightly into the gloom. Now it was late September 1885. The daylight hours were shortening and the mornings on the southern prairie were chilly, with occasional frost, but the days were often bright and sunny, even warm. He had only recently arrived in Regina, now the headquarters of the North West Mounted Police, and soon would be leaving for eastern Canada. As Dickens dressed, he felt a sense of gratitude that he had finally been granted invalid leave from his postings in the West. He shuddered at the thought that without leave he might have been required to spend yet another bitter winter in the drafty cold barracks that were the lot of the police, furnished too sparsely to keep the officers of the Queen comfortable. Eleven damnable winters in this country were enough! He grumbled to himself that his father, then his sisters, had somehow condemned him to extremes in weather in his life's work. From the excruciating heat and stifling humidity of Bengal to the painful ice-bound, wind-blasted winters along the Saskatchewan, his body, frail by nature, had been undermined by the conditions he had been forced to endure.

Even his trip to Regina had been a trial for Dickens. Accompanied by the guide Josie Alexander, and young Constable Laurence O'Keefe, he had left Battleford during the second week of September, once his leave had come through. The trio of riders had crossed the Eagle and Bear Hills, skirted the Bad Hills and White Bear Lake, and forded the big river at Saskatchewan Crossing.

Dickens would have preferred riding in silence but Alexander, whose grizzled features spoke of both his father's white heritage and his mother's Indian origins, was amiable and keen to talk. Normally taciturn at the posts, Alexander was happy to be on the trail. He spoke at length of young Metis women he remembered fondly, whether there might be Cree renegades still lurking in the hills only too eager to ambush a trio of lonely riders, asked when was the last time Dickens had seen a buffalo, and in excruciating detail described where the sweetest water could be found along the trail. The moody policeman was preoccupied and only heard parts of the guide's chatter. O'Keefe, anxious to rejoin family back east, was well ahead of the others.

Alexander was rattling on about Moose Jaw hop beer.

"They'll be some in Regina, y'know. But best not to try it, sir. Packs a wallop, it does. Purty nigh killed me last time I drank it."

Dickens turned to the scout with a brief forced smile. He rode on in silence.

"Will yuh be comin' back, cap'n?" The only question Dickens really had an ear for. How would he answer?

"Possibly. But I'm hoping for a suitable government position in the east. Have you been east, Josie?"

"No, sir. I want to go east some day. Only fer a visit, mind. Can't stand to live too crowded. Y'know, lots of people steppin' on yer toes." Alexander paused. "If yuh don't come back, who's to look after yer dog?"

Ah, yes. The dog. Connemara was Dickens's truest, most constant friend in his lonely life on the plains, beyond doubt. They had made their last hunting expedition together shortly before Dickens left Battleford. He wouldn't see that beloved animal again and felt badly.

"Inspector Morris has him. He is in good hands." Dickens spoke slowly, sadly.

"I'd take him if the inspector don't want him, and be all the happier fer it," the guide said cheerfully. "I likes dogs."

"Thank you, Josie. Ask Morris when you return."

Dickens spurred his horse on. He did not want to talk further on the painful subject.

The ride south to the rail line at Swift Current should not have been a burden for an experienced policeman in the west but Dickens' health was already precarious and his spirit depressed. By the time Swift Current was attained, he had fallen seriously ill. He recalled nothing of the train journey to Regina, except that he was told he had been delirious, ranting about a pension not yet granted, cursing the names of John A. Macdonald, William McLean and Inspector Morris. Alexander was circumspect enough not to tell anyone that police Superintendent Leif Crozier was another target of Dickens' subconscious venom, but he did mention it to Frank, with an astute warning to be more subtle in his raving denunciations, as though the inspector could have controlled them during his illness.

But all that was two weeks ago. His frame of mind was much improved. Today, Dickens thought, he would wear full dress uniform. He preferred mufti, feeling more comfortable in casual gear, but this was a special occasion and he had no doubt that other officers would be dressed formally. Certainly Superintendent Deane, once of the Royal Marines and his commanding officer in Regina, would expect it. Deane's views of the men under his command were not complimentary — it was he who had described the police as an "armed mob."

No one had told Dickens that he had to attend the sentencing of Big Bear, and his duties had been very light since he arrived in Regina, but he felt a personal obligation to go to the court. Indeed, he felt some sympathy for the man to be sentenced today. Others clearly had too. Even the jurors had recommended mercy for the accused when they brought down their guilty verdict. When the trial had occurred, Dickens was still in Battleford, preparing for his journey, and while he could have provided some useful evidence to the court, his superiors felt there were others whose testimony would be more crucial. Still, now that he was here, he wanted to see the final outcome.

This could be the final occasion that he would wear full police dress. Dickens had begged for work in the civilian bureaucracy, and had some influential people working on his behalf in Ottawa. Getting the ear of the prime minister, whose nickname was Old Tomorrow, was always a problem. Getting it when the Canadian leader was sober was even more of a gamble. Still, Dickens hoped that when he left for the east in a few weeks he would not only receive his retiring allowance but would be granted a secure government job. Surely, it was evident to all that his health would not permit active police work any longer. Commissioner Irvine had noted that Dickens's work habits were improving but did mention that the inspector's deafness was worsening.

Dickens took out his inspector's dress uniform, the red serge jacket with the gold fringes, and the gold braid on the pockets, lower sleeves and shoulders. His blue collar sported brass buttons marked "NWMP", and his blue pants had broad yellow stripes down the outside of the leg. He wiped a speck of dust from his high black boots, adjusted the golden sash over his shoulder and attached the scabbard of his three-and-a-half-foot sword to his belt. He drew the weapon he had never used in battle and examined the blade. His fingers ran over the name of the manufacturer, Maynes, Harris & Grice of London, a connection to the city where he had spent his early years. Then he put on his blue pillbox hat with the yellow stripe. There was no need today, he thought, to bring the Enfield Mark II revolver he'd been issued recently when he needed it least.

A rap came at the door, but Dickens did not react. His hearing was much worse since his frightening ordeal six months earlier. At times, taking testimony from witnesses in Battleford over the summer, he missed entire sentences and lost track of what people were saying. He did not know then whether it was his mind that was wandering or whether he simply was unable to hear. He sometimes had to ask them to repeat themselves and so missed some of the earlier, subtler nuances that witnesses buried in their statements.

The knock at the door was repeated. This time, the door was pushed open and Sub-Constable Prior appeared with a tray.

"Good morning, inspector. Tea, sir. Best kind available. I have your eggs and toast, too."

"Oh, thank you, Prior." Dickens was startled, as though the sudden appearance of this man would allow his thoughts to be read. "Leave it on the table, please."

"Will you be going to the sentencing today, sir?"

"Yes, I will," Dickens said. "I do hope British justice will treat the chief fairly."

"Fairly, sir?"

"Anyone who knows the convicted man as I have will know he is no criminal. A pest, possibly. Troublesome, assuredly. But no criminal."

# Chapter 42

The man reputed among some whites to be a killer and the terror of the northwest frontier was smaller than many in the inquisitive crowd had imagined. Here was Mistahi-Muskwa, known to the whites as Big Bear, the chief who many believed had challenged the authority of the world's mightiest empire with a small band of fearsome warriors. Yet now he stood alone, surrounded by the agents of those whom he had for so long defied, a man into his sixties, short but barrel-chested, with deep crevasses in a dark, pockmarked face, shackled and chained, once wild black hair, flecked with gray, now shorn like a white man's.

A small crowd had collected near the Regina courthouse. There were more than the usual number of uniformed police about. Some civilians, clad in flannel shirts and wide-brimmed hats or bowlers lounged about, waiting for events to begin. A scattering of Indians stood at a distance, nervous about getting too close. None were of Big Bear's band. Regina was not traditional territory for his followers, and his band was scattered and no more. Many of the militants had fled south to the bluecoats' country, or were in chains in white men's prisons. Others had run to join bands led by chiefs who had refused to join the uprising in the previous spring.

A few white men gathered about the chief shouted curses as Big Bear entered the Regina courthouse under warm, sunny skies for sentencing. Most of the curious, however, remained silent, some even felt sympathetic, as the man guarded by red-coated policemen moved slowly toward the prisoners' dock. Big Bear looked back toward the sun and raised his arms in a gesture of gratitude for the glory of the day.

"A fine day," he said in his deep voice to his captors. Few understood what he was saying in Cree.

"Not as many here now as for the trial," a fellow officer told Dickens. "There were no seats available then, I tell you."

"The hunger for revenge has been gratified, then?" Dickens said. "Now, we're settling in for the port and cigars?"

"Mood seems different, too," Dickens' companion said. "Perhaps because most of the witnesses who testified at the trial were favourable to Big Bear. Even the whites. No telling what the judge is thinking though. Yesterday in this same court Big Bear's war chief, Wandering Spirit, was sentenced to hang. Wonder if that will influence the judge."

Dickens looked around the courthouse. The building was so new that the court still smelled of the fresh wood. Despite its newness, the courthouse had been heavily employed in recent weeks, with the trial of Louis Riel and Big Bear's Cree friend Poundmaker, and One Arrow, the leader of the rebellious Stoneys. Regina was a young settlement, too, for that matter, a place on the flat, featureless prairie, broken only by the modest creek Wascana. The site was known to the Indians as Pile of Bones because of the leavings of an old buffalo kill. It was dusty in dry spells and mud-encrusted after the tempestuous summer electrical storms. The Cree thought the white men had made a mistake when they chose this strange place on the open prairie to make their big camp.

"There's the prosecuting lawyer, Scott," said Dickens' fellow officer. "His colleague is Hamilton. Over there is Robertson, defence lawyer. Despite his age he conducted an able defence, considering the circumstances. Richardson, the judge, will be here soon. And there's Peter Houri, interpreter for Big Bear."

"I know Houri," said Dickens.

Hampered by leg irons, the leader of the last of the buffalo hunters, shuffled toward the place set for him. Nemesis to the government of Canada for years, Big Bear and his followers had refused demands by the new white rulers of the plains to abandon their nomadic life and settle on reserve land picked out well away from the American border. When rebellion began in the spring, Big Bear's River Cree band was one of a surprisingly few Indian bands that risked destruction and joined the fighting on the side of their mixed-race Metis cousins. All the killings, looting and mutilation, the taking of civilian prisoners, threatened lives and forced marches had been blamed initially on Big Bear.

There were white people, witnesses, who knew better: That Big Bear had not counselled violence, that he tried to prevent murder, that he had lost control of his band to the angry militants. Several witnesses said so at his trial earlier that month. Dickens knew that he and scores of others owed their lives to the old scarred chief who made his way through the courthouse. It was true that members of Big Bear's band had taken up arms against the Canadian authorities, but some in the government were determined to seek vengeance against the most visible leaders in the West and cared little for the subtleties of native politics.

Big Bear had now reached the prisoner's box. He reached out and gently placed a hand on the shoulder of one of the North West Mounted Police officers accompanying him and made a gesture of thanks, then turned to face the crowd. His high cheekbones and broad forehead were raised proudly, not so much in defiance as with a sense of a man who knew his place in the world. Big Bear had often joked that he was old and ugly, but no one would describe him that way today.

At first, his eyes seemed to look beyond the throng of onlookers, as though he was surveying an unknown future. But now that he had turned and looked at those who had come to see him tried they flickered with recognition and even humour at those whom he considered had done him favour in the past.

Houri, the interpreter, whispered to Big Bear, who scanned the courtroom. Dickens coughed, and Big Bear cast him a kindly glance, and quick nod. The policeman forced a fleeting smile. To Dickens, the Cree chieftain resembled nothing less than one of those portraits of the proud but defeated leaders who were taken by the victors to Rome in chains. Had he been a literate man, Frank mused, he might have been the Charles Dickens of his people.

Were the events of the last few months inevitable, Dickens wondered? Would lives have been spared and Big Bear now be in the court if the government and its agents in the east had been less stiff-necked and listened to warnings?

But now Judge Hugh Richardson was in the court and all eyes turned to him.

Big Bear's trial had come in September, two months after the fugitive chief was captured after a chase through the northern forest and muskeg. Cameron, the sole white man to survive the Frog Lake killings, and others, testified on behalf of the old chief. Big Bear's own son, Imasees, said others, had rebelled against his father's authority and treated him with contempt. Now that the rebellion was crushed, those who were able had fled south across the medicine line into the United States, and would not return. The only witness who had testified against the old chief was Stanley Simpson, and his evidence was based on a conversation in Cree that the young Simpson understood imperfectly.

The defence witnesses were not enough to turn a vengeful jury in Big Bear's favor, but they might have saved him from the noose. The jury deliberated for only 15 minutes before bringing in a verdict of guilty but with a recommendation of mercy.

Dickens was en route from Battleford to Regina when the trial occurred. But when the time came for Big Bear's sentencing late in the month, he had recovered some of his stamina.

Before the sentence was ordered, Big Bear was given a chance to speak.

The chief knew scarcely any English but the powerful, deep vibrance and expressive tone of his voice was such that he could move even those who could not understand his words. His aristocratic bearing and his expressive manner enhanced his speech. He would plead not for himself, but for his people. He gave a quick toss of his head and began:

"I wish to speak about what happened that brought me here in chains," he said, raising his shackled hands for all to see.

"No one can say truthfully that I ever ordered the death of any white man, whether agent, priest or soldier. I am a warrior, a hunter of buffalo — that has been my life. I am not a coward who slays the unarmed, the weak and defenceless. I did not tell my people to take part in the rebellion; I advised against it. When those who joined my band despised me for not joining the Metis rebellion I held strong. I did not join the fight, neither did I take anything that belongs to the white men nor the half-breeds. There are good and bad among all our peoples. I believed, though some white men had been cruel to us, that many white men would help my people in our times of greatest need, and so I offered them protection, brotherhood and friendship.

"I have spoken harshly at times to the white man. Some of you know this. Never have I threatened any with death or injury. At those times I was speaking only for my rights. This country once belonged to my people and to myself. We went where we wanted to go, hunted where the best hunting grounds were, gathered the good things of the earth to use as we saw fit. Then we saw it taken and sold without our knowledge, and without any benefit to us. Suddenly, there were places we had been all our lives, and all our grandfathers' lives, where we could no longer go. The young men asked why, and I could give them no answers. The white man now ruled our land."

His voice lowered and he looked to the floor.

"Today, my heart is on the ground, and I am dead to my people. They scatter in fear through the lands that we once owned and roamed freely at our will. I do not know where they are. They are starving and outcast, afraid to show themselves in the sun. If the Great-Grandmother's men do not come to help them with food and shelter before the winter comes, surely they will die. Despite all that has happened, I do believe that good white men will come to stop that starvation that has afflicted my people since the buffalo have gone. I know that one day, the Great-Grandmother will know that my people and the other nations of this land will be of service to her. That is why I have confidence in the days to come."

With this, Big Bear thrust his hands forward in supplication.

"I appeal to you, the powerful and strong, the chiefs of the white man's laws, to take pity and help the outcasts of my band. I am old now, and ugly, and have tried to do good for my people. Now I am helpless and have only the words of my tongue to offer. As a friend of the white man, I beg you, pity my people, pardon them, feed them and protect them. I have spoken."

There was silence in the courtroom. Those few white people who could understand Cree were stunned. Even some who had endured the threats and the hardships of imprisonment in the Cree camp were affected and would be haunted by Big Bear's speech for years.

After a time, the judge, Hugh Richardson, leaned forward. He spoke quietly but firmly.

"Big Bear. You have never owned the land. This country belongs to the Queen and she has allowed you to make use of it. Now that the great herds of buffalo are gone, she has been generous in offering your people some of the best places to live. You have dragged your feet in picking out land that has been offered you. While you have not killed anyone yourself, you have been found guilty of causing trouble for the Queen and her government. I sentence you to three years imprisonment in Stony Mountain penitentiary."

Dickens had left the court depressed. So it was over now for Big Bear. Could the humiliated old man survive three years in a white man's prison? Dickens doubted that. He felt that now, more than ever, he wanted to leave this place of cruelty, bitterness and death.

# Chapter 43

*Until I peered into the mirror in my room on the day I dressed in uniform for the sentencing of Big Bear, I had not realized the toll that our recent adventures had taken on me. I had certainly felt exhaustion and depression, but now the man looking back at me seemed much older than his early forties. He looked drawn and haggard. Was this an irreversible toll?. Or had I always looked that way, I wonder? Pain, both physical and emotional, was evident in that man's eyes, and he wore a sad, wearied expression that robbed his body of life and, rather cruelly, his dignity.*

*How would Pa have described my appearance today, I wonder? I am looking a decade older and more washed out than I was when I passed the mirror at Fort Walsh. My work has made me old before my time. My receding hair is counterpoint to an increasingly bulging stomach. My blotchy complexion is offset by my graying beard. I feel as though someone crept upon me as I slumbered and poured a container of whitewash onto my face. Not a flattering portrait, I dare say.*

*When I began dressing, I had felt proud and capable. Now, having seen my image, I felt depressed and feeble. What if life had been different? What if father had been more patient, forgiving and charitable? Would I have had a career in the professions in England like young brother Henry, or a place in* the publishing industry of London like brother Charley, with respect from my colleagues and family, and a cottage to repair to in the shires for weekends and holidays, or a maison in the south of France. Would I have married a sweet-hearted, gentle woman, and raised brilliant children endowed with my father's talents who would love me and cuddle with me, and eagerly await my return home, as I did with my own father, who so often did not have the time to spare? Well, it was not to be so why dwell on it? Still, I am only forty-one, perhaps those possibilities remain open.

When I am truly low, I think of the dead: Quinn, Sleigh, Cowan, Cut Arm, too, who had shown us his friendship. Rutledge, the hero of our river flight, came down with typhoid and died shortly before I left Battleford. Police surgeon Rolph believed Rutledge had carried the disease within him from the moment he swallowed the river water on the first day of the trip. Only the constable's strong constitution had kept him alive throughout the summer.

When will this pain and frustration end?

There are days now when I feel that I might be next. I find myself breathless, with pains in my chest, agitated and beset by severe headaches, many times I can't hear what happens about me.. I have written repeated letters to my senior commanders and to Fred White, the police comptroller in Ottawa, requesting extended leave.

After eleven years, I want more than a few months leave. I would like a retiring gratuity, a job as a bureaucrat in Ottawa, something I can handle. I am at least owed back pay. White has kindly said he will make interventions on my behalf and says the prime minister, Sir John Macdonald, wants to know the full particulars of my illness. At any rate, I have been given some time and will travel east on the new railroad to Ottawa, hoping for a reply.

In the meantime, I will live hand-to-mouth, relying on my meager savings and never knowing when my last penny will be spent. I borrowed from a friend and, feeling compelled to offer a guarantee for the loan, gave him the precious watch I inherited from my father.

The unfortunate and unwise decision to lend a month and a half's pay to Crozier has brought me nothing but grief. When I have requested repayment, my letters and messages have been returned with silence. Desperate, I wrote a letter to his brother-in-law, hoping for an intervention. His reply, to say the least, was disconcerting: "I sincerely hope that you have not lent the Colonel a substantial sum, because he has played this same despicable trick on others."

My begging, for that's what it amounts to, seems to be of no avail. It is like pulling teeth from a tiger to get an answer from the government. Or perhaps more aptly, like entering a sloth in a horse race.

# Chapter 44

When Dickens received promises without any follow through month after month, he lobbied family friends and political connections to advocate on his behalf.

Frederick Chesson was a friend of the Dickens family in England and a highly regarded reformer active in the emancipation movement, the prevention of contagious diseases and other worthy causes. He wrote early in 1886 to Sir Charles Tupper, head of the Canadian diplomatic mission to London, reminding him that Dickens had been appointed an officer through the good graces of Lord Dufferin, still a rising star in the imperial firmament. Now, after years of service, the officer faced financial and physical ruin. "I know that many persons of great influence in this country would be exceedingly glad if anything could be done for him," Chesson added.

It happened that John Macdonald was arriving in London for a conference early in the year, and Tupper chose to take the matter up with the prime minister once he arrived.

Tupper read from Chesson's letter: " 'You will no doubt remember that Mr. Dickens behaved with great gallantry during the recent rebellion in the North West. After engaging the rebels who were in greatly superior force, he retreated from the fort carrying with him some of the settlers (sic), the guns and ammunition, and the whole of his little force. He was reported to have been massacred with all his men, and appears to have had a very narrow escape. He was much praised in the Canadian papers for his conduct.' "

Perhaps another position could be found for this exceedingly well-read and educated man? Chesson suggested.

Macdonald listened closely to Tupper, then snorted.

"Hah! Some in Canada say Dickens's abandonment of Fort Pitt was simply another humiliation for the police. Irvine holed up in Prince Albert, Morris's refusal to ride out from Battleford to confront the rebels, Crozier's defeat…all damned fiascoes. I was gravely disappointed in the ineffective performance of the police during the uprising. Now, Charles, are we to transform, by feats of legerdemain, a headlong retreat into a glorious victory? Absurd! Were it not for the volunteer militia from the east, the west might have been lost."

"I see your point, Sir John," said Tupper. "But the fact is that many people regarded the successful retreat by Dickens from Fort Pitt to Battleford as the first good news from the northwest. Until then, there was nothing of note but panic, loss and defeat. And I might remind you, John, that one of your own nephews was a constable in the retreat. Even the first military actions were, at best, stalemates. I have been told that people at Battleford were jubilant when Dickens's party arrived. It revived their spirits and renewed their hope."

"Very well, then, Charles. I'll be busy this week with meetings. Send Chesson's letter on to me in Ottawa and I'll look into doing something for our Mr. Dickens upon my return. What's next?"

Tupper followed the prime minister's advice, enclosing a reminder that he had told Chesson the matter would be pursued once Sir John returned to Ottawa. But Old Tomorrow lived up to his reputation. There would never be a government sinecure for Frank Dickens.

# Chapter 45

Frank was eating alone in a hotel dining room in Montreal when a man approached and stood by his table. Feeling unsociable and miserable, Dickens stared at the wall.

"May I share your table?" the man asked politely in an American drawl. "There are very few settings available."

Dickens, with his mouth full, waved his fork, implying assent. After many years in North America he had become accustomed to the casualness of Yankee acquaintances.

"Dr. Alexander Jamieson, from Moline, Illinois," said the newcomer, offering his hand.

"Frank Jeffrey Dickens," the gloomy diner replied.

"Dickens! Not a relation of Charles, I trust?" Jamieson inquired, smiling.

"My father," said Frank.

The doctor started.

"How astonishing! I'm delighted. I saw your father read in Boston, in '67 or '68, I believe. Had to line up ten hours just to get a ticket. What a night! What power and eloquence! So impassioned, your father was, superb acting, playing all the parts of his characters. They say he used to exhaust himself in such performances, giving his all to his audiences."

"Then you saw him more recently than I," said Frank. "My father died while I was serving with the Bengal Mounted Police in India. I never saw him after 1863."

"How sad! He had mixed feelings about us Americans, I gather."

"Occasioned by the criticism he received at the hands of some of your countrymen when he had the temerity to suggest that he might be paid copyright fees for works sold in America. Otherwise, he enjoyed his visits to this side of the Atlantic, and he certainly profited from them."

"I can understand his opinion," said the doctor. "He was simply doing what a good American businessman would do, trying to be paid for his efforts."

Jamieson ordered his dinner.

"And what brings you here?" he asked.

"I have recently completed many years of service with the North West Mounted Police. I'm awaiting approval of my retirement gratuity."

Jamieson drew the quiet, morose man into conversation. As Dickens told his tales of the west and of life with his father, his personality was transformed. He became animated and passionate, waving his hands to make a point, ardently expressing his versions of events with eloquence and dramatic flair. His resemblance to his remarkable father became more apparent. Oblivious to Frank, people at nearby tables began listening, whispering quietly and nodding in approval. None of this was lost on the astute doctor.

"I must go now, but want to hear more," said Jamieson. "Can we meet tomorrow?"

He thought a moment: "You know, Frank, you could make a career of your experiences. Travel around and give lectures on your father and first hand accounts of your connections with the Blackfoot, Sitting Bull, Crowfoot, the police, the Cree, Louis Riel. You could embellish them with recollections of your seven years in India. There is a great thirst among Americans for stories about the west. What an opportunity this could be for you!"

Dickens looked at the American physician with acute interest. Jamieson could be right, he thought. The doctor certainly seemed fascinated by his anecdotes. There was much more he could add.

"Come with me to Moline," Jamieson continued. "I am a member of a historical society. We would be delighted to hear you speak. You could practice your talk there and then strike out...Chicago, St. Louis, St. Paul, New Orleans, then east to New York, Philadelphia, Boston. The possibilities are endless."

Jamieson pulled some coins from his pocket and left them on the table. Dickens made a half-hearted motion toward his own pocket.

"Oh, no, Frank," the doctor said. "Allow me. I've greatly enjoyed your company."

Dickens relaxed. The truth was, he did not have the money to cover his new companion's dinner, and barely enough to pay for his own. He had left behind a trail of unpaid debts — charges for a new pair of dress pants ordered in Toronto to replace his threadbare clothing, hotel and food charges run up with a promise to repay.

As the doctor departed, Dickens thought that perhaps at long last he had an opportunity of pulling himself out of the jaws of debt. Before coming to Montreal, he had spent weeks in Ottawa lobbying for the retirement allowance he believed he deserved. During this time, his financial resources had been limited and after some weeks, feeling he had made all the progress he could with the bureaucracy, he quit his residence at the Russell Hotel. He had left without paying his account of $111, one-third of it for the wine that he moodily consumed sitting in the darker corners of the hotel tavern. The Russell was one of the livelier drinking establishments in the town, but while Dickens had been a regular, he had kept to himself, not joining in the raucous nightly activities favoured by most of the tavern's habitues. The hotelier was reluctant to see Dickens leave without paying a portion of the account, but his desperate client pleaded that he was expecting a pension for his time with the police and, in any case, his family would be good for any outstanding bills. The innkeeper thought about calling in the local constabulary, but due to the nature of his business he preferred to have as little contact with the law as he could, and so he decided against that alternative. Instead, he extracted a signed commitment from Dickens that his bill would be paid from his police pension, or failing that, could be settled directly with the Dickens family in London. As Dickens scuttled out the door, heading for the Montreal train, the innkeeper grumbled aloud about ne'er-do-well sons from the Old Country running up accounts that took months to collect.

He went to the door and shouted at Dickens's retreating back.

"Don't come back here, you English bastard, understand, unless you are prepared to make payment before you cross the threshold."

A few weeks after Dickens met Jamieson, the two men boarded the train for Toronto, where they would make connections for a trip on to Chicago and thence to Moline. Dickens was embarrassed that he had to ask the doctor to cover the cost of his fare. He promised that he would make good on the loan once they reached Toronto because Fred White, the police comptroller, had told Dickens a draft would be waiting for him when he arrived. At least White, Frank thought, was a friendly face in the grey wall of the bureaucracy.

Dickens stared out the window as the train chugged through the St. Lawrence River valley on its way westward. The woodland was being transformed into rolling farmland, with green sprouts of corn and buckwheat now springing from the soil. They passed by acres of apple trees, now past blossoming and with fruit beginning to set. There were miles of pastureland with herds of cattle and sheep. Here and there, farmers were still ploughing or burning off the last of stubble from the previous year's crops. It had been eighty years since most of this land had been turned from thick forest into agricultural land, and Dickens had greatly missed these pastoral scenes during his time in the west. Settlers would now be flooding into the western prairie much as they did here years ago, setting up farmsteads and forever altering the natural patterns of life that had been established for eons. Surveying the countryside along the river and north of Lake Ontario, Dickens found it hard to reconcile that a little over a year earlier he feared for the lives of himself and his comrades in the last great uprising in the Canadian west. The murders, the pitched battles, and the starvation and disease that led up to those events seemed so distant to him now.

His reverie was broken by Jamieson's voice.

"Do you intend to call on your friend, the Colonel, when you arrive in Toronto?"

Frank felt the anger boil up in him at this reference to the "friend", Crozier, who had never repaid the money he had borrowed. Perhaps the doctor feared he would not be paid back the advance he had made to allow Dickens to make this trip. He felt embarrassed at the obligation he was under to Jamieson. Perhaps the doctor did not believe his story. Red-faced, Dickens lost his composure.

"No," he snarled. "I shall try to forget it and I ask you as a favour never to mention the circumstance to me again."

Dr. Jamieson was startled. He had not seen this flash of temper from Frank before.

"I am sorry, Frank. I shall never raise it again."

The two travelled in silence for some time, Dickens sheepish that he had erupted so violently, Jamieson angry with himself for causing offence. When the train reached Toronto, Dickens found that some promised money had been wired from Ottawa and while the amount, fifty dollars, was less than he had hoped, he promptly repaid Jamieson for the advance on his fare.

# Chapter 46

On the afternoon of June 11, 1886, a black carriage drawn by two brown horses trotted along the banks of the Mississippi, heading into the city of Moline, Illinois. The three occupants were in fine humour. Dr. Jamieson listened smiling as his guest gently teased his young daughter, Louise.

The day was hot and sultry, and the travellers had left the doctor's estate at Richwood Farm, four miles southeast of the town. They were to visit Samuel Kennedy, editor of the Moline *Republican* newspaper, dine with him and then repair to the Friday Club, a meeting of the local literary association, to hear readings by the doctor's guest, Frank Dickens.

"Moline is a young city by your standards, Frank," the doctor said. "Our Riverside cemetery over there still has plenty of space for those who have gone to rest. But I'd reckon that there are not many graveyard sites, in our United States or in Europe, that boast as fine a view as this one does."

Frank looked to his left. The cemetery sat on a high bluff overlooking the mighty river. On a clear day, one could look west well into the Iowa prairie, or down upon the tree-lined river bank where houses had been springing up over the decades since Black Hawk's Sauk and Fox warriors had been suppressed by the power of the burgeoning American state. The centre of town was the location of the factory established by John Deere, who had invented the steel plow capable of breaking up tough prairie sod and dealing with tall grasses, enabling the opening of the plains to agriculture and putting Moline on the map.

The visitor mused that his parents had passed by these high banks along the river as they travelled by paddlewheeler north from St. Louis more than four decades earlier. Charles might have looked up at this very spot while on his first American tour, nervous over the unseen perils that lurked in the once-expansive forests, fretting over the hidden obstacles in the mighty river, logs and sandbars. Father had been awed by America but had never been wholly comfortable here.

"We'll soon be at Kennedy's home," the doctor remarked. "He's a fine editor, well-read and with a good grasp of the transformations that are happening throughout North America. You'll enjoy his company, and this is a wonderful start for your lecture tour."

The carriage turned down a lane and into a drive. There stood a whitewashed house with gables and blue-painted shutters. A tall, bony man with his wife and two young daughters stood outside, expectantly awaiting the arrival of their visitors.

The agile Jamieson jumped from the carriage. Dickens though younger than the doctor, clambered down slowly, puffing from the exertion. Frank felt small beside the two rangy American men who were his hosts. He wore a dark new suit, which even though cotton, was ill-chosen for this sweltering day. He wiped his perspiring brow with a handkerchief that he pulled from his suit jacket.

"Sam," Jamieson said, drawing his guest along with a hand on his left arm. "I'd like you to meet my new friend Captain Frank Dickens, late of Canada's North West Mounted Police. I believe his official rank is Inspector, but that's the equal of our Captain."

"Delighted, sir, to make your acquaintance," said Kennedy. "We look forward to hearing you this evening. This is my wife, Betsy, and my two girls, Alice and Lina. Come in. It's an unusually hot day for this early in June, and we have a pitcher of iced lemonade to quench your thirst."

Frank put two fingers of his right hand in the collar of his shirt to allow air to his sweating neck, gave a pat to the rump of one of the horses, and followed his hosts into the house.

"We should have a good turnout at our Friday Club tonight," said Kennedy. "It's not often that we in Moline have a speaker with such intimate connections to a great author, and with a wealth of experience on the western frontier to boot. You are Charles's third son, are you not, Captain?"

"Correct, Mr. Kennedy. And I'm very happy to be here. I'm looking forward to a new career, travelling throughout America to tell my stories. The credit must go to Dr. Jamieson here, who found me in a bit of a funk, I confess. He encouraged me to cut myself adrift from my personal troubles and to use my knowledge and experience for the edification and enjoyment of others."

"Please, call me Sam," said Kennedy. "Did you have a good journey? Have you seen our great Mississippi before? "

"Twice before, Sam. I passed through St. Paul on my way west in 1874 to join the police, then again upon my return. It is magnificent country. I have connections to Illinois, you know. My Uncle Augustus, father's brother, worked for the Illinois Central Railway until his death in 1866. And my brother Henry's brother-in-law lives in Chicago. His name is Roche and he is a prominent attorney, I believe."

The Kennedys led their visitors through the house to a shaded porch on the back of the house where a breeze drifted eastward off the Mississippi, affording some relief from the scorching afternoon sun. Kennedy beckoned Jamieson and Dickens to sit, while Betsy Kennedy fetched lemonade. When she returned she made a request.

"Captain, you must do a reading from your father's works for our girls. They would enjoy it so much and would remember it all their lives. Your father loved children so much, did he not?"

Dickens hesitated. "I'm sorry, Mrs. Kennedy. One of the consequences of my experiences in the west is that I am somewhat deaf."

"Would you be so kind as to read for our children?" she said, louder this time. "They will remember this occasion for the rest of their lives, I am sure."

"Of course, I've brought a book and would be delighted."

"But first, we'll have a bit of a rest," said Kennedy. "Captain, would you indulge a newspaperman's curiosity? The doctor tells me you spent eleven years in the northwest, and before that seven years in India, but you are in your mid-forties, are you not?"

"And three years in England between services," said Dickens. "I'm forty-two. If I appear older, it is my weary body that betrays my chronology."

"Now, tell me how you and our mutual friend Jamieson came to meet?"

"I have been on leave from the North West Mounted on account of the severe breakdown of my health," said Dickens. "I spent, as you say, eleven years with them, devoted to my duty, and then when my system collapsed as a result of my time in service, I appealed to the Canadian government for a retirement pension. It's only recently that I have received a small portion of what I am owed from the Canadian government. That I am sure is entirely due to the fact that I told the comptroller that I had the prospect of paying work in the United States and needed money for expenses."

"Well, we are so fortunate to have benefited from your chance meeting with the doctor and so pleased you are here," said Betsy Kennedy. "Now, would you read to the children? They have great expectations of your reading."

Frank Dickens smiled at her little joke. He produced a small, battered leather-bound book, with golden lettering embossed on the cover.

"I thought I would read them something from Sketches by Boz, which my father wrote anonymously early in his career. You know Boz has a peculiar Illinois connection. It was the family nickname of Uncle Augustus. My father used the name to cover his identity so that he could move without notice among the people who were the models for his work. This reading may seem inappropriate for this time of year, but my father, as you know, was the world's foremost Christmas enthusiast and we always awaited that holiday season with great joy and excitement. I would like to share that joy."

The girls gathered around and Frank opened the book and read:

" 'Who can be insensible to the outpourings of good feeling, and the honest interchange of affectionate attachment, which abound at this season of the year. A Christmas family party! We know nothing in nature more delightful. There seems a magic in the very name of Christmas...'"

As Frank read, his body changed. He became less restrained. He seemed younger, his health restored. His ruddy, sweating face cleared. He smiled throughout and laughed when the children giggled as he read the part about mischievous grandpapa kissing old-fashioned grandmamma under the mistletoe, and she calling him — but with pleased expression — an impudent young dog, and the children in the story laughing, and grandpapa laughing more than the others.

" 'And thus the evening passes, in a strain of rational goodwill and cheerfulness, doing more to awaken the sympathies of every member of the party in behalf of his neighbour, and to perpetuate their good feeling during the ensuing year, than half the homilies that have ever been written by half the divines that have ever lived.'"

Frank closed the book. He addressed the adults.

"I'm glad my father never wrote anything that was harmful for young or old to read."

"Now, girls, off with you," said Sam Kennedy. "It's time for we adults to have our time with Captain Dickens. Now, sir, we would like to hear your opinions on the recent rebellion in the Canadian West."

# Chapter 47

"How do you assess blame in that uprising, Captain?" Sam Kennedy asked. "You suggested that warnings to the government about the halfbreed and Indian questions were ignored. We hear so much about the Indian fighting in our own western reaches but little about the events that led to war on the Canadian side. We, of course, know about Sitting Bull and the Sioux taking refuge there for some years, to the consternation of our military, and that Chief Joseph of the Nez Perces tried to attain the border but was stopped by our troops."

"Everyone and no one was to blame," Dickens replied. "Our own police commanders repeatedly told the government what was happening, but they were largely ignored. I cannot say whether that was simple neglect by the politicians or a considered decision to do nothing. Neither would surprise me. And the leaders of government failed to comprehend the urgency of the needs in the west. Certainly, some of our officers and government agents on the frontier pushed the Indians too far with unfortunate results. Even some of my friends and colleagues whom I respected were guilty of that. The initial good will of the Indians toward our own officers as their protectors faded as the buffalo herds disappeared and those people of the hunt realized we were not there to protect them so much as to prepare the way for newly arriving white settlers. The halfbreeds allowed themselves to be duped by what many believe to have been a madman, and some of the more susceptible Indians followed along with brutal results. The natives failed to adjust to changing realities, did not recognize they could no longer live as they once had. Some tried to turn from their lives of nomadic hunting and become farmers, but they failed, whether because they were ill-taught or because of some deeper fault that existed in their own nature. And the company had no particular interest in the arrival of settlers who would upset their monopoly business of two centuries."

"So, everyone must share the responsibility?"

"No one wished to take responsibility for the causes of the rebellion," Dickens continued. "The fighting in the Canadian west was nobody's fault, just as the failed institutions and injustice in the England described by my father three decades ago was nobody's fault. No one would step forth and take the action needed to solve the problems yet the failures were evident everywhere they looked. I do not exempt the police, or myself, from that failure. As my father wrote: 'Every failure teaches a man something, if he will learn.' The question is, will we learn?."

Dickens looked at Jamieson and the Kennedys.

"My father understood from the depth of his being that all of us, no matter what our position in society might be, are imprisoned by our own faults, our own prejudices and attitudes, our own nature. So when something is no one's fault, it is everyone's fault. We too readily accept the imposition of imprisoning institutions. Often we are happy to see restrictions binding others, but seldom do we wish them on ourselves. The chains that restrict us in our lives will not be loosened until we take pains to understand that there are chains that bind others, as well. And that those chains may keep those unfortunate others from understanding us, and prevent them from escaping their own prisons.

"There is a widespread sense that we are all trapped in confining cells of our own making and can do nothing to improve society.

Father captured that sense when he had a character in *Little Dorrit* sum it all up: 'As to who was to blame, Mr. Plornish didn't know who was to blame for it. He could tell you who suffered, but he couldn't tell you whose fault it was. It wasn't his place to find out, and who'd mind what he said, if he did find out.'

"You know, in spite of my career, I have never been of a military frame of mind. Looking back, I consider myself to be much more like my father than I would have ever imagined. Like him, I have seen injustice, inequities in society, ignorance and want. My burden, perhaps, is that unlike father I have not had the means nor the extraordinary talent to do something about it. At times, when I have had the luxury of pondering on my experiences, I thought that my role as a policeman was to make a difference. I have seen no point in dominating the Indian, sneering at his ways, bullying him. I have met reasonable men, Crowfoot, Poundmaker, Big Bear, who have seen their way of life come to an end, and who have borne the injustice of that catastrophe with immense patience."

"Tell Sam about Big Bear," said Jamieson.

Dickens described Big Bear's speech in the court after he was found guilty.

"I personally hold no animosity toward Big Bear," Dickens said. "He is now in prison serving a term for his supposed misdeeds. He was to me a cantankerous and difficult old man, a troublesome leader as far as the government was concerned. But he must be credited with trying to find the best course for his people. Had the government in Ottawa not taken such a hard line with the Cree perhaps the worst would not have happened. For my part, I believe he returned favour for favour, giving us time to retreat from Fort Pitt. And there are half a dozen witnesses who said he tried to stop the killings at Frog Lake. Give the man some sympathy; he had lost control of his band. My belief is that his authority, and that of other chiefs, had been undermined by the hard line taken by the superintendent of Indian affairs, unfortunately adhered to in the strictest of terms by the agents, including a close friend of mine who lost his life for his intransigence."

As Big Bear's speech played through his mind, Dickens was increasingly aware that he had left his past behind him. There would be no more of Western Canada, of Bengal, likely no more of England. He was now in Moline, Illinois, talking to newfound friends. His words were flowing like a spring freshet, he heard his voice telling the story, but his body seemed in some distant place, drifting across a continent, perhaps an ocean, around the world. He hoped he had been coherent. Then, he found his voice weakening, frequent clearings of his throat necessary, his breathing becoming more difficult. Did the others notice?

"My experience of Big Bear at Fort Pitt was a lesson in the rewards of kindness. On several occasions, I did what I could to fulfil requests made by Big Bear. They were small things: Some tea and a blanket here, sugar and some meat another time. It was largely through Big Bear's intervention that my men were allowed to go. If I had refused those petty requests in the past, do you think the chief would have risked challenging the war chief, Wandering Spirit, to let us depart without further loss of life? The Cree chief was grateful and sympathetic, he repaid those small kindnesses many times in allowing us to escape at Fort Pitt. At the time, there was little in it for him, no prospect of reward for him in letting us go.

"I contrast this with the behaviour of an officer colleague who borrowed a considerable sum from me with a promise to repay," Dickens said with bitterness. "This was a man who ridiculed the 'savage' practice of demanding gifts of food and other desirable goods. But I ask the question, which man was more 'civilized'? The chieftain, whose followers stare starvation in the face and who begs for food for his kin? Or the comfortable gentleman officer who cadges a friend for money, and then fails to repay."

As he said this, Mrs. Kennedy caught his eye.

# Chapter 48

*Mrs. Kennedy has just asked me the most extraordinary question. After the children left the parlour, I surveyed my surroundings. The comfortable ambience and the attentive demeanour of newfound friends was so far removed from the tense anger and hostility I had felt in the Canadian northwest and in recent months.*

*How can I make these people understand the set of circumstances that have shaped my life, my experiences, my failures and my modest victories? But to Mrs. Kennedy's question:*

*"I am curious," she asked. "Is there a character in your father's works that you feel very akin to, who might be a parallel to your own life?"*

*Her eyes sparkled as she asked this question, and while I might have disdained to reply to another, I felt I owed this charming woman a response.*

*"An amusing question for speculation, Mrs. Kennedy," I said. "Father often took characters from life and worked their peculiarities into his works. Do I see myself portrayed in any of them?"*

*I felt a twinge in my upper chest and tapped it gently. My hesitation gave me time for reflection and my mind raced through the vast array of odd and memorable personalities conceived by father's active imagination. I thought of David Copperfield's musings about whether he would be the hero of his* own life's story. I considered whether my last active role as a police officer, the retreat down the Saskatchewan, was my most ennobling, comparable in any way to the final gesture of Sydney Carton. I chuckled at the thought.

Betsy Kennedy was poised expectantly. Jamieson and Kennedy both smiled, awaiting my reply.

"Clennam," I blurted, the name leapt to my lips. I would have liked to have come up with a more heroic figure. But the character to whom I feel most akin is Arthur Clennam, from Little Dorrit. "He would not have been modelled after my own life, of course, my father created him before my career began," I said. "My real life, however, seems to have some parallels to his fictional one."

Betsy Kennedy gave me a puzzled look. "Why so? If I remember correctly, Clennam is so serious and reserved, helplessly weighed down by life. Watching you read to the children, I would not have thought you so."

The two men leaned back on their chairs, faces expressionless.

I told them Clennam spent many years in the Orient, apart, virtually banished, from his family, returning to an England that was little changed for the better after the death of his father.

I found my voice heavy, strained, almost choking and suddenly charged with emotion. My own arrival in England after the death of Father seemed to have been foreshadowed by the opening scenes of the book. It was as though, in writing those lines many years earlier, Papa had a premonition of my own melancholy and impotence in the face of life.

"There are differences, to be sure," and my stutter returned. "In Arthur Clennam's fictional life, he was rejected by his mother. My father...my family..."

I paused. Had I gone too far in betraying my innermost thoughts, the ultimate sadness of my life?. Was I being unjust, in seeking to blame my failings, my lack of confidence, my problems on the way I was treated by my father and family? Surely it was time that I take responsibility for the burdens that I myself have placed upon my own life, my own soul. I must, after all, accept that much of my life was wasted and misspent; my assets — both personal and financial — squandered. The mental torment punishing me as I sat, for the moment, silent in that parlour in this home in the American Mid-West only worsened the physical pain that was mounting ever more oppressively upon my chest.

I have struggled, often, to find the meaning in my itinerant life, with all its travels and travails, measuring its grand disappointments against its modest achievements. Have I expected too much? Do I feel it is my due as the son of a great father? I search for ways to justify my passing into a paradise beyond this life. In scrutinizing my past zealously and systematically, I find little comfort in that respect. I hope for a new enterprise that can set this mediocre past to rights. Yet perhaps the very process of self-examination is sufficient to find the grace I yearn for. Such is my hope.

Betsy Kennedy's voice broke into my thoughts, betraying some concern.

"Captain Dickens," she said. "Are you quite all right?"

Then, I felt better and continued. I desperately wanted to change the direction this conversation was taking but felt compelled to go on, as though I was trying to work my way through my own feelings of despair.

"In my case, my exile, if you like, was India. I felt beaten down, oppressed, beset by sadness. Like poor Arthur, I was uncertain how my life would proceed after my return to England. That path was determined for me, by my family, the vagaries of fortune and truth be told, by my own folly. Once here, I ran into an institution in the Canadian government, which reminds me of nothing less than the monstrous Circumlocution Office my father wrote about: everything goes into the bureaucracy and nothing comes out. People punished for creativity and invention. Warnings and advice ignored. In some ways, I feel, like my fictional counterpart, that I have lived my life in a kind of prison from which there is little chance of escape, with little chance of parole or opportunity to set things right."

Having revealed this, I took a deep, shuddering breath. I had to get off this dolorous, pessimistic path, expel the deep misery that was overtaking me.

"But there is a difference between Arthur Clennam's life and mine."

"What is that? Please go on," said Mrs. Kennedy.

"I have yet to find my Amy Dorrit." The words were spoken in a quick burst and I intended to voice them in a jesting tone, but the ache in my breast was there again. I winced and tears came to my eyes. I put my left hand to my heart and stared over my hosts, struggling to regain control. I was looking out the window of the house and a cart drawn by two black horses passed by. Despite the bright sunshine, the vehicle had a funereal appearance.

"But, Captain Dickens, you are still young," Mrs. Kennedy exclaimed, with a smile, believing that the jest showed that my moment of pain had passed. "Perhaps on your tour you will find a fine American lady, your Amy, and settle here, as your Uncle Augustus did."

"I would like to think that's so," I heard myself reply. But my thoughts drifted off to hot, steaming Bengal, halfway around the world. I wanted to say: "I found her once, but then I lost her."

# Chapter 49

One of the Kennedy girls had entered the parlour.

"Dinner is ready," she said.

"We'll dine and then head out to the Friday Club where you can regale us with more of your stories and opinions, Captain," said Sam. "But tell us more of the adventure of the place. Your listeners might not be quite so inclined as we are to listen to philosophy on a Friday evening."

Frank was feeling the heat again. His throat felt raw and his voice was cracking.

"Might I have a glass of water?" he asked, as the party headed toward the dining table.

"Of course, Frank. Lina, bring the captain some cold water. Quickly now, before we eat."

Lina hurried back with a glass of ice water, condensation dripping from the cold tumbler. Dickens swallowed it down rapidly, taking large gulps. Almost immediately, he felt a sharp stabbing pain in his chest. He cried out and pounded his chest with his open hand.

Jamieson rushed to his side. "Are you all right, Frank?"

Dickens struggled to catch his breath.

"Yes, yes," he gasped. "The cold water was a shock."

He paused to catch his breath. "Please, please go to dinner. I'll sit by the window for a bit and will join you later."

"I'll stay with you," said Jamieson.

"No, doctor, go to table. I will be quite fine."

"We'll check on you in a few minutes," said Sam, worried about his guest.

Dickens sat, struggling for breath and life, the stabbing in his chest excruciating. Sometimes the pain waned, then it surged again. He groaned.

"Too fast," he thought, trying to catch his wind. His head swirled.

As he rested, his head back on a pillow, his mind wandered. He had a fleeting vision of Walter's sudden collapse in India. He remembered the agony in Dutta's eyes when the old Brahmin told the young policeman of Darshani's death. There was a fleeting memory of the grace and power of her dance, ended with the egg broken dramatically on the ground. He recalled the pain of Clarence Loasby in the boat, how he had wept when he wrote Ralph Sleigh's father of his only remaining son's death in battle and of the quiet acceptance by the old man that surely masked deep despair. He saw the wizened old woman carving the corpse of the rotting horse in upper Bengal, in the same vision standing beside once-proud Cree and Blackfoot chiefs holding out their hands begging for food. Then there was Rutledge, whose heroism on the river brought him little reward but death. He thought of Tom Quinn, his stubbornness and untimely murder, and proud Wandering Spirit, too, ultimately crushed in spirit, quietly going to his fate, his body dancing at the end of a rope. He had a vision of his father, a young lad, humiliated by working in the window of that dark, rat-infested factory, yearning to be free from the chains of debt; his mother's pain at the breakdown of her marriage. Again, a dream of his father came, shaking with laughter over the ghost in the moonlit grove at Gad's Hill, followed by the many scoldings he gave Frank for his failures. He thought of the watch, now turned over to a Canadian friend in exchange for a loan, lost to him, likely forever. Strangely, in the wave of pain that engulfed him, lines from *The Chimes*, the Christmas book that gave him that cursed nickname of Chickenstalker, sprang to his mind:

"I know that our inheritance is held in store for us by Time. I know there is a Sea of Time to rise one day, before which all who wrong us or oppress us will be swept away like leaves. I see it, on the flow."

Then, Darshani came to him again, her dark eyes flashing, smiling and dancing. Red silk with gold trim rustled and swirled as it carried her along. Words came back: "I found her once, but then I lost her." The empty glass slipped from his hand and crashed to the floor.

Ten minutes later, young Lina came back into the parlour. She looked at Dickens, semi-conscious and deathly pale, his fingers twitching uncontrollably. She shrieked, and ran out to call the others.

Jamieson rushed in. Dickens was convulsing, his whole body shaking and his eyes rolling back in his head.

"Frank, hold on, man. Hold on," he heard himself saying as he tried to take his friend's pulse. Dickens gasped twice, could not speak, then his respiration failed. Jamieson tried to start him breathing again to no avail.

"My God, he's gone," the doctor said, looking with horror at Kennedy.

"His constitution was not strong, the cold water must have paralyzed his heart."

# Epilogue

Messages were exchanged, sent to Ottawa and to Charley Dickens in London. The people of Moline appealed for Frank to be buried in their town, in the beautiful cemetery that overlooked the broad Mississippi. The inventor John Deere had been buried in the same cemetery just a month before Dickens. Sam Kennedy and other citizens of Moline paid the funeral expenses upfront and a few years later Frank's relatives in England sent funds for a modest tombstone. Final services were held in the Congregational Church. Twenty-five carriages were in the funeral procession, including that of the recently bereaved Deere family. Dickens' pall-bearers included the mayor of Moline, representatives of local charitable organizations and senior officers in the American military. A year or so later, brother Charley visited the gravesite and stayed a short time. No others from the family ever came.

The inscription on the tombstone read: "Take Ye Heed, Watch and Pray, For Ye Know Not When the Time Comes."

In 2002, the old tombstone was replaced by a new one, thanks largely to the fund-raising efforts spearheaded by David and Jean

Carter of Elkwater, Alberta. A Royal Canadian Mounted Police escort took part in the installation ceremony.

In a tragic coincidence, a cheque with a least a part of Frank's retiring allowance, arrived in the Moline post office on the same day he died. He did not have the pleasure, nor the apprehension, of opening it.

Volunteers who had fought in the Northwest Rebellion were issued medals for their service but the federal government resisted giving medals to the police who had seen action. The argument was that they were only doing their job, so did not deserve special recognition. Dickens was among those who argued that a medal should be issued to the police. Eventually, the government relented but too late for Frank.

More than forty years after his death, the red and blue ribbon and medal that would have been issued to Dickens for his service in the Northwest Rebellion was sent to his last surviving brother, Henry Fielding Dickens, known to the family as Harry. The medal had been found languishing in a strong box in a drawer in Ottawa. The medal he never saw and the sword he never wielded in battle are exhibited in the Royal Canadian Mounted Police museum in Regina.

A lake in northern Saskatchewan is named in his honour.

# Afterword

Not everyone can be a hero, otherwise heroism would be meaningless, the central character of this book muses. But a measure of success or failure is how one stands up to trying circumstances. An ordinary person can not be expected to be heroic in every act; nor indeed can an extraordinary one. And we all in some way have measures of the ordinary and the extraordinary within us.

Jane Smiley, a biographer of Charles Dickens, said he was the first modern celebrity. One wonders what today's scandal sheets and social media would make of Charles' family life, and the antics of his often aimless and debt-ridden sons.

Francis Jeffery Dickens was the offspring of a giant of English literature, yet was a flawed common man, an anti-hero. I have, through this work of fiction, delved into events that shaped the personality of a man who is regarded as a minor and — by many — not very successful character in the history of the Canadian West. Most of the Canadian portion of Frank Dickens' story, and a good part of his early life, is based on actual events but I have taken the liberty to examine forces which might have made him the man he was. My goal has been to explore the relationship between Frank and his father. I believe his family history, his relationship with Charles would have created ambivalent feelings — a yearning to be acceptable in his father's eyes yet a fear of his father's dominant paternal authority. Frank was in awe of his father's matchless skill but also in some ways aware that the idol whom he both loved and feared also had some underpinnings of clay. I regard this work as a departure from the hagiography that Frank's sister Mamie wrote thirty years after Charles' death. My Father as I Recall Him. Mamie's work refers obliquely to "inevitable changes" in the family home life over time, apparently hinting about Charles' painful separation from his wife Catherine. She also writes "woe betide" the child who left a chair out of place, or a crumb on the floor, the sole explicit reference that indicates Charles could be a martinet with his children.

The soliloquies in which Frank engages in this book with respect to his father are my own imaginings but they attempt to reveal truths about forces that moulded the son's character. In the end, Frank in his final act of field service with the North West Mounted Police was able, not only to survive, but to lead those under his command to safety when many feared they were lost. Would Charles have beamed with pride at Frank's success?

Frank was a member of the Bengal Mounted Police, but I could find no records about his service. My account of his time in India is entirely fictional, save the facts that he learned of his brother's death upon arrival in Calcutta, that he suffered severe sunstroke, and that indigo as a cash crop induced great suffering and resulted in violence during the time he was in Bengal.

As for Frank Dickens' Canadian service, there are many documents in the National Archives in Ottawa referring to his career. He is mentioned, often not favorably, in many documents and books about the Rebellion of 1885.

I would like to thank certain individuals who helped in the long gestation of this book, notably Maureen Monette of Ottawa, to whom I express grateful thanks for her work in extracting records from the National Archives, but who also never stopped believing in the project. I also express my deepest thanks and love to my wife Lorraine who made many worthy suggestions and urged me onward.

I must stress that though this is a work of fiction, much of it is based on fact and on real people from Canadian history. I take full responsibility for any errors in fact or misrepresentations.

# Selected Bibliography

Cameron, William B.; *Blood Red the Sun*, and *The War Trail of Big Bear*. Two similar books written by the sole white male survivor of the Frog Lake massacre.

Carter, David J.; *Inspector Francis J. Dickens of the North-West Mounted Police: The Christmas Carol Baby*. 2003 A compilation of documents and references to Dickens' life, most of which were also consulted independently by the present author.

Denny, Cecil; *The Law Marches West*, and *Riders of the Plains*. Books written by an original member of the NWMP, which have been reprinted.

Dempsey, Hugh (ed.); *Men In Scarlet*, 1973.

Dickens, Mamie; *My Father as I Recall Him*; reprinted in 2005 by Fredonia Books

Horse, John & Fred, reminiscences by an aboriginal father and son. John Horse, then 11, was a witness to the murder of Tom Quinn by Wandering Spirit. John's father was Kamistatum, referred to in this book as a friend of Cameron. Saskatchewan Indian Federated College.

LaChance, Vernon; The Diary of Francis Dickens, *Queen's Quarterly*, *37, May, 1930.*

Manning, John; *Colorado Quarterly*, Volume VIII, No. 1, Summer 1959.

McLean, William; Reminiscences by the rival of Frank Dickens at Fort Pitt, National Archives of Canada., also the Hudson Bay Co. archives.

Library and Archives Canada, Ottawa; Assorted documents about Frank Dickens. E.g. Sessional papers, Copy of Records and Proceedings, Report of the Commission of the North-West Mounted Police, 1885. Witness testimonies recorded by F.J. Dickens in his own hand and articles written about Dickens over the years..

Neavitt, R.B.; *A Winter at Fort Macleod*, 1973 reprint.

Steele, Sam; *Forty Years in Canada*, 1973 reprint.

Stonechild, Blair and Waiser, Bill; *Loyal Until Death: Indians and the North-West Rebellion*. 1997.

Turner, John P.; *The North-West Mounted Police, 1873-1893*.

Wiebe, Rudy; *The Temptations of Big Bear*, 1973, McClelland & Stewart

I consulted several biographies of Charles Dickens, in particular looking for refernces to his relationships to his children, notably Frank. These included the works by Peter Ackroyd, Edgar Johnson, Jane Smiley and Claire Tomalin.

I also sought out books describing the British experience in India in the mid- to-late 19th century. One was *Lives of a Bengal Lancer*, by F. Yeats-Brown.

# Other Books Published by Vic Parsons

Vic Parsons is the author of two previous books of non-fiction, many articles and some short stories.

What critics said about *Bad Blood: The Tragedy of the Canadian Tainted Blood Scandal* published by Lester Publishing: Finalist for the Gordon Montador award and the Ottawa-Carleton Non-fiction prize.

"It's a horrifying account of bureaucratic bungling, collective denial and false economies...Parsons writes clearly on difficult technical matters in a book about hemophiliacs' AIDS nightmare." *The Globe and Mail*

"A veteran Ottawa journalist, Parsons builds an unflinching case against a top-heavy blood bureaucracy...that operated a system riddled with flaws." *Maclean's Magazine.*

About *Ken Thomson: Canada's Enigmatic Billionaire* published by Burgher Books:

"Parsons has solidly researched how the (Thomson) empire has grown and changed during Ken's watch." *Quill and Quire*

Printed in Canada